THE FUTURE OF THE
ENVIRONMENT

THE FUTURE OF THE ENVIRONMENT

Ecological Economics and Technological Change

FAYE DUCHIN

GLENN-MARIE LANGE

with Knut Thonstad and Annemarth Idenburg

New York   Oxford
OXFORD UNIVERSITY PRESS
1994

Oxford University Press

Oxford   New York   Toronto
Delhi   Bombay   Calcutta   Madras   Karachi
Kuala Lumpur   Singapore   Hong Kong   Tokyo
Nairobi   Dar es Salaam   Cape Town
Melbourne   Auckland

and associated companies in6
Berlin   Ibadan

Published by Oxford University Press, Inc.,
200 Madison Avenue, New York, New York 10016

Oxford is a registered trademark of Oxford University Press

Library of Congress Cataloging-in-Publication Data
The future of the environment: ecological economics and
technological change / Faye Duchin . . . [et al.].
p.   cm.   Includes bibliographical references and index.
ISBN 0-19-508574-4
1. Sustainable development.
2. Technological innovations—Economic aspects.
I. Duchin, Faye, 1944–   . II. Title.
HC79.E5F88   1994   363.7—dc20   93–43254

1   3   5   7   9   8   6   4   2

Printed in the United States of America
on acid-free paper

Preface

This book attempts to tell several different stories. In many ways, the most important one consists of our practical conclusions about what needs to be done to forestall increasingly serious environmental problems. This story leads us to examine technological considerations governing how a wide range of economic activities are carried out in all parts of the world now and how they might be done differently in the future. We then go on to assess the economic and environmental consequences of following a particular path over the next several decades. To do this, we build a framework that makes it possible to "weigh ends and means together in order to set [objectives] that are reasonable in relation to the efforts necessary to achieve them" (Sagoff, 1988, p. 220). We believe that too much attention is generally given to targets and too little to the possible means of achieving them. Here the emphasis is on the means and their relation to the ends.

The contribution of this work lies not only in its specific conclusions but also in their relationship to the other story lines. The conclusions we reach are based on asking a new set of questions and on developing the concepts and building the analytic framework needed to address them. We believe that the new field of ecological economics, with its focus on issue-oriented rather than single-discipline-based research, can provide a suitable home for this kind of analysis. In return, this approach can provide for ecological economics a conceptual and empirical framework with which to evaluate alternative theories and build alternative visions of the future. We try to make our case convincing enough that more analysts, as well as informed citizens, will want to join us in asking these kinds of questions. We hope that the conclusions of our practical story, which is mainly what the present volume is about, will reinforce our more abstract arguments about methodology.

Probably the questions most frequently asked today about environmental pollution and the economy are the following: How much would it cost to clean up? How much would it cost to adapt to certain environmental changes (like an irreversible change in climate) instead of cleaning up? What would be the financial costs (and benefits) of limiting carbon dioxide emissions from human activities to specific target amounts? These appear to be sensible questions, like asking how much it would cost to buy and drive a fuel-efficient car rather than an ordinary one. Answers to these questions have in fact been estimated, but we believe that single, bottom-line answers to such complex questions are simply not credible. It is like claiming that it would cost $300,000,000,000 a year (or any other figure) to eradicate half the poverty in the world when we do not have a clue as to how to do it (without getting into the question of what half of the poverty in the world actually means). On a more modest scale, it is like putting a dollar figure on how much it would cost to find a cure for cancer when it would probably turn out to be far more fruitful to work on prevention, which needs to be "costed out" rather differently.

Before we can say how much it would cost, we need to know how to do it. Once we have an idea of how we might clean up the environment, how we might adapt to certain changes, or how we might reduce emissions, we can evaluate whether we as a society would like to proceed in those ways, based both on estimates of how much it might cost and on whether the full range of likely accompanying changes in our quality of life are desirable or acceptable.

This book comes at a relatively early stage in the inquiry into how we might reduce the environmental degradation associated with the everyday activities on the planet. We approach this challenge by classifying these activities, selecting what appear to be the most important ones, and looking into the alternative ways in which these activities could actually be carried out—examining, for example, choices about how electricity is generated in different economies or the materials from which buildings are constructed. A large part of the book is devoted to these case studies which are indispensable for the subsequent investigation and which should prove informative for many other purposes as well. From a methodological point of view, these case studies represent a systematic way to collect a vast amount of economic and technological information about the present and projections about the future.

As economists, we also bring to the investigation a framework for assembling all these pieces into one coherent picture. This role is played by our mathematical model, which is basically a so-called input-output model of the world economy. While a simple (static) form of the input-output model of a single economy has been widely used for several decades, the input-output model of the world economy and other equally promising theoretical extensions are today known mainly among specialists only. If this study succeeds in demonstrating the potential power of the approach through the interest of its empirical conclusions, modern dynamic input-output models can be made available to various kinds of users through existing networks for a multitude of practical purposes.

We economists have had a tendency to partition ourselves into macroeconomists, who study the big picture in broad and aggregated terms, and microeconomists, who study smaller parts of the economic system in great detail. The authors of this volume identify themselves as *structural economists* who feel the need to study the big picture in terms of the interrelationships among its moderately detailed parts. All economists use models (theory) as well as data (empirical content), and there is, not surprisingly, significant overlap in theory and data among the different kinds of economists. But there are also some fundamental differences about what constitutes an operational, issue-oriented theory of how the world economy actually works.

In this book, we sketch our vision of how economists can use the power of a formal approach combined with real empirical content to address what we consider to be some of the most important questions about the economy and the environment. To do this, we stake out the domain for a structural economics that overlaps with both macroeconomics and microeconomics but also is conceived to accept, and indeed to require, the inputs of other fields as well. The data work in our case studies crosses the invisible boundaries separating a number of different fields. We consider that our theory is operational in that there is an unusually close correspondence between our verbal description of it and its expression in mathematical form. Most of all, there is a tight integration among the questions we ask, the data we collect, the variables and parameters of our model, and the conclusions we draw.

Economists distinguish between a *positive* analysis, which describes things as they are or will be, and a *normative* analysis, which prescribes how they should be. Researchers need to be prepared to do both kinds of work. However, this book is intended as a contribution to positive economics in that it is an effort to understand how the system can work in the future in light of the constraints under which it operates. We see this work as a prototype for an ambitious and thoroughly contemporary style of investigation that is issue-oriented and science-based. Our effort is crude and uneven in many ways, but we hope it will provide a counterweight to what we believe are oversimplified answers to crucially important questions and a substantial step toward a more integrated technological and economic analysis of real options. Such analysis is necessary to inform the social and political deliberations from which collective action needs to spring.

New York   F. D.
August, 1994

Acknowledgments

This volume is based on a study, "Strategies for Environmentally Sound Economic Development," prepared for the United Nations over the three-year period ending at the time of the Earth Summit in Rio de Janeiro in June 1992. The authors would like to thank Statistics Norway, and the University of Twente as well as the Netherlands Organization for Scientific Research, which supported Knut Thonstad and Annemarth Idenburg, respectively, during their stay at the Institute for Economic Analysis at New York University. We also benefited from Statistics Norway's support of Torgeir Johnsen, who participated in the early stages of this work.

We are grateful to Olav Bjerkholt, Assistant Director General of Statistics Norway, for his role in initiating this project and his ongoing interest in it, and to the Norwegian government for its financial support. We also appreciate the input of Anatoly Smyshlyaev of the United Nations and the financial support provided by the United Nations. The computer work was carried out with the support of the U.S. National Science Foundation at the Cornell University Center for Supercomputing. We would like to thank William Dean for making the model operational on the Cornell supercomputer.

The results of this study were presented at the International Symposium sponsored by the state and city of Rio de Janeiro at the time of the Earth Summit and at the meeting of the International Society of Ecological Economics (ISEE) in Stockholm several months later. ISEE members Martin O'Connor of the University of Auckland (New Zealand) and Jack Ruitenbeek of British Columbia (Canada) subsequently read the manuscript, and each provided wide-ranging comments about the scope and usefulness of this work from which we have benefited substantially. Will Baumol, our colleague at New York University, offered advice, which we have tried to heed, for improving the readability of the manuscript, and several other colleagues also made helpful suggestions. All remaining defects, large and small, are obviously our own responsibility. We are particularly grateful to our colleague Wassily Leontief, who introduced us to this type of intellectual endeavor.

Contents

I

METHODS AND RESULTS

1

Can Technology Assure Environmentally Sound Economic Development?

The Nature of the Problem

The large-scale use of the technologies developed since the beginning of the Industrial Revolution, and especially since World War II, has placed considerable stress upon the environment mainly in the industrialized economies. This is due in part to steeply increasing rates of extraction and processing of natural materials, accompanied by the generation of a wide range of waste products. In addition, the new technologies have involved the dissipation of naturally occurring materials and the synthesis of materials which are not found in nature. Widely dispersed materials, whether natural or synthetic, are not easy to collect. Even if collected, many of the new materials cannot be reused or recycled at reasonable cost after their initial useful life is over.

Poverty, especially coupled with the rates of population growth typical of many developing countries, also generates characteristic patterns of pollution. Main0ly associated with improperly treated human sewage and the degradation of land, these problems tend to be localized, although they affect large numbers of people. Today's concerns about the global environment are a response to the massive scale on which modern technologies are now utilized and the certainty that they will spread to the developing countries in the decades ahead.

At the same time, modern technology is responsible for the elevated material standard of living that has been achieved by a significant fraction of the earth's population. As we approach the twenty-first century, most parts of the developing world are attempting to improve their material standard of living both in absolute terms and relative to the industrial countries. This effort involves the development of new technologies, particularly those that have a biological basis, and the widespread diffusion of both old and new technologies.

People in rich and poor countries alike value increased levels of comfort, which tend to be associated with increased material throughput. Two good examples are the automobile and air conditioning. There are significant differences in their use in different countries at the present time. In the United States both are used more intensively than in other affluent societies. The differences are attributable to cultural preferences and historical circumstances, as well as population density, climate, and other factors. The automobile is already very popular in developing countries, and air conditioning will be increasingly sought, especially in cities with a tropical climate.

While increased affluence based on the further spread of modern technologies can be expected to place even greater pressures on the global environment, it is also true that new technologies can be vastly more efficient and cleaner, in terms of the use of energy and materials and the generation of waste, than the ones they displace. These potential benefits may still be largely untapped because, until now, the costs of raw material inputs and the penalties for generating pollution and degrading the environment have been low relative to likely future costs and penalties.

Another factor that could reduce future pressures on the environment is the prospect for selectively curtailing some types of activities and expanding others that are more environmentally benign. For example, industrial countries appear to have reached a number of plateaus: population growth and the use of materials tend to level off as affluence increases. Many activities run into limits, as in the case of traffic congestion or the exhaustion of landfills, because they elicit social responses before irreversible physical barriers are breached. Over the next several decades, reliance on benign technologies and prudent practices is likely to grow.

This book explores some important aspects of the relationships among increasing affluence, pollution, and technological choices. The analysis considers the situation in the world economy over the next several decades.

The Significance of the Brundtland Report,
OUR COMMON FUTURE (OCF)

The Brundtland Report, *Our Common Future* (World Commission on Environment and Development, 1987), popularized the definition of *sustainable development* as humanity's ability "to ensure that it meets the needs of the present without compromising the ability of future generations to meet their own needs" (p. 8). To achieve this outcome, the Report continues, "the international economy must speed up world growth while respecting the environmental constraints" (p. 89) by the appropriate management of technology and social organization. The Brundtland Report is comprehensive in identifying the areas of economic and environmental problems, and it describes different technological and organizational measures that might be taken in each area to contribute to sustainable development.

The Brundtland Report is an important point of departure for the study described in this volume because it reflects a progressive and moderate position about how both economic prosperity and preservation of the environment could be achieved. It implicitly argues that they are mutually supportive in that we cannot have one without the other. According to this view, people will not be willing or able to afford to preserve the environment unless they have a high material standard of living, nor will they be able to maintain that standard of living (let alone continually increase it) unless they ensure the continued provision of environmental services. Of course, it is also true that the two objectives can compete with each other because meeting environmental goals generally requires resources that could otherwise be allocated for growth (which could be achieved at least in the short term), and vice versa. The Brundtland Report takes the position that both economic and environmental objectives can be achieved if reasonable choices are made regarding technology and social organization. This book undertakes to evaluate this proposition.

The Brundtland Report has had to reconcile a relatively wide range of views. This characteristic makes it a volume that sometimes sounds like the work of a committee (of course, it is the work of a committee), but this feature is also its great strength: the members, many of whom are influential individuals in different parts of the world, were willing and able to arrive at a consensus. Thus the conclusion that we will reach—that the position taken in the Brundtland Report is not realistic—underscores the need for significant rethinking about how to achieve environmentally sound economic development in both rich and poor countries.

To make the challenges of sustainable development concrete, we focused in this prototype study on global environmental problems, in particular emissions of carbon dioxide. These are directly related to the use of energy, which plays a crucial role in economic development. The emphasis on fuel use made it easy to examine the emissions of oxides of sulfur and nitrogen as well.

Framework for This Study

In order to analyze the position of the Brundtland Report, the numerous recommendations directly or indirectly related to energy and air pollution that are sprinkled throughout it needed to be assembled, and further developed with more detail and concreteness, into an integrated scenario that is free of at least surface contradictions: we have called this the *Our Common Future* (OCF) *scenario*. For comparison, a *Reference scenario* was constructed in which no technological change takes place after 1990. Subsequently, additional scenarios, comprised of alternative technological and organizational assumptions, were also developed. An analytic framework was needed to evaluate the economic and environmental implications and the feasibility of the scenario. The model and data base we have used —called the *World Model* and the *World Data Base*— are well suited to this task because, in the assumptions that are inevitably built into them, they represent a pragmatic view of how an economy does and can work. Technological choices for each sector of the economy are described in the data base in physical terms, such as those an engineer might use. This characteristic makes it natural to relate them directly to material inputs and to the generation of pollutants and other wastes. They are also represented by the model in value terms, allowing for a direct relationship with changes in income and wealth. The first version of this modeling system was constructed by Wassily Leontief and his colleagues (Leontief, Carter, and Petri, 1977).

Building the scenario required a systematic, quantitative description of the technologies currently in use in the different parts of the world economy and identification of the kinds of options intended by the Brundtland Report but generally not explicitly identified. This information was then incorporated into the World Data Base, which is a repository of information about technological options, a generalized input-output data base that can now be used for various purposes. The bulk of the World Data Base has been built over a number of years; while it is crude in many ways, its prior existence made this study possible.

To analyze the scenario, we made use of an input-output model of the world economy, the World Model; the basic mathematical structure of the current version of the model is given in Appendix A. It divides the world into sixteen geographic regions, each described in terms of about fifty interacting sectors. Regions are linked within each time period by the trade of commodities and flows of capital and economic aid; they are linked over the period 1980–2020 by the accumulation of capital and international debt or credit. Use of energy and materials is directly represented, and flows of pollutants have been incorporated. Public and private consumption and sector-level investment are also represented, both in terms of detailed goods and services and in the aggregate. The output of agricultural products and of minerals and emissions of pollutants are measured in physical units; most other quantities are measured in constant U.S. prices. The data base describes the inputs and outputs associated with alternative technologies specified by the OCF scenario.

A conventional textbook might describe the economist's objective as identifying those alternatives, and in the process determining the corresponding "right" prices, that ensure optimal allocation of resources and maximum utility for consumers in a global economy in equilibrium. This theoretical position, and the actual models that are based on it (general equilibrium models), are appealing for their comprehensiveness and simplicity of objective. However, any theory or model of an economy has its shortcomings, and some of the major ones of this perspective are that a real economy is never in equilibrium; that social welfare is not the same as the "utility" of consumers; and that most environmental problems cannot reasonably be associated with prices that would make it possible to simply add them to calculations of utility because any such prices would be arbitrary. The challenge we have tried to face is to go beyond criticism of mainstream economic models, and beyond qualitative description alone, to build a formal framework that is capable of representing the activities of a real economy and to arrive at quantitative results while avoiding these shortcomings.

The World Model and Data Base are strong candidates as the starting point for this undertaking. While the theory and the model can be criticized, mainly for all that is still left out, we believe they are well suited to this kind of investigation for a number of important reasons.

The World Model does not attempt to determine a unique and optimal path to sustainable development, but simply to evaluate the implications of a set of technical and organizational choices that are made outside the model (by the

Brundtland Report, in this case). Freed of this impossible burden, it does not need to resort to a constraining notion of equilibrium based on the assumption of market-type behavior alone. Economic well-being is gauged by a number of variables, not by gross domestic product (GDP) alone, and many environmental variables are measured in physical units (e.g., tons of carbon emissions) with no attempt or need to put a price on them. There is not a single bottom line; weighing the relative importance of the economic and environmental outcomes is considered to be a social and political responsibility. We believe this is a realistic position about what an economist can hope to contribute to these questions.

The theoretical framework of the World Model and Data Base is well suited to this type of inquiry precisely because the underlying theory is understood to be necessarily incomplete. The empirical content of the data base—that is, the description of the technological choices—takes on an importance (in terms of the allocation of research effort) that it is not accorded in frameworks in which all of the major relationships are represented by mathematical equations. In addition, the openness to fundamental multidisciplinary collaboration is greater because this is recognized as a major avenue for the further development of the theory.

In a conventional economics textbook, the prominent policy questions focus only on monetary and fiscal options, the most familiar example being the design of a carbon tax, in fact an "optimal" carbon tax. These kinds of instruments are clearly important and necessary. But the design of a carbon tax and the assessment of its effects are most fruitful *following* a different type of analysis, such as that described below. The first stage of analysis needs to focus on the implications of the technological options for achieving specific targets. If the objectives still appear desirable, the economic incentives needed to make the shift voluntary can be explored at later stages.

Evaluation of the OCF Scenario

Under the assumptions of the OCF scenario, clean and efficient modern technologies associated with the use of energy and materials are adopted in all parts of the world economy over the next several decades. The specific technologies and the timing are different for different regions, but overall the assumptions appear to us rather optimistic. The results are analyzed first from an economic and then from an environmental point of view.

From an economic point of view, the scenario is attractive in that it is cost-saving: global consumption (at overall rates of economic growth that are approximately those of the Brundtland Report) is higher than under the Reference scenario. The advantages are very unevenly distributed, however, and it is a matter of judgment whether or not most of the developing countries are better off. For these countries, the new technologies represent a capital-intensive path; the capital is paid for by holding down consumption and by increased debt and aid relative to the Reference scenario. This outcome is feasible only if these loans and aid are actually forthcoming.

From an environmental point of view, the OCF scenario reduces emissions of the three pollutants that are tracked significantly below what they would be under the Reference scenario. But the problem is that these emissions still increase substantially between 1990 and 2020; in particular, annual carbon emissions rise by 60 percent. In addition, the locus of pollution shifts decisively from the industrial countries, where historically most of it has originated, to the developing countries, where most of the world's people live and where most of the future increase in population will take place. Material use and emissions are still much lower than in the industrial countries on a per capita basis, which augurs badly for the more distant future since people in developing regions can be expected to aspire to the material standards of living of those in the developed regions. The effect on the economy of potential environmental damage due to these elevated levels of emissions has not been taken into account in this study, in part because the relationships are not yet well understood.

Certain conclusions about long-term global strategies follow directly from these results, and there are policy implications as well. It appears that the economic and environmental objectives of the Brundtland Report cannot be achieved simultaneously. To the extent that our results about the physical reality are convincing, no amount of social organization and political will, not even cleverly designed carbon taxes, can make the OCF scenario work. This leaves two paths for action, and the authors of this volume feel that it is important to pursue both of them.

Two Directions for the Future

A scenario about much bolder technological and social changes might bring the basic objective of the Brundtland Report, sustainable development, within reach. Going well beyond the aim of more fuel-efficient vehicles, it may be necessary to replace a large number of private automobiles in developed countries by practical, convenient systems of public transport. New designs for communities would reduce the need for motorized transport. Developing countries could adopt similar approaches instead of pursuing the route of expansive highway networks, suburbanization, and unrestrained use of individual cars.

Another opportunity for technological innovation is large-scale, region-specific reliance on renewable sources for energy and materials. This is a far-reaching proposition because it would involve not only the phasing in of materials with significantly different properties from those they would displace, but also significant changes in the use of land and potential competition with agriculture. Of course, developing countries already make substantial use of renewable materials (biomass), but generally in relatively unprocessed forms. Research and development in this area is likely to be promoted by the emerging field of engineering known as *industrial ecology*.

Industrial ecology is a set of ideas that has taken root in the engineering community in many industrialized countries. It involves life-cycle planning of products for durability, reuse, and recyclability. At the corporate level, major objectives are better customer acceptance and greater efficiency in satisfying present and potential future environmental regulations. These concepts need to be generalized by other institutions, with a global mission and a longer-term perspective, to identify and promote promising technological options that might not otherwise be explored.

The areas just described are also in the spirit of the Brundtland Report; we call them bold because they differ in two major ways. First, they require a far greater break with present practices, which means that they would be harder to achieve both socially and politically, in part because particular interests would be threatened at least in the short term. Second, they require breakthrough achievements—not so much scientific ones, like achieving superconductivity at room temperature, but rather in technical design, like innovative transportation plans, which are expensive to develop and for which there is no evident institutional and financial support. It is not clear who will take the initiative for planning a second Brundtland Report along these more ambitious and more technical lines, but we hope that the results of our analysis can help by establishing the need for such an undertaking.

A second line of analysis also needs to be pursued: a new practice of development economics that is based more on the specifics of each situation and less on general principles than are, say, current international lending and advisory practices. Modernization of the nature, and at the pace, of the ocf scenario reflects the conviction that there is basically one path to development, and that it entails free markets for the movement of all factors of production to the privately most profitable alternatives for exploiting them. This path does not coexist easily with more traditional social relationships and is implicated, at least indirectly, in the rise of both religious fundamentalism and urban misery in the developing world. Perhaps some of the technical innovations described in the last few paragraphs can not only achieve economic and environmental objectives but can also do so with less social disruption to traditional societies that do not now have modern infrastructure in place.

Plan of the Book

The book is divided into two parts. Part I (Chapters 1–3) provides an overview of the methods and assumptions used to build the scenarios and presents the conclusions of the study. Part II (Chapters 4–13) includes a detailed discussion of the case studies on which the scenarios are based.

Chapter 2 describes the ocf scenario, and several scenarios about other technological options, in terms of concrete assumptions regarding each region and each sector. We present a summary of the case studies and other important assumptions such as the future growth of GDP and population, future oil prices, and changes in economic assistance to developing countries.

Chapter 3 contains the economic and environmental results and our conclusions about the ability of the ocf scenario (and the other scenarios) to alleviate the serious environmental problems we are now facing in a way that is economically feasible. The relationship between future levels of carbon emissions and potential climatic change is discussed. Consumption, investment, and the balance of trade, and their relative changes over time, are reported for each region. We calculate levels of fossil fuel use and the associated atmospheric emissions of carbon, sulfur, and nitrogen, as well as the regional distribution of the pollutants over the four-decade period. Changes over time in the output and trade in specific goods and services are analyzed for four major groups of regions: the rich, developed regions, newly industrializing regions, other developing regions, and Eastern Europe and the former Soviet Union.

Part II of the book begins with the case study describing the conditions under which carbon, sulfur, and nitrogen are released into the atmosphere in the course of production. Since these pollutants were not included in the original World Model, both the methodology and the actual numerical values had to be developed. For the other case studies, we selected sectors that make intensive use of materials or energy since the processing of materials is energy-intensive and the combustion of fuels is directly associated with the generation of emissions. These sectors include electric power, metal processing, construction, cement, pulp and paper, chemicals, households, and motor vehicle transportation; there is also a chapter on industrial energy conservation in all sectors. Each case study provides a description of the sectors involved and their importance in the different regions of the world economy. It also includes an account of current and expected future technologies that is translated into the detailed assumptions that are incorporated in the World Model and Data Base.

The appendixes describe the mathematical structure of the World Model (Appendix A) and the methodology that we have attempted to utilize in all of the case studies (Appendix B). The geographic and sectoral classifications are shown in Appendixes C and D, respectively.

2

The OCF Scenario

The content of the OCF scenario was developed in the course of carrying out ten case studies that provide the bulk of the data for this project. In order to examine likely future changes in emissions of carbon dioxide and oxides of sulfur and nitrogen, we focused on the most energy-intensive sectors. The technologies of greatest interest to us would promote development by their efficient use of energy and materials and their potential for low pollution and commercial implementation on a significant scale. Data collection for a case study covers one or several related sectors (e.g., iron and steel) and requires identifying the technological choices faced both in producing the output (in the iron and steel sector itself) and in using it (in the metal-fabricating sectors). The description of each technological alternative (e.g., electric arc technology) involves quantifying the major inputs per unit of output.

Economic models provide a conceptual framework for examining the effects of possible future climatic change. Some of these models, however, treat technology in a highly aggregate and essentially symbolic way. Even in more detailed studies of this type, future technological changes that do take place respond to changes in prices only. The underlying logic is that if we tax pollution and if energy prices rise as we exhaust energy reserves, energy-conserving technologies will become relatively less costly than energy-intensive ones in terms of current-account money outlays and will for this reason be adopted. While this mechanism is clearly important, there are additional important mechanisms for technological change—for example, strategic business investments aimed at profits for the long term, or voluntary changes in personal behavior as a result of changed values or additional information. Restrictive legislation is another mechanism. Our approach is able to include the kinds of changes that might result from all of these mechanisms.

At the other extreme from the abstract models are the end-use studies, which are rich in technical detail. These studies often develop data about new technologies, including those that have not yet been demonstrated on a commercial scale, and about the rate at which they might be adopted. Unfortunately, many of these studies provide only a description or at best a partial analysis because they lack a framework to account for full costs and indirect implications (like the energy required for the production of the equipment in question). There is also a tradition of end-use studies, especially about energy, using

11

input-output models to provide a comprehensive analysis (for example, Hirst and Hannon, 1979, Hannon and Joyce, 1980; see also Idenburg, 1993). The World Model and Data Base, based on an input-output framework, provide a unique opportunity to incorporate the extremely valuable end-use data work into a comprehensive economic framework.

We have attempted to chart a moderate course in defining the assumptions for the OCF scenario. We believe that the barriers to the adoption of many efficient technologies will be overcome at low cost (with the transmission of information and the establishment of standards, for example). For this reason, our scenario is not only explicit in its technological assumptions but also fairly optimistic about the prospects for technological change. On the other hand, there are generally considerable time lags, and often unbreachable gaps, between knowledge about a new technology, its technical demonstration on a commercial scale, cost reductions that make it economically feasible, its diffusion in the developed countries where new technologies have generally in the past been adopted first, and its spread to developing countries. We believe, for example, that photovoltaics are unlikely to be used on a significant scale to produce electricity in developing countries within the time horizon of this study (i.e., by 2020).

While we have undertaken to define a comprehensive and moderate, realistic scenario, this is easier said than done. We have been able, however, to take significant first steps in developing and analyzing such a scenario. It is important to clarify the nature of the difficulties to be faced in order to lay the groundwork for effectively overcoming them in the future. First, a global perspective requires coverage of the entire world economy, and most technical information and projections are available for selected regions only. Based on the information available for some regions, we have made rough estimates for other regions.

Second, even in the case of the economy for which the most technical information was available to us, that of the United States, this information takes the form of characteristics of individual pieces of equipment or individual production processes. Many additional assumptions must be made in order to represent the ways in which this equipment and these processes function within the economy as a whole. Part of the power of our conceptual framework is that it requires explicit assumptions; when assumptions are explicit, they can be discussed, debated, and changed. We have reported these assumptions in the case studies.

Basic Description of the OCF Scenario

The technical assumptions underlying the OCF scenario are spelled out and documented in the case studies. These assumptions cover the direct changes in inputs per unit of output in a given sector. (The modeling framework ensures that indirect changes will be captured and that the levels of different activities will be consistently calculated.) Several alternative scenarios have also been constructed for comparison with the ocf scenario and are described at the end of this chapter.

In all scenarios, we assume that levels of economic activity (as measured by GDP) will increase by about 2.8 percent a year for the world as a whole (see Table 2.1); this is generally consistent with the view underlying the Brundtland Report, though this report sets higher targets for growth rates in some developing countries. We also assume that the relative price of petroleum will gradually rise above its level of the 1980s to $44 per barrel (in 1987 prices) by 2020. The increased real price of energy directly affects regional balances of trade, as well as enhancing the attractiveness of energy-saving alternatives. Population projections are shown in Table 2.2.

The case studies cover the likely future changes in the use of energy in households, transportation, electricity generation, and industrial production and also examine pollution control options. We have made assumptions about the changing use of materials in processing and fabricating industries, as well as for construction. The changes in the use of energy, materials, and other inputs are achieved either costlessly, through current-account substitutions of some inputs for others, through investment in new types of capital goods, or through some combination of these. In the case of investment, we assume that the new capital goods are phased in through the expansion of production that relies on new technology or through the normally planned replacement of capacity in place. In general, we have not assumed accelerated replacement of operational capital, although the consequences of this avenue for modernization are explored in one of the other scenarios (for China and India). We have also made assumptions about population growth and urbanization and about changing trade shares in world markets. Accelerated introduction of electronic

Table 2.1. Projected annual rates of GDP growth for World Model regions, 1990 to 2020 (percent)

	1990–2000	2000–2010	2010–2020
High-income North America	2.4	2.2	1.9
Newly industrializing Latin America	4.3	4.1	3.9
Low-income Latin America	3.7	3.8	4.0
High-income Western Europe	2.2	2.1	1.9
Medium-income Western Europe	3.3	2.9	2.2
Eastern Europe	2.4	2.5	2.9
Soviet Union	2.1	2.2	2.2
Centrally planned Asia	5.0	4.6	4.2
Japan	3.5	3.1	2.5
Newly industrializing Asia	6.2	4.5	3.5
Low-income Asia	4.9	4.9	5.0
Major oil producers	3.3	3.3	3.4
North Africa and other Middle East	3.2	3.2	3.2
Sub-Saharan Africa	3.1	3.4	3.9
Southern Africa	1.2	1.4	2.0
Oceania	2.2	2.2	2.3
World	2.9	2.8	2.7

Source: Prepared for this study by UN/DIESA and Statistics Norway.

Table 2.2. Population and urban population for World Model regions in 1990 and projections for 2020

	Population		Urban population (%)	
	1990	2020	1990	2020
High-income North America	279,595	332,191	74.3	77.3
Newly industrializing Latin America	287,403	459,527	75.7	87.3
Low-income Latin America	139,133	237,878	60.1	74.6
High-income Western Europe	297,052	296,615	79.9	86.1
Medium-income Western Europe	140,214	176,366	57.2	72.3
Eastern Europe	116,535	127,116	63.0	72.4
Former Soviet Union	287,991	343,212	71.8	75.9
Centrally planned Asia	1,160,660	1,502,269	22.4	40.8
Japan	123,457	129,916	77.0	79.9
Newly industrializing Asia	326,483	454,381	36.5	57.3
Low-income Asia	1,318,432	2,238,136	26.8	47.4
Major oil producers	246,742	569,849	47.0	66.1
North Africa and other Middle East	224,536	445,872	35.7	52.1
Sub-Saharan Africa	264,604	645,164	30.9	53.2
Southern Africa	37,124	64,271	58.8	75.3
Oceania	27,765	39,972	67.6	71.3
World	5,277,726	8,062,735	42.7	57.5

Source: Medium projection, MEDS database, UN/DIESA.

equipment is accompanied by improvements in overall productivity. Projections assume the speedy and successful transition of the former Soviet Union and Eastern Europe to modern market economies. The following paragraphs convey a quantitative sense of the assumptions, which are summarized in abbreviated form in Table 2.3.

Table 2.3. Summary description of the OCF scenario in 2020 relative to 1990

1. Petroleum price		$44 by 2020; same in reference scenario (RF)
2. GDP and population		See Tables 2.1 and 2.2; same in RF
3. Household energy		
	A. In-house use	Small increase in investment requirements
	B. Developed	50 percent energy savings
	C. Developing	200–400 percent increase in energy per capita (including fuel for transportation); greater increases in electricity per capita
4. Transportation		
	A. Motor vehicles	Changing material inputs, 20 percent increase in capital costs
	B. Transportation services	50 percent less fuel per mile
	C. Households	50 percent less fuel per mile, 16–450 percent expansion in vehicles per capita in developing countries
5. Electricity		
	A. Fuel mix	Displacement of 15 percent of coal and oil by gas in most regions Unchanged share of non-thermal electricity in most regions after 2000
	B. Conversion efficiency	
	Developed (including pollution control)	15 percent improvement 20 percent increase in capital

Eastern Europe, former Soviet Union and other regions	25 percent improvement, 20–25 percent increase in capital
6. Emissions	
A. Carbon	Reduction of emissions only through lower energy use
B. Sulfur and nitrogen	
Developed	Scrubbers provide 90 percent removal after combustion; 10 percent increase in electricity use and 10 percent increase in capital; installation in 100 percent of power plants in Japan, 50 percent in Europe, 20 percent in Eastern Europe, 25 percent in former Soviet Union, 33 percent in North America; installation in 50 percent of industries in Western Europe and Japan; 30 percent reduction of coal sulfur in Eastern Europe and former Soviet Union through coal washing; Sulfur content of petroleum products reduced 33–50 percent; 33–50 percent reductions of nitrogen with 100 percent installation of catalytic converters in motor vehicles
Developing	No use of scrubbers; 35 percent decrease in coal sulfur content in centrally planned Asia and low-income Asia due to increased coal washing with increase in capital requirements; little use of catalytic converters
7. Industrial conservation	Small increase in investment requirements
Developed	20 percent energy savings on average
Eastern Europe and former Soviet Union	20–50 percent energy savings (depends on sector)
Developing regions	20–50 percent energy savings (depends on sector); 10–30 percent of fossil-fuel use displaced by electricity
8. Construction	
A. Maintenance vs. new construction	Share increase of 50 percent
B. Materials	Copper inputs decrease by 33 percent; aluminum inputs increase 15–33 percent; wood inputs unchanged; cement inputs decrease 15–25 percent; finished chemical inputs (mainly paint) increase 35 percent
Developed	Steel inputs decrease 25 percent
Developing	Steel inputs decrease 50 percent, more highly processed inputs
9. Metal-fabricating sectors	Virgin material inputs decrease 15 percent
10. Paper	Recycled content reaches 60 percent in developed regions
11. Electronics	
A. Investment	
Most regions	Value share in total investment goods rises to 56 percent
Poorest regions	Share remains at 1990 value
B. Production	
Developed and newly industrializing	65 percent decrease in inputs
Other regions	45 percent decrease in inputs
12. Capital coefficients	
Developing regions	Increases in various sectors

Notes: 1. Developed economies include high-income North America, Japan, high-income Western Europe, Oceania, medium-income Western Europe, and southern Africa. Newly industrializing economies include newly industrializing Latin America and newly industrializing Asia. Developing economies include low-income Latin America, centrally planned Asia, low-income Asia, major oil producers, North Africa and other Middle East, and Sub-Saharan Africa. "Poorest" regions include the African regions, low-income Latin America, and low-income Asia.

2. This rough summary is discussed in the text. See case studies for the underlying detail.

Source: Institute for Economic Analysis.

15

Detailed Technological Assumptions

For households in developed regions, the emphasis was on conservation of energy without sacrifice of convenience. It was assumed that new technologies would be used in lighting, major appliances, space heating and cooling, and building construction. The new equipment was assumed to be competitive (i.e., small additional capital cost) and achieved an energy saving of nearly 50 percent by 2020 per unit of consumption relative to households' use of energy under the Reference scenario.

Future use of purchased energy by the average household in developing regions will increase with urbanization, the substitution of commercial fuels for biomass, and improvements in the standard of living. These increases will be to some extent offset by increased energy efficiency. While the figures vary among geographic regions, per capita consumption of commercial fuels in households in developing countries is assumed to rise as much as four times between 1990 and 2020. Per capita electricity use is projected to increase even more rapidly.

Transportation is an extremely important and complex area; we have focused mainly on the production and use of motor vehicles. We assume that the fuel mix will remain unchanged but that an improvement in the average fuel efficiency of the fleet of 50 percent is achieved by 2020, with an increase in capital costs per average new vehicle of about 20 percent. We assume that the number of motor vehicles per capita and the number of miles driven per vehicle in most developed countries remain fairly stable, with an expansion of between 16 percent (Sub-Saharan Africa) and 450 percent (newly industrializing Asia) in vehicles per capita in developing countries.

A major use of energy is for the generation of electricity. There have been several estimates in the literature of likely changes in the mix of fuels and the use of nuclear and hydroelectric power for the generation of electricity in 2000 for major groupings of countries, and we have used these. After 2000, we assume a greater use of natural gas in every region. By 2020, 15 percent of the electricity produced using coal or oil (whichever is dominant in a region) in 2000 will be provided using natural gas, both in new capacity and due to fuel switching in existing capacity.

The share of nuclear energy is not expected to expand in developed countries after 2000 and in fact is most likely to fall, except in Japan. Counteracting this trend, some increases in hydroelectric, geothermal, wind, municipal solid waste, and small installations of solar electric power facilities are expected to keep the share of nonfossil fuel electric capacity fairly constant after 2000.

In developing countries there will be increases in nuclear capacity, especially in Asia. Hydroelectric capacity will also increase. The expansion of both of these technologies, however, will be sufficient only to maintain the share of nonfossil fuel-generating capacity between 2000 and 2020. The installation of geothermal, wind, municipal waste, or solar facilities is expected to be small.

Increased use of scrubbers and other retrofit devices for removing sulfur from the waste stream will increase the electricity sector's own use of electricity by 10 percent and increase capital costs by 10 percent. We have assumed that this equipment, with a 90 percent sulfur removal rate, will be adopted in 100 percent of coal and oil installations in Japan, at least 50 percent in Western Europe, nearly 30 percent in Eastern Europe and the former Soviet Union, and 33 percent in North America by 2020. Similar percentage reductions in nitrogen emissions are projected for developed regions. Developing regions are not expected to introduce postcombustion emission controls in significant quantities.

We have assumed an increase in average conversion efficiency in the use of fossil fuels to generate electricity in developed countries of about 15 percent between 1990 and 2020, bringing efficiency to about 40 percent. The investment needed to achieve these improvements, including a mix of new techniques and equipment such as adjustable-speed drives, will increase capital requirements per unit of output by an average of 20 percent in developed countries when the additional costs of retrofitted pollution-control equipment are also taken into account. In Eastern Europe, the former Soviet Union, and the newly industrializing regions of Asia and Latin America and other developing regions, conversion efficiency is assumed to increase by 20–25 percent, raising capital requirements by 25 percent. Some of the improvement is assumed to result from more thorough and systematic maintenance, which generally turns out, on balance, to be costless.

Energy conservation has been the source of significant energy savings in the developed market economies since the 1970s. Savings have been achieved in industry through such measures as practically costless improvements in "housekeeping," recovery of waste heat, and electronic controls for a variety of processes. More intensive and widespread reliance on these techniques is expected to achieve an additional 20 percent savings of energy per unit of output in these regions between 1990 and 2020. Based on rough calculations about past costs, it is assumed that these savings will be realized at the cost of additional capital equipment amounting to 0.5 percent more in value than the equipment assumed in the Reference scenario.

Industrial energy conservation also holds significant potential for energy savings in other regions that generally did not respond in this way to the oil price increases of the 1970s. For the OCF scenario, we have assumed that conservation measures are implemented in selected industrial and commercial sectors in developing countries, Eastern Europe, and the former Soviet Union. These measures achieve energy savings per unit of output ranging from 37 percent in petroleum refining in the former Soviet Union to 50 percent in cement production. Electricity displaces 10–30 percent of fossil-fuel use in these sectors. Continued energy conservation is also projected for developed regions.

New procedures in the production and use of metals and nonmetallic materials offer another avenue for increased efficiency and energy savings, as the newer technologies and uses tend to require less material per unit of output. With higher energy prices, we assume a general substitution away from processes and products that rely most heavily on fossil fuels.

In the very large, material-intensive construction industry, the share of maintenance and repair construction is expected to grow by about 50 percent in all regions over the next several decades, with compensating reductions in the share of new construction. By 2020, the share of maintenance in total construction will reach 50 percent in industrial Europe and North America, for example, while in the developing countries of Africa, at the other extreme, it will attain 15 percent. This continues a long-term trend in the developed economies and a trend that will begin in developing countries as their stock of structures expands and ages. This assumption is significant because replacement and maintenance construction activities are considerably less material-intensive than new construction, although they require increased inputs of chemical products, mainly paints.

We expect an increased level of fabrication for inputs to construction, especially in the developing countries. Examples of this are the substitution of ready-mixed or prefabricated concrete for concrete mixed on site, an increase in the degree of fabrication of metal inputs, and a substitution of processed wood for wood in the rough state.

With income growth and urbanization in developing countries, there will be a significant expansion in the construction of buildings, which use more cement, concrete, and wood, relative to infrastructure and engineering construction, which are metal intensive. The anticipated increase in fossil fuel prices will reduce the competitiveness of steel for bearing structures relative to cement and wood. Copper is expected to face increased competition from fiber optics, plastics, and aluminum. Aluminum will increasingly be produced in developing regions with cheap hydroelectric power and will substitute for many other materials.

The combined effect of these assumptions about construction is a reduction in the physical quantity of raw materials required per average structure. In the construction industry as a whole, we anticipate that inputs of steel per unit of output will decline by 25 percent in most developed regions and by about 50 percent in most developing regions by 2020. Copper inputs should decline by about one-third in most regions. Aluminum inputs are expected to increase by 15–33 percent, depending on the region. For most regions, cement inputs per unit constructed are assumed to decline by 15–25 percent, while inputs of wood (in terms of raw wood content) are assumed to remain unchanged. All these changes will contribute to a substantial indirect savings of energy per unit of output in the construction sector.

In metal-fabricating industries, the use of more intensively processed materials will achieve similar or even superior properties with less material and lighter weight. Aluminum will increasingly substitute for other metals in fabricated items because of its desirable physical properties, as well as the cost advantages made possible by increased reliance on hydroelectric power for its production.

An important area for material saving is recycling. With slower growth in total metal production and use, the size of the stock of available old scrap relative to new demand will increase, and significantly less energy will be required to process scrap than virgin metals. (This is also true for nonmetallic materials.) Both of these factors will lead to lower shares for virgin materials in processed goods. Under the OCF scenario, we assume that virgin material inputs of several major metals will be reduced by about 15 percent in 2020 relative to their use in 1990, increasing the share of recycled metal by a world average of 40 percent for most metals. Considering that perhaps half of all metals are tied up in buildings and other long-standing structures, this is a sharp increase. This figure cannot be directly compared, for example, with much higher recycling rates for individual items, like aluminum cans.

The share of paper that is recycled is expected to continue to increase, reaching 60 percent by the year 2020 in the developed regions. This rate was achieved in a few European countries in the late 1980s, but it is substantially above the average for the European regions and North America, which had recycling rates of approximately 40 percent and 30 percent, respectively, at that time. Recycling will also increase in developing regions.

Electronic components have undergone rapid and continuing advances in capability and reductions in cost since they were first introduced on a commercial scale. The anticipated future importance of this sector in all economies, and its spread in developing economies in particular, are represented in the OCF scenario by an increase in its share (in value at constant prices) among investment goods. In developed economies, including the former socialist economies, we have increased the share from 35 percent in 1990 to 56 percent by 2020. In developing economies, the share was estimated to be 31–37 percent in 1990; we have assumed that it would rise to 56 percent for newly industrializing economies by 2000 but remain at the 1990 level for other developing economies.

The material inputs for the production of electronic equipment can be expected to continue to decrease. In the developed and newly industrializing economies, we assume that input requirements will fall by 65 percent between 1990 and 2020. These improvements in productivity will amount to about 45 percent in the other developing regions, as well as in Eastern Europe and the former Soviet Union.

It has not been possible to include a case study of agriculture and forestry. These are priority areas for further work, since the future productivity of agriculture, especially in developing countries, may have a strong impact on the standard of living, investment priorities and trade.

Economic Assumptions

The balance of payments is calculated in current prices in 1980. For subsequent years, an attempt has been made to capture the effects of changing relative prices (notably the relative prices of fuels). Future prices of fuels, based on the moderate projections of the World Energy Conference, are given in Table 2.4. Future petroleum export shares, from the same source, are given in Table 2.5.

The parameters governing the international inflows and outflows of official development assistance (EE40 and MM40) have been reestimated for historical years. New, optimistic projections were made under the OCF scenario for 2000–2020, assuming significant increases in aid as a percentage of donor region GDP. These are shown in Table 2.6, and the recipient regions' shares are shown in Table 2.7.

Table 2.4. Fuel prices used for calculation of the
balance of payments in the World Model (1980 prices
in 1980, 1987 prices in 1990–2020)

	Oil		Gas	Coal
	$/bbl	$/tce	$/tce	$/tce
1980	33	158	83	54
1990	20	96	84	51
2000	25	120	84	54
2010	33	160	84	54
2020	44	209	84	54

Source: Romain-Frisch (1989).

Parameters representing imports and exports were calculated for 1980 and
1990 from data obtained from the UN COMTRADE data base, the Food and Agriculture Organization, and other sources, and projections were made for the
future. Some of these parameters are discussed in the case studies. The complete set of parameters is reported in Duchin, Lange, Thonstad, and Idenberg
(1992) (see Appendixes C and D).

Parameters governing households' investment in structures in developed
regions in 1980 were adjusted so that the share of plant stock held by households matched those reported in OECD (1987). Since these shares remained more
or less constant over the period 1960–85, we assumed they would also remain
constant in the future. No similar information was available for the developing
regions. Detailed data on consumption for many countries from the International Comparison Project were aggregated to World Model regional and sectoral classifications by Meagher (1994) and were used to verify the composition
of household expenditures for each region in 1980. The same mix was assumed
for future coefficients.

It can be assumed that achieving the GDP targets in many of the developing
regions will require the use of more modern technologies in a number of sectors
besides those explicitly addressed in the case studies, such as agriculture.
Selected input requirements were changed in these cases under the OCF scenario:
the figures were reported in the original World Model study and are not repeated here, as we have not been able to carry out new work in these areas.

Table 2.5. Future net export shares for petroleum
(percentage)

Region	2000	2010	2020
Newly industrializing Latin America	15.2	17.6	20.1
Low-income Latin America	0.5	1.3	1.8
Former Soviet Union	10.0	7.5	4.0
Centrally planned Asia	0.7	0.0	0.0
Major oil producers	70.8	70.3	70.3
North Africa and other Middle East	0.8	0.8	0.8
Sub-Saharan Africa	2.0	2.5	3.0
All other regions	0.0	0.0	0.0
Total	100.0	100.0	100.0

Source: Based on projections by Romain-Frisch (1989).

Table 2.6. Official development assistance as a percentage of donor region GDP, 1970–2020

	1970	1980	1990	OCF scenario 2000	2010	2020
High-income North America	.32	.25	.20	.40	.60	.80
Japan	.22	.30	.31	.40	.60	.80
Oceania	.55	.40	.33	.40	.60	.80
High-income Western Europe	.42	.48	.50	.60	.80	1.00
Medium-income Western Europe	0	.08	.15	.20	.25	.30
Former Soviet Union	.25	.14	.10	.10	.30	.40
Eastern Europe	0	.06	.10	.10	.30	.40
Major oil producers	3.00	4.50	5.80	3.00	3.00	3.00
Centrally planned Asia	.45	.09	.04	.05	.05	.05
Low-income Asia	.05	.10	.08	.05	.05	.05
Newly industrializing Latin America	0	0	0	.10	.10	.10
Newly industrializing Asia	0	0	0	.10	.10	.10

Note: The 1990 values are repeated in 2000, 2010, and 2020 for the reference scenario.

Source: Institute for Economic Analysis, based on OECD, 1991, Table 2, pp. 172–73: former Soviet Union in 1970: OECD, 1972, p. 39; centrally planned Asia in 1970: OECD, 1972, p 70; former Soviet Union, Eastern Europe in 1980: OECD, 1981, p.122; IEA projections for 2000 through 2020.

Representation of Investment

Investment is represented in the World Model in terms of three sets of parameters for each region and time period: sectoral capital-to-output ratios for plant and equipment, the ratio of gross investment (for growth and replacement) as a share of the stocks of plant and equipment, and the sectoral composition of gross investment in plant and equipment. The capital-to-output ratios of the original World Model have been maintained except in two cases where explicit

Table 2.7. Shares of official development assistance by recipient regions, 1970–2020 (percentage)

	1970	1980	1990	OCF scenario 2000	2010	2020
Sub-Saharan Africa	17.6	25.6	34.8	40	40	40
Centrally planned Asia	0.0	0.1	4.4	8	12	14
Newly industrializing Asia	17.1	5.0	6.2	5	5	5
Low-income Asia	32.0	25.5	20.4	20	17	15
Oceania	4.7	3.2	3.8	3	3	3
North Africa and other Middle East	7.9	26.4	15.8	11	10	10
Newly industrializing Latin America	3.8	0.8	0.8	1	1	1
Low-income Latin America	12.0	10.0	12.0	10	10	10
Medium-income Western Europe	2.7	3.5	1.9	2	2	2
Major oil producers	2.2	0	0	0	0	0
World	100.0	100.0	100.0	100.0	100.0	100.0

Note: The 1990 values are repeated in 2000, 2010, and 2020 for the reference scenario.

Source: Institute for Economic Analysis, based on OECD, 1991, Table 20, pp. 190–91, and Table 37, pp. 210–11; OECD, 1972, Table 19, pp. 238–39; IEA projections for 2000 through 2020.

new assumptions were made. We have assumed that electric power generation will require more capital per unit increase in output in the future as techniques to conserve energy are adopted and that increased fuel efficiency of motor vehicles will be achieved at the cost of additional capital. These assumptions are quantified in Chapters 5 and 13, respectively.

Rates of gross investment as a share of capital were revised for 1980 and 1990 based on data on investment from the UN National Income Accounts. The trends of these rates were projected for future years. Investment control figures (as a share of GDP) are shown in Table 2.8, and the investment to stock ratios are given in Table 2.9.

We found it necessary to revise the composition of gross investment in equipment, even for 1980, because there had been a systematic underestimation of the diffusion of electronics. It would have been hard to anticipate in the 1970s that by 1988, electrical machinery, dominated by electronics, would account for over half of the value of total investment in equipment in any country, yet this proportion was reached in the United States.

The composition of investment in equipment in the United States, according to the National Income Accounts, is shown for 1980 and 1987, aggregated to World Model sectoral categories, in Table 2.10. The table shows that in 1980, electric machinery accounted for 60 percent of the combined investment in all machinery (codes XX21 and XX22 in the table); this proportion rose to 82 percent by 1987. We used the 1987 composition, as shown in the table, for 1990 to 2020. In keeping with the conventions of the World Model, margins for trade, transportation, and other services are explicitly represente,d although they are not included in the National Income Accounts.

Table 2.8. Gross investment as a share of GDP for World Model regions in 1970, 1980, and 1987

	1970	1980	1987
High-income North America	0.182	0.174	0.192
Newly industrializing Latin America	0.223	0.285	0.189
Low-income Latin America	0.184	0.212	0.169
High-income Western Europe	0.254	0.217	0.197
Medium-income Western Europe	0.275	0.266	0.231
Eastern Europe	0.298	0.241	0.269
Former Soviet Union	0.298	0.241	0.277
Centrally planned Asia	0.255	0.338	0.191
Japan	0.390	0.345	0.346
Newly industrializing Asia	0.226	0.292	0.210
Low-income Asia	0.172	0.204	0.146
Major oil producers	0.250	0.260	0.270
North Africa and other Middle East	0.188	0.234	0.185
Sub-Saharan Africa	0.199	0.213	0.170
Southern Africa	0.280	0.311	0.182
Oceania	0.268	0.239	0.223
Total	0.257	0.227	0.275

Source: UN National Income Accounts.

Table 2.9. Gross investment in equipment and plant as a share of capital stock for World Model regions in 1990

	Equip.	Plant
High-income North America	0.155	0.049
Newly industrializing Latin America	0.138	0.094
Low-income Latin America	0.112	0.104
High-income Western Europe	0.151	0.070
Medium-income Western Europe	0.171	0.112
Eastern Europe	0.199	0.102
Former Soviet Union	0.191	0.151
Centrally planned Asia	0.138	0.144
Japan	0.282	0.141
Newly industrializing Asia	0.181	0.226
Low-income Asia	0.159	0.137
Major oil producers	0.207	0.179
North Africa and other Middle East	0.176	0.158
Sub-Saharan Africa	0.175	0.162
Southern Africa	0.116	0.089
Oceania	0.148	0.101

Source: UN National Income Accounts and capital stock computed by the World Model, as described in the text.

For most other regions, we revised the two coefficients for machinery (XX21) and electric machinery (XX22) by decreasing the former and raising the latter, such that the latter was 60 percent of the combined total in 1980. This revision was not made for the five poorest regions. We assumed that the developed regions had the same composition of investment as North America by 1990, that most other regions also did by 2000, and that this composition would not change between then and 2020. All of these assumptions are summarized in Table 2.11.

Table 2.10. Composition of gross investment for high-income North America under the ocf scenario, 1980–2020

Code	Sector	1980	1990–2020
XX8	Furniture	.033	.026
XX17	Motor vehicles	.132	.105
XX18	Ships, other transportation equipment	.032	.013
XX19	Aircraft	.023	.023
XX20	Metal products	.030	.013
XX21	Machinery except electrical	.236	.118
XX22	Electrical machinery	.332	.556
XX23	Instruments	.085	.061
XX24	Miscellaneous manufacturing	.028	.019
XX27	Trade	.046	.045
XX28	Transportation services	.009	.009
XX30	Other services	.013	.013
	Total	1.000	1.000

Source: U.S. National Income and Product Accounts for 1980 and 1987 (adjusted because of the inclusion of trade, transportation, and other service margins in the World Model definition of investment inputs). 1987 values are repeated for 1990–2020.

Table 2.11. Summary of assumptions about the composition of gross
investment in World Model regions under the OCF scenario, 1980–2020

	1980	1990	2000–2020
High-income North America	NA80	NA	NA
Newly industrializing Latin America	M	M	NA
Low-income Latin America	nc	M	M
High-income Western Europe	M	NA	NA
Medium-income Western Europe	M	M	NA
Eastern Europe	M	NA80	NA
Former Soviet Union	M	NA80	NA
Centrally planned Asia	nc	M	M
Japan	M	NA	NA
Newly industrializing Asia	M	M	NA
Low-income Asia	nc	M	M
Major oil producers	M	NA80	NA80
North Africa and other Middle East	nc	M	M
Sub-Saharan Africa	nc	M	M
Southern Africa	M	M	NA
Oceania	M	NA80 NA	

Notes: nc: no change from old coefficients. M indicates that the two machinery coefficients have
been revised so that electrical machinery is 60 percent of the total of the two. NA80 and NA indicate
the composition of investment for high-income North America in 1980 and later years, respectively,
as shown in Table 2.10.

Alternative Scenarios

In a study such as this, based on detailed case studies, each involving projected
values for many parameters, it is difficult to use a formal approach to sensitivity analysis that varies parameter values one at a time. Instead, the spirit of a
sensitivity analysis is embodied in the design of several alternative scenarios
that differ in the values of sets of parameters chosen for substantive reasons.
Intended for comparison with the OCF scenario, these include a Reference scenario, which is essentially a "no technical change" scenario, and four scenarios
based on more extreme assumptions about energy savings than the OCF scenario.
All scenarios use the same projected values for GDP and population.

Under the Reference scenario, all regions continue to use 1990 technology
through 2020; this provides a "worst case" scenario in terms of resulting energy use and pollution, for comparison with the results of the OCF scenario. The
four more optimistic scenarios were constructed to explore further some of the
possibilities outlined in the Brundtland Report and to examine more extreme
approaches to reducing global emissions of carbon, sulfur, and nitrogen than
were considered under the OCF scenario.

These alternative scenarios are summarized in Table 2.12. Scenarios OCF/HN
(Our Common Future/Hydro-Nuclear) and OCF/S (Our Common Future/solar)
assume increased reliance on nonfossil-fuel electric power—hydroelectric and
nuclear (OCF/HN) and solar (OCF/S). Scenario OCF/CI (China-India) assumes more
rapid modernization of industry in China and India, and scenario OCF/HNCI combines the assumptions of scenarios OCF/HN and OCF/CI. These four scenarios
depend on a number of technological assumptions. The OCF/HN and OCF/S scenar-

Table 2.12. Description of five alternative scenarios relative to the ocf scenario

Scenario	Technical assumptions
Reference	No technical changes after 1990
OCF/HN	Larger share for nuclear and hydroelectric power with greater capital costs; other assumptions same as OCF
OCF/S	Larger share for solar electric power, but at no additional cost; other assumptions same as OCF
OCF/CI	Rapid modernization of technology in energy-intensive sectors of China and India; other assumptions same as OCF
OCF/CIHN	Combination of scenarios OCF/HN and OCF/CI

ios are described in Chapter 5. Under scenario ocf/ci, modern technology, represented by the technology used in Japan, is introduced into the energy-intensive sectors of the two major coal-burning developing regions, centrally planned Asia (China) and low-income Asia (India), between 1990 and 2020. The results must be regarded as preliminary since it was not possible to conduct full case studies for these scenarios.

3

Results and Conclusions

This chapter contains the results of computations of the OCF scenario and the Reference scenario that were described in Chapter 2. The principal findings about consumption, investment and international exchange and credit, about energy use and emissions, and about sectoral production and trade are reported, as well as summary results for several alternative scenarios. A number of conclusions about economic assistance and the development and transfer of new technology are discussed. In the first appendix to this chapter, our results are compared to those of other studies that have investigated some part of this story.

Under the Reference scenario, substantial increases in GDP are assumed to be achieved between 1990 and 2020 in all regions in the absence of structural changes. Thus, the scenario naturally entails large increases in worldwide production and use of fuels, materials, capital goods, and labor, accompanied by correspondingly sharp increases in the generation of pollutants. Annual use of fuels and materials would more than double, and their cumulative extraction may not be consistent with known reserves in some cases.

Even if the scenario is deemed physically feasible, there is the further question about the intraregional arrangements that would be required to achieve it. Volumes of world trade would increase substantially over the period, made possible by the extension of international credit at levels that are massive by today's standards.

In this chapter, we do not present a detailed analysis of the Reference scenario but instead explore the extent to which the kinds of actions described in the Brundtland Report can provide a more promising basis for sustainable development. Specifically, we ask whether the OCF scenario can reduce the economic burdens relative to the Reference scenario and assess the extent to which it is physically more advantageous in terms of reduced factor inputs, especially fuel and materials, and reduced emissions.

At a global level and in each region, the changes associated with the OCF scenario and the more extreme alternative scenarios will significantly reduce the use of energy, of materials more generally, and of the wastes that are associated with their processing and use below what could be expected on the basis of present practices (represented by the Reference scenario). In addition, at a global level, the benefits will outweigh the costs, from an economic as well as an environmental point of view: while a similar volume (but different mix) of goods and services will be produced, higher levels of consumption can be achieved with lower investment requirements and significantly lower emissions.

At a regional level, however, it becomes clear that the ocf scenario requires significant increases in investment in the developing regions, accompanied, in most cases, by increases in net imports. It is unlikely that these countries will be inclined to undertake the path to sustainable development described in that scenario, or that they would be able to obtain the credits if they wanted to, in the absence of economic assistance of a magnitude that dwarfs even optimistic assumptions about the proportion of GDP that donor nations are inclined to devote to economic aid. Yet the rich nations clearly have an interest in providing assistance because it seems very likely that most paths to economic development, like those analyzed here, will involve steep increases in the share of global pollution originating in the developing economies.

Clearly, a development strategy that is sufficiently ambitious to satisfy both material and environmental objectives will have to rely not only on aid but mainly on the much larger economic engine of commercial market forces. The aid that can realistically be provided by the international community, while of relatively small magnitude, needs to be used to play a strategic role that includes the identification and development of suitable technologies and the facilitation of their effective adoption.

At the same time, it is clear that the scenarios based on our interpretation of the prescriptions in the Brundtland Report are not adequate to arrest the growth in global emissions of the pollutants that were examined. On the basis of this analysis, we believe that far more strenuous actions need to be taken that—unlike the assumptions of the ocf scenario—may be politically difficult or may require technological breakthroughs. In the first category are options like substituting common transport for much of the use of personal automobiles. In the second category are discoveries that make it possible to reduce sharply the costs of photovoltaics or the use of fuels from biomass. Both outcomes will require concerted action if they are to be fruitful in the next several decades or at all. The consequences of these actions can be analyzed in new World Model scenarios.

Global and Regional Economic Implications

Global Economic Results

The ocf and Reference scenarios both assume the same rates of increase in overall economic activity (GDP). Each region faces different tradeoffs among consumption, investment, the balance of trade, and international debt, and these are explored below. First, we present results about the economic implications for the world as a whole.

Selected comparisons of the scenario outcomes in 2020 are shown in Table 3.1 in constant 1970 U.S. prices (the constant-price unit used throughout the database), along with a rough conversion to 1990 prices. Under the OCF scenario, personal consumption is $250 billion higher than under the Reference scenario, about 1 percent of total world consumption. In addition, the total debt of all debtor regions is $2,400 billion lower, about 1.8 percent of total world debt. One can conclude that for the world as a whole, the OCF scenario describes a development path that is not more costly than under present technological arrangements.

According to Table 3.1, international debt (summed over World Model regions) is nearly five times as large as the value of world consumption. Valued at 1970 prices, the volume of world exports is slightly lower under the OCF scenario but is some thirty times greater than the total of economic aid. The latter is also minuscule compared to interest on the debt.

Regional Economic Results

Table 3.2 compares the results of the two scenarios for World Model regions in 2020 with respect to consumption, investment, the balance of trade, and international credit.

For the world as a whole, it is possible to consume more, because it is necessary to invest less, under the OCF scenario. In all regions, both consumption and investment grow substantially in the decades after 1990 (see Table 3.3), and per capita consumption (not shown) grows significantly in all regions except Sub-Saharan Africa.

In North America, Japan, Eastern Europe, and medium-income Western Europe, the OCF scenario makes it possible to maintain or increase consumption because investment requirements are reduced (see Table 3.2). These reductions result from significant savings in energy and materials and associated capital requirements. These regions also increase their volume of exports relative to

Table 3.1. Worldwide consumption, international debt, economic aid, and exports under the OCF scenario and the reference scenario in 2020

	Billions of dollars in 1970 U.S. prices			Billions of dollars in 1990 U.S. prices		
	OCF	Reference	Difference	OCF	Reference	Difference
Consumption	$8,924	$8,841	$83	$26,736	$26,488	$249
International debt	41,611	42,200	−789	124,667	127,031	−2,364
Aid outflows	81	40	41	243	120	123
Exports	2,500	2,694	−194			

Notes: 1. The U.S. GDP inflator of 2.996 was used to convert 1970 U.S. prices (the basis for constant prices in the data base) to 1990 prices. In principle, different inflators should be used for consumption and exports. The composition of exports is sufficiently different from that of total final deliveries that we have not attempted to convert these figures to 1990 U.S. prices using the GDP inflator.

2. Debt is summed over all World Model debtor regions.

Source: Institute for Economic Analysis.

Table 3.2. Consumption, investment, and international exchange under the OCF scenario relative to the reference scenario for World Model regions in 2020

Region	Consumption (constant prices)	Investment (constant prices)	Balance of trade (constant prices)	International credit (current prices)
High-income North America	+	−	+	+
Newly industrializing Latin America	+	+	−	−
Low-income Latin America	−	+	−	−
High-income Western Europe	−	−	+	+
Medium-income Western Europe	=	−	+	+
Eastern Europe	+	−	+	+
Former Soviet Union	=	+	−	−
Centrally planned Asia	−	+	+	+
Japan	+	−	+	+
Newly industrializing Asia	=	−	+	+
Low-income Asia	+	+	−	−
Major oil producers	+	+	−	−
North Africa and other Middle East	−	+	=	−
Sub-Saharan Africa	+	+	−	−
Southern Africa	+	=	−	−
Oceania	+	−	−	−
World	+	−	=	+

Notes: 1. Consumption, investment, and the balance of trade are measured in constant 1970 U.S. prices. International credit is measured in current U.S. relative prices. Improved credit includes the case of reduced debt.

2. The entry + means that the value is higher for the OCF scenario than for the reference scenario; − indicates a lower value. If the last two columns have different signs, the terms of trade changed for that region relative to other regions. Note that GDP is the same under both scenarios.

Source: Institute for Economic Analysis.

imports (i.e., the balance of trade is higher) and improve their international credit (or reduce their debt) under the OCF scenario.

A second set of regions is also able to increase consumption relative to the Reference scenario, but these regions cannot finance this increase solely through savings in investment. Southern Africa, Oceania, and low-income Asia increase their imports and their debt.

The OCF scenario assumes the adoption of modern, generally more capital-intensive technology, so it is not surprising that in some regions investment is higher than under the Reference scenario. (Consumption still grows significantly over the time horizon of the scenarios under the OCF scenario; see Table 3.3.) This is true for the former Soviet Union, which experiences virtually no change in consumption relative to the Reference scenario, and in centrally planned Asia, low-income Latin America, and northern Africa, where consumption is lower than under the Reference scenario. In most of these regions, more investment requires increased net imports and increased debt.

The OCF scenario makes it possible to increase consumption while also increasing investment relative to the Reference scenario in several resource-rich regions—newly industrializing Latin America, the oil-rich Middle East, low-income Asia, and Sub-Saharan Africa. But these regions have to increase net imports, reducing their credit positions.

Any scenario specifying rapid economic growth could be expected to

Table 3.3. Rates of growth of consumption and investment under the OCF scenario (percentage average annual rate of growth between 1990 and 2020)

Region	GDP	Consumption	Investment
High-income North America	2.2	2.1	1.8
Newly industrializing Latin America	4.1	4.2	4.1
Low-income Latin America	3.9	3.9	4.5
High-income Western Europe	2.1	1.8	1.8
Medium-income Western Europe	2.8	2.9	2.7
Eastern Europe	2.6	2.6	2.4
Former Soviet Union	2.2	2.5	1.4
Centrally planned Asia	4.6	4.5	5.1
Japan	3.0	3.4	2.6
Newly industrializing Asia	4.7	5.3	4.9
Low-income Asia	4.9	5.1	4.9
Major oil producers	3.3	3.2	4.9
North Africa and other Middle East	3.2	3.1	3.9
Sub-Saharan Africa	3.5	3.5	4.7
Southern Africa	1.5	1.5	1.6
Oceania	2.2	2.4	1.6
Rich developed economies	2.3	2.2	2.0
Newly industrializing economies	4.4	4.7	4.6
Other developed economies	4.4	4.3	4.9
Eastern Europe and former Soviet Union	2.3	2.5	1.7
World	2.8	2.9	2.8

Notes: 1. GDP growth rates are exogenous; personal consumption and investment are endogenous.

2. In most cases, the growth rate for GDP falls in between the other two. This is not always the case, however. Trade and various categories of government spending, which are also included in GDP, are not shown in this table.

Source: Institute for Economic Analysis.

involve more debt for most developing regions. In general, the Reference scenario results in increased polarization, with the creditors accumulating more credit and the debtors more debt with the passage of time. The next question is whether this trend is moderated under the OCF scenario relative to the Reference scenario.

In Figure 3.1, the sixteen World Model regions are divided into four categories according to whether they are creditor or debtor regions and whether the credit or debt grows larger or smaller over the period 1990–2020 under the OCF scenario. Panel A shows that only four regions are creditor regions in 1990*, and their credit grows over the period; all remaining regions are debtor regions, and their debt grows larger. The newly industrializing regions, Eastern Europe, and the former Soviet Union are in the debtor category. The developed countries as a whole are shown as a net creditor because the size of the credit of high-income Western Europe and Japan offsets the debt of North America and the other developed regions. The credit of the oil-rich Middle East is likewise large enough to offset the debt of all other regions included in other developing economies.

* Sub-Saharan Africa is a debtor region in 1990 but achieves a small credit by 2020 largely because of the increased price of its oil exports. While this may seem surprising, the region did, in fact, have a net surplus in the merchandise trade in the late 1980s according to the UN COMTRADE data base.

A, OCF *Scenario in 2020 relative to 1990*

		Bigger			Smaller
Credit	WEH			DC	
	OIL			ODE	———
	JAP				
	TAF				
Debt	WEM	EEM	OCH	NI	
	NIA	LAL	ASC	ER	———
	ASL	SAF	RUH		
	NAH	NILA	AAF		

B. OCF *Scenario in 2020 Relative to Reference Scenario in 2020*

				DC	OIL	ODE
Credit	WEH					
	JAP					
Debt	NIA	OCH		NI	WEM	
	ASL	RUH		ER	NAH	
	LAL	AAF			EEM	
	SAF				ASC	
	NILA					

Notes: 1. Region code names are identified below. DC is all rich, developed regions; NI are the newly industrializing regions; ODE are all other developing regions; and ER includes Eastern Europe and the former Soviet Union.

2. Within each box, regions are ordered according to declining magnitude of the credit (or debt) in 2020 under the OCF scenario.

3. Region code names are: high-income North America (NAH); newly industrializing Latin America (NILA); low-income Latin America (LAL); high-income Western Europe (WEH); medium-income Western Europe (WEM); Eastern Europe (EEM); former Soviet Union (RUH); Japan (JAP); centrally planned Asia (ASC), newly industrializing Asia (NIA), low-income Asia (ASL); major oil producers (OIL); North Africa and other Middle East (AAF); Sub-Saharan Africa (TAF); southern Africa (SAF); and Oceania (OCH).

Figure 3.1. Comparison of International Credit and Debt of World Model Regions Under the Reference Scenario and the OCF Scenario (*Source*: Institute for Economic Analysis)

Under the Reference scenario, the results are similar in direction to those shown in panel A of Figure 3.1, with one important exception. The former Soviet Union ends the period as a small creditor rather than a debtor. This difference follows from the significant savings in fuels and other raw materials, in individual countries and in the world as a whole, under the OCF scenario relative to the Reference scenario and the fact that the former Soviet Union is resource-rich but an importer of electronics and other important investment goods.

The results for 2020 under the two scenarios are compared directly in panel B of Figure 3.1. This panel shows that the credits of the oil-rich Middle East and of sub-Saharan Africa are reduced under the OCF scenario, as are the debts of a number of debtor regions. On balance, there is a significant improvement in the position of the developed economies because of the increased credit of Japan and high-income Western Europe and the reduction in the North American debt. Among the largest changes are a steep reduction in the debt of China but substantial increases in the debts of the former Soviet Union and newly industrializing Latin America. There is also a sharp increase in the credit of Japan and a reduction in that of the oil-rich Middle East.

The OCF scenario moderates the massive international flows of credit required to support the specified rates of GDP growth and tends to shift the advantage from countries that are resource-rich to ones that are technology-rich. Nevertheless, indebtedness in many regions increases substantially by 2020 relative to 1990 despite increases in economic aid that are steep by historical standards.

Energy Use and Emissions of Carbon, Sulfur, and Nitrogen

World GDP is projected to increase by 130 percent over the next three decades, and the increased volume of economic activity implied by the GDP assumptions involves substantial increases in energy use and pollutant emissions.

Worldwide, fossil fuel use under the OCF scenario increases 61 percent over this period to 16 billion tons of coal equivalent a year (see Table 3.4). This con-

Table 3.4. Fossil fuel use under the OCF scenario for regional groupings, 1990–2020 (millions of tons of coal equivalent)

	Oil	Gas	Coal	Total
1980				
Rich, developed economies	2302	1113	1180	4595
Newly industrializing economies	323	91	38	451
Other developing economies	398	97	588	1083
Eastern Europe and former Soviet Union	619	556	908	2083
World	3642	1857	2714	8213
1990				
Rich, developed economies	2578	1090	1251	4919
Newly industrializing economies	393	143	80	616
Other developing economies	639	266	1011	1916
Eastern Europe and former Soviet Union	655	865	869	2389
World	4265	2364	3211	9839
2000				
Rich, developed economies	2554	1226	1319	5099
Newly industrializing economies	689	225	125	1039
Other developing economies	1149	530	1482	3161
Eastern Europe and former Soviet Union	719	964	923	2606
World	5111	2945	3849	11905
2010				
Rich, developed economies	2603	1257	1229	5089
Newly industrializing economies	857	319	167	1343
Other developing economies	1437	699	2150	4286
Eastern Europe and former Soviet Union	789	1059	976	2824
World	5686	3334	4522	13542
2020				
Rich, developed economies	2642	1242	1142	5026
Newly industrializing economies	1113	508	220	1841
Other developing economies	2003	986	2825	5814
Eastern Europe and former Soviet Union	931	1216	1040	3187
World	6689	3952	5227	15868

Source: Institute for Economic Analysis.

trasts with an increase of 151 percent under the Reference scenario. Much of this growth under the OCF scenario occurs in the newly industrializing and other developing economies, where fossil fuel use triples, even with substantial improvements in energy efficiency, because of increased production in energy-intensive sectors and increases in the consumption of energy services by households. The mix of fossil fuels does not change very much after 1990, despite projected increases in the use of natural gas in most regions, mainly because of the rapid growth of two major coal-consuming developing regions, centrally planned Asia and low-income Asia. Improved energy efficiency in transportation is offset by the rapid rise in the use of transportation services in developing regions.

Worldwide, production of electricity grows only slightly faster than fossil-fuel use between 1990 and 2020. However, there is considerable variation among the regions. In the developed regions, energy conservation results in slow growth of electricity use (similar to the growth in the use of fossil fuels), and their share of world production of electricity falls from 67 percent in 1990 to 38 percent in 2020. Despite strong energy conservation measures, increased household use of electricity and the displacement of some fossil-fuel use by electricity result in much more rapid growth of electricity than of fossil fuels in developing regions and, to a lesser degree, in Eastern Europe and the former Soviet Union.

Carbon emissions increase under the OCF scenario roughly 60 percent, to 9 billion tons (of carbon) per year by 2020 (see Table 3.5). High-income North America and Western Europe manage to stabilize carbon emissions slightly below 1990 levels under the assumptions of the OCF scenario. Sulfur emissions increase only 16 percent to 147 million tons, even though the combustion of coal increases substantially, reflecting the greater use of pollution control

Table 3.5. Emissions of carbon dioxide, sulfur oxides, and nitrogen oxides under the OCF scenario, 1980–2020

	1980	1990	2000	2010	2020
A. *Carbon dioxide (millions of metric tons)*					
Levels of emissions					
Rich, developed economies	2592	2790	2877	2850	2799
Newly industrializing economies	249	339	573	738	997
Other developing economies	678	1180	1906	2605	3515
Eastern Europe and former Soviet Union	1211	1323	1435	1548	1733
World total	4730	5632	6791	7740	9044
Regional distribution					
Rich, developed economies	0.55	0.50	0.42	0.37	0.31
Newly industrializing economies	0.05	0.06	0.08	0.10	0.11
Other developing economies	0.14	0.21	0.28	0.34	0.39
Eastern Europe and former Soviet Union	0.26	0.23	0.21	0.20	0.19
World total	1.00	1.00	1.00	1.00	1.00
Per capita emissions (kg)					
Rich, developed economies	3067	3070	2978	2671	3073
Newly industrializing economies	492	552	795	899	1091
Other developing economies	250	352	463	532	624
Eastern Europe and former Soviet Union	3210	3269	3351	3433	3681
World total	1066	1067	1089	1078	1122

Table 3.5. (continued)

	1980	1990	2000	2010	2020
B. *Sulfur oxides (millions of metric tons of SO_2 equivalent)*					
Level of emissions					
Rich, developed economies	51	45	42	38	35
Newly industrializing economies	5	8	13	15	20
Other developing economies	19	29	41	50	59
Eastern Europe and former Soviet Union	50	45	41	37	34
World total	125	127	137	140	147
Regional distribution					
Rich, developed economies	0.41	0.36	0.31	0.27	0.24
Newly industrializing economies	0.04	0.06	0.10	0.11	0.14
Other developing economies	0.15	0.23	0.30	0.36	0.40
Eastern Europe and former Soviet Union	0.40	0.35	0.30	0.27	0.23
World total	1.00	1.00	1.00	1.00	1.00
Per capita emissions (kg)					
Rich, developed economies	61	50	43	37	33
Newly industrializing economies	11	13	18	19	22
Other developing economies	7	9	10	10	11
Eastern Europe and former Soviet Union	131	111	96	83	71
World total	28	24	22	20	18
C. *Nitrogen oxides (millions of metric tons of NO_2 equivalent)*					
Levels of emissions					
Rich, developed economies	35	35	35	34	32
Newly industrializing economies	5	6	11	15	20
Other developing economies	10	17	26	35	49
Eastern Europe and former Soviet Union	19	21	22	24	27
World total	69	78	94	108	127
Regional distribution					
Rich, developed economies	0.51	0.45	0.38	0.32	0.25
Newly industrializing economies	0.07	0.08	0.12	0.13	0.16
Other developing economies	0.14	0.21	0.27	0.32	0.38
Eastern Europe and former Soviet Union	0.28	0.26	0.24	0.22	0.21
World total	1.00	1.00	1.00	1.00	1.00
Per capita emissions (kg)					
Rich, developed economies	42	38	37	34	30
Newly industrializing economies	10	10	15	18	22
Other developing economies	4	5	6	7	9
Eastern Europe and former Soviet Union	1	51	52	54	56
World total	16	15	15	15	16

Source: Institute for Economic Analysis.

equipment in developed regions and coal washing in developing regions. Nitrogen emissions are 63 percent higher than in 1990; the increased use of emission controls for both stationary and mobile sources is offset especially by the expanded use of automobiles in developing countries.

In the absence of structural change (i.e., under the Reference scenario), achieving the same GDP in 2020 would require nearly 56 percent more energy than under the OCF scenario, with a higher share (39 percent vs. 33 percent) contributed by coal, the fuel with the highest carbon and sulfur contents per unit of energy. Annual emissions of carbon, sulfur, and nitrogen would increase nearly two and a half times between 1990 and 2020 under the Reference scenario.

Over the period 1980–2020, there is a decided shift in the use of fuels, and in associated emissions, from the developed to the developing regions; this is seen in Tables 3.4 and 3.5, respectively. The rich, developed economies accounted for 55 percent of carbon emissions due to the combustion of fossil fuels in 1980 (and a greater share in earlier years); this is projected to fall to 31 percent by 2020 (Table 3.5). Their share of sulfur emissions drops from 41 percent to 24 percent, and that of nitrogen emissions from 51 percent to 25 percent. On a per capita basis, the emissions are still highest in the rich economies, Eastern Europe, and the former Soviet Union. The reduction in emissions that could be achieved under several alternative scenarios will be examined after a discussion of sectoral results under the OCF scenario.

Growth of Individual Economic Sectors

Production

Individual sectors naturally grow at different rates, and these differences cannot be adequately reflected in aggregate statistics. Sectoral rates of growth, relative to growth in GDP and in population, respectively, are tabulated for four groupings of regions, for the world as a whole, and for forty-four sectors in Tables 3.6 and 3.7.* Some of the highlights of these tables, including the underlying details for the sixteen World Model regions, are summarized below.

On a worldwide basis, eleven of the forty-four sectors grow faster than total world product. These are textiles and apparel; furniture and fixtures; miscellaneous manufactures (consumer items); fruits, vegetables, and cash crops (called "other agriculture"); cement; services; construction; transport equipment (other than motor vehicles and aircraft); printing and publishing; electric machinery; and construction.

In almost all regions, the extraction of fuels and agricultural crops grows faster than population but slower than GDP. Notable exceptions are the production of natural gas, which grows very rapidly (even faster than GDP) throughout Asia and in the oil-rich Middle East, and production of fruits, vegetables, and cash crops (other agriculture), which increases steeply in a number of developing regions. In most regions, per capita use of iron, lead, nickel, and copper falls between 1990 and 2020. However, there is increased per capita use of bauxite and, to a lesser extent, zinc.

Most manufacturing sectors in the rich, developed economies, and to a lesser extent in Eastern Europe and the former Soviet Union, grow at about the same rate as overall GDP; while there is regional and sectoral variability, the growth is much more even than in the developing regions. Among the fastest-growing sectors in the rich countries are transportation equipment (including

---

* Sometimes the average for a grouping of regions is larger than that for any region in the group. This result may appear counterintuitive; the reason for it is shown in Appendix 2 to this chapter.

Table 3.6. Growth in sectoral output relative to growth in GDP between 1990 and 2020 under the OCF scenario (growth of sectoral output divided by growth of GDP)

		Rich, developed regions	Newly industrializing regions	Other developing regions	Eastern Europe and former Soviet Union	World
Resource outputs						
SE5	Copper	0.48	0.39	0.36	0.52	0.50
SE6	Bauxite	1.04	0.68	0.64	0.75	0.93
SE7	Nickel	0.56	0.41	0.40	0.55	0.52
SE8	Zinc	0.74	0.50	0.47	0.50	0.64
SE9	Lead	0.45	0.43	0.44	0.50	0.49
SE10	Iron	0.56	0.36	0.45	0.37	0.52
SE11	Petroleum	0.44	0.71	0.57	0.52	0.68
SE12	Natural gas	0.59	0.93	0.98	0.66	0.72
SE13	Coal	0.51	0.47	0.76	0.60	0.71
Sectoral outputs						
FS1	Fish	0.56	0.34	0.34	0.54	0.51
SE1	Livestock	0.73	0.67	0.77	0.72	0.85
SE2	Oil crops	0.78	0.66	0.69	0.79	0.91
SE3	Grains	0.73	0.73	0.66	0.76	0.86
SE4	Root crops	0.70	0.51	0.59	0.66	0.78
XX1	Other agriculture	0.99	0.76	0.96	0.88	1.10
XX2	Other resources	0.97	0.90	0.89	0.76	0.94
XX3	Food processing	0.84	1.22	1.37	0.79	0.81
XX4	Petroleum refining	0.30	1.08	1.11	0.52	0.57
XX5	Metal processing	0.80	0.65	0.70	0.58	0.71
XX6	Textiles, apparel	1.15	0.77	0.99	1.07	1.16
XX7	Wood	0.90	0.88	1.13	0.78	0.96
XX8	Furniture, fixtures	0.96	1.13	1.23	0.68	1.20
XX9	Paper	0.97	1.08	1.22	0.98	0.93
XX10	Printing and publish.	1.03	1.64	1.44	1.18	1.00
XX11	Rubber products	0.94	1.16	1.24	1.00	0.91
XX12	Industrial chemicals	0.98	0.86	1.01	0.97	0.97
XX13	Fertilizer	1.02	0.46	0.68	0.83	0.86
XX14	Finished chemicals	1.00	1.03	1.37	0.98	0.95
XX15	Cement	0.89	0.83	1.10	0.62	1.11
XX16	Glass	0.92	1.01	1.19	0.85	0.96
XX17	Motor vehicles	0.73	1.00	1.65	1.13	0.76
XX18	Other transportation equip.	1.10	0.47	1.09	0.80	1.04
XX19	Aircraft	0.99	0.98	0.99	0.95	0.90
XX20	Metal products	0.90	0.86	1.10	0.85	0.88
XX21	Machinery	0.96	0.63	1.13	0.68	0.87
XX22	Electrical machinery	1.01	1.19	1.23	1.31	1.01
XX23	Instruments	1.00	1.14	1.21	0.78	0.92
XX24	Miscellaneous manufactures	1.09	0.78	1.10	1.28	1.12
XX25	Electricity	0.58	1.24	1.05	0.78	0.78
XX26	Construction	0.94	1.13	1.22	0.83	1.01
XX27	Trade	0.92	1.27	1.25	0.94	0.95
XX28	Transportation	0.98	1.00	1.01	0.93	1.00
XX29	Communications	0.91	1.12	1.13	0.96	0.91
XX30	Services	1.03	1.12	1.17	1.13	1.04

Notes: 1. For each sector, the reported figure, X, is calculated as $(X_{2020}/X_{1990})/(GDP_{2020}/GDP_{1990})$.

2. There is considerable diversity in the relative growth rates among the regions that make up a regional group.

3. The growth rate for the regional groups, or for the world as a whole, may lie outside the range of growth rates for the component regions. See Appendix 2 to this chapter for an explanation of why this occurs.

Source: Institute for Economic Analysis.

Table 3.7. Growth in sectoral output relative to population growth between 1990 and 2020 under the OCF (growth of sectoral output divided by growth of population)

		Rich, developed regions	Newly industrializing regions	Other developing regions	Eastern Europe and former Soviet Union	World
Resource outputs						
SE5	Copper	0.82	0.94	0.78	0.90	0.76
SE6	Bauxite	1.78	1.66	1.39	1.30	1.40
SE7	Nickel	0.96	0.99	0.87	0.94	0.78
SE8	Zinc	1.26	1.21	1.01	0.86	0.96
SE9	Lead	0.77	1.03	0.95	0.86	0.74
SE10	Iron	0.96	0.87	0.96	0.63	0.78
SE11	Petroleum	0.75	1.73	1.24	0.90	1.02
SE12	Natural gas	1.01	2.27	2.12	1.14	1.09
SE13	Coal	0.88	1.14	1.65	1.04	1.07
Sectoral outputs						
FS1	Fish	0.95	0.84	0.74	0.93	0.77
SE1	Livestock	1.24	1.62	1.67	1.24	1.29
SE2	Oil crops	1.33	1.60	1.50	1.36	1.37
SE3	Grains	1.25	1.78	1.42	1.31	1.30
SE4	Root crops	1.20	1.24	1.28	1.13	1.17
XX1	Other agriculture	1.68	1.84	2.08	1.51	1.66
XX2	Other resources	1.65	2.20	1.93	1.31	1.42
XX3	Food processing	1.43	2.97	2.96	1.35	1.23
XX4	Petroleum refining	0.52	2.63	2.41	0.89	0.86
XX5	Metal processing	1.36	1.57	1.51	1.00	1.08
XX6	Textiles, apparel	1.96	1.88	2.14	1.83	1.75
XX7	Wood	1.53	2.15	2.45	1.34	1.44
XX8	Furniture, fixtures	1.63	2.74	2.67	1.18	1.82
XX9	Paper	1.65	2.61	2.64	1.68	1.40
XX10	Printing and publish.	1.75	3.98	3.12	2.02	1.51
XX11	Rubber products	1.61	2.82	2.67	1.72	1.37
XX12	Industrial chemicals	1.67	2.09	2.19	1.67	1.47
XX13	Fertilizer	1.74	1.12	1.46	1.43	1.30
XX14	Finished chemicals	1.70	2.50	2.97	1.69	1.44
XX15	Cement	1.52	2.01	2.38	1.07	1.67
XX16	Glass	1.56	2.45	2.57	1.45	1.45
XX17	Motor vehicles	1.24	2.43	3.56	1.94	1.14
XX18	Other transportation equip.	1.88	1.13	2.36	1.38	1.56
XX19	Aircraft	1.68	2.37	2.14	1.64	1.36
XX20	Metal products	1.54	2.10	2.38	1.46	1.32
XX21	Machinery	1.64	1.53	2.45	1.16	1.32
XX22	Electrical machinery	1.72	2.88	2.65	2.24	1.52
XX23	Instruments	1.71	2.78	2.61	1.34	1.39
XX24	Miscellaneous manufactures	1.86	1.90	2.37	2.20	1.69
XX25	Electricity	0.99	3.01	2.27	1.34	1.18
XX26	Construction	1.61	2.74	2.64	1.43	1.52
XX27	Trade	1.57	3.09	2.71	1.62	1.43
XX28	Transportation	1.67	2.42	2.18	1.59	1.51
XX29	Communications	1.54	2.71	2.45	1.65	1.37
XX30	Services	1.76	2.72	2.54	1.93	1.56

Notes: 1. For each sector, the reported figure, X, is calculated as $(X_{2020}/X_{1990})/(POP_{2020}/POP_{1990})$.

2. There is considerable diversity in the relative growth rates among the regions that make up a regional group.

3. The growth rate for the regional groups, or for the world as a whole, may lie outside the range of growth rates for its component regions. See Appendix 2 to this chapter for an explanation for why this occurs.

Source: Institute for Economic Analysis.

motor vehicles) and miscellaneous manufacturing, which includes a wide array of mainly consumer items such as watches and clocks, toys, and sporting equipment; and services.

International Trade

Worldwide, exports and imports grow at about the same rate as GDP under the Reference scenario and slightly less under the OCF scenario. The total volume of trade is lower under the OCF scenario than under the Reference scenario, largely because of reduced sectoral requirements for fuel and nonfuel minerals and a correspondingly lower volume of trade in these commodities. Trade in agricultural commodities, like production, grows more rapidly under the OCF scenario than the Reference scenario, but both increase less than GDP because the increased per capita incomes over the period are accompanied by a reduced share of food in total consumption. Trade in most manufactured consumer goods is somewhat higher under the OCF scenario, reflecting the higher level of consumption. Trade in electrical machinery is higher, under the OCF scenario, reflecting the increasing importance of electronics projected for this scenario relative to the Reference scenario. Worldwide, trade grows most rapidly in electrical machinery, textiles, printing and publishing, and cement under the OCF scenario; the last two sectors, however, account for very little of world trade.

Changes in trade patterns are different for each region. Under the OCF scenario, exports grow more rapidly than imports in the developed economies, Eastern Europe, and the former Soviet Union, while the reverse is true in the newly industrializing regions and in other developing economies. This pattern of trade partly reflects some conservation of primary materials, especially fuel and nonfuel minerals, and the increasing importance of a number of manufactured goods, exported mainly by the developed regions. These are finished chemicals, transportation equipment other than motor vehicles, electrical machinery, professional instruments, services, and miscellaneous consumer items.

In the developed regions exports of almost all manufactured goods grow more rapidly than GDP, and most imports grow more slowly than GDP. In the Newly Industrializing regions, virtually all exports grow less rapidly than GDP, while most imports grow more rapidly. In other developing economies, Eastern Europe, and the former Soviet Union, both exports and imports of many commodities grow more rapidly than GDP; however, on balance, import growth outstrips export growth in the developing countries, while the reverse is true in the other two regions.

Results of Alternative Scenarios

Four alternative scenarios were described in Chapter 2—the OCF scenario coupled with more reliance on hydroelectric and nuclear power (OCF/HN), the OCF scenario with more use of solar energy (OCF/S), the OCF scenario with more rapid modernization of the energy-intensive sectors in China and India (OCF/CI), and a final version which combined the last scenario with more reliance on hydroelectric and nuclear power (OCF/HNCI). The results show that increased use of nuclear and hydroelectric power, or of solar technologies for electricity generation and rapid modernization of productive capacity in developing countries can reduce carbon and other emissions at relatively low cost (that is, with a tradeoff of consumption for investment that is relatively small on a global scale) although with increased investment and increased debt in the countries in question. However, these measures still do not stabilize global emissions at the 1990 level, and other aspects of the associated environmental damage—notably the accumulation of nuclear waste and the flooding of inhabited lands—that are not tracked by the model need to be taken into account in a full assessment of these scenarios.

Greater Use of Nonfossil-Fuel Electricity Technologies

Global consumption and investment requirements are virtually the same under the OCF/HN and OCF scenarios since the more expensive nuclear and hydroelectricity generating capacities are phased in over a ten-year period between 2010 and 2020 and the costs are partly offset by reduced investment requirements in fuel extraction and refining sectors. Global carbon and nitrogen emissions are about 4 percent lower than under the OCF scenario, and sulfur emissions are about 6 percent lower (Table 3.8). Under this scenario, the assumed shares of hydroelectric and nuclear power are much higher than is probable over this time horizon; still, these technologies would have to be introduced on an even more massive scale to prevent the increase in emissions. Reductions in carbon, sulfur, and nitrogen emissions under the OCF/S scenario, with greater use of solar energy, are virtually identical to those under the OCF/HN scenario: about 4 percent less carbon and 6 percent less sulfur and nitrogen by 2020 than under the OCF scenario.

More Rapid Introduction of Modern Technology in China and India

Scenario OCF/CI involves the rapid modernization of energy-intensive sectors in China and India. We assumed that by 2020 they have the same input structures as the comparable sectors in Japan. Carbon, sulfur, and nitrogen emissions are 8–10 percent lower for the developing regions and 3–4 percent lower for the world as a whole relative to the OCF scenario in 2020. Under this scenario, global consumption and investment are nearly the same as under the OCF scenario in 2020. However, in centrally planned Asia (China) and low-income Asia (India), consumption is about 3 percent lower, investment 7 percent higher, and the balance of trade worsens (10 percent) as these regions import more capital goods.

Scenario OCF/HNCI combines the assumptions of Scenarios OCF/HN and OCF/CI, greater use of nuclear and hydroelectric power throughout the world and

Table 3.8. Emissions of carbon dioxide, sulfur oxides, and nitrogen oxides in 1990 and 2020 under five alternative scenarios

	OCF		Each scenario outcome as a percentage of OCF in 2020			
	1990	2020	OCF/HN	OCF/S	OCF/CI	OCF/HNCI
Carbon dioxide						
(10⁶ metric tons of carbon)						
Rich, developed regions	2791	2799	95	96	100	95
Newly industrializing regions	339	997	95	96	100	95
Other developing regions	1179	3515	95	96	82	78
Eastern Europe and former Soviet Union	1323	1733	96	96	100	96
World	5632	9044	96	96	93	89
Sulfur oxides						
(10⁶ metric tons of SO₂ equivalent)						
Rich, developed regions	46	35	91	91	100	91
Newly industrializing regions	8	20	90	90	100	90
Other developing regions	29	59	95	95	80	76
Eastern Europe and former Soviet Union	45	34	94	94	100	94
World	127	148	93	93	92	86
Nitrogen oxides						
(10⁶ metric tons of NO₂ equivalent)						
Rich, developed regions	35	32	94	94	100	94
Newly industrializing regions	6	20	95	95	100	95
Other developing regions	17	49	96	96	84	80
Eastern Europe and former Soviet Union	21	27	93	93	100	93
World	78	128	95	95	94	88

Notes: 1. See text for description of the alternative scenarios: HN (hydro and nuclear), S (solar), CI (more rapid modernization of industry in China and India).

2. Regional figures may not sum to the world total because of rounding.

3. Rich, developed economies include high-income North America, Japan, high-income Western Europe, Oceania, medium-income Western Europe, and southern Africa. Newly industrializing economies include newly industrializing Latin America and newly industrializing Asia. Other developing economies include low-income Latin America, centrally planned Asia, low-income Asia, major oil producers, North Africa and other Middle East, and Sub-Saharan Africa.

Source: Institute for Economic Analysis.

rapid modernization of the energy-intensive sectors in China and India. Global investment is 2 percent higher and consumption 1 percent lower in 2020 relative to the OCF scenario and costs, in the tradeoff of investment for consumption, to centrally planned Asian and low-income Asia are similar to those under the OCF/CI scenario. Global carbon emissions are 11 percent lower than under the OCF scenario but are still 43 percent higher than in 1990; the story is similar for nitrogen emissions. Sulfur emissions, however, are reduced by 14 percent relative to the OCF scenario and are approximately the same as in 1990.

These results suggest that the development decisions made in China, India, and other developing countries, on the basis of the technologies that have been discussed, have considerable significance for the global environment. It may be possible for the international community to influence these decisions if this advice is accompanied by financial assistance in the acquisition of new capital goods.

Appendix 1. Comparison of Results with Other Studies

In this section, we compare our projections of future energy use and the associated emissions with those made in other studies. To make the comparisons most useful, it is necessary to distinguish the underlying assumptions about growth, in both the overall levels of economic activities and population, from the assumptions about technological change. In the numerous studies about future energy use and carbon emissions that appear in the literature, the assumptions of the first kind generally are explicitly reported. However, assumptions about technological change are usually extremely aggregate and not well documented; no other study of the world economy reports technical parameters that can be directly compared with the sector-level assumptions developed for this study. In addition, none of these studies makes projections for the entire world that are as disaggregated as the sixteen-region World Model projections.

We have selected three widely cited studies that are global in scope and represent a spectrum of assumptions about future energy use. These are briefly described below, and their results are subsequently compared with those obtained using the World Model.

Romain-Frisch's report (1989) to the Congress of the World Energy Conference (WEC) about projected world energy use in the year 2020 reports results for a Moderate Growth scenario and a Low Growth scenario. These differ in their assumptions about average annual GDP growth rates (3 percent and 2 percent, respectively, for the world as a whole), as well as about population growth and projected future energy prices. The Moderate Growth scenario is similar to the World Model OCF scenario in terms of GDP and population growth rates. Energy conservation and the introduction of more efficient technologies are assumed in both WEC scenarios, but specific assumptions are not discussed, with one exception: only modest growth is anticipated in the use of renewable energy sources and nuclear power. The structure of the model used for projections is not described in the report.

A study for the U.S. Environmental Protection Agency (EPA, 1989) includes four scenarios, two versions of a Slowly Changing World (SCW) and two versions of a Rapidly Changing World (RCW). The SCW scenario assumes very slow GDP growth coupled with minimal technological changes, while the RCW scenario assumes rapid GDP growth, the effects of which are moderated by rapid introduction of new technology. The RCW scenario corresponds fairly closely in intent to the OCF scenario analyzed with the World Model. More extreme approaches to reducing carbon emissions, aimed at stabilizing emissions of carbon (and other greenhouse gases) at 1985 levels, are included in the alternative versions of the SCW and RCW scenarios (labeled "with stabilizing policies"). These assumptions include, for example, the widespread use of solar energy and biomass. The EPA study does not include a "no-change" scenario comparable to the Reference scenario of the World Model.

The EPA study divides the world into three regions: the developed countries, Eastern Europe and the former Soviet Union, and the developing countries.

There is a detailed discussion of alternative energy-using technologies. Unfortunately, the technical discussion is not directly associated with parameter changes. Indeed, the EPA report acknowledges at the outset that the various parts of the study are "linked" but not truly integrated.

A study of the U.S. Working Group on Global Energy Efficiency (WGGEE) (Levine et al., 1991) makes use of the model developed by Edmonds and Reilly (1985) and distinguishes nine regions and five end-use sectors. Two scenarios are analyzed: a Reference scenario (not the same as the World Model Reference scenario since theirs includes moderate technology changes) and an Efficiency scenario. Both scenarios are based on a 2.5 percent average annual rate of growth of world GDP over the period 1985–2025 (our scenarios assume 2.8 percent growth). The technological changes are described in narrative fashion and, as in the EPA study, the technical discussions are not directly associated with parameter changes. Nonetheless, the assumptions underlying the Efficiency scenario appear to be in the same spirit as those of the OCF scenario. Forecasts of energy demand for individual regions were conducted by three separate research groups, each using its own methodologies. These forecasts were then linked, in a way that is not described in the paper, to the model of Edmonds and Reilly.

Projections of Fossil Fuel Use

The projections of fossil fuel use in 2020 are comparable for the OCF scenario of the World Model (16 billion tons of coal equivalent [tce]), the Moderate Growth scenario of WEC (15 billion tce), and the RCW scenario of the EPA (18 billion tce); these are shown in Table 3.9. (The WGGEE study reports only total primary energy consumption, which is not directly comparable because it includes the energy content of electricity from nuclear and hydroelectric power plants, as well as fossil fuel use.) Much of the difference among these three projections of fossil fuel use is explained by the different assumptions about GDP growth. As to the future mix of fossil fuels, the World Model projects a somewhat larger share for natural gas and a smaller share for coal than the WEC study and the EPA studies.

Climate Change and Projection of Carbon Emissions

Studies conducted by the U.S. National Academy of Sciences since the late 1970s have consistently concluded that a doubling of the concentration of carbon dioxide in the atmosphere relative to the preindustrial concentration would result in climatic change. The concentration in 1985 was 350 ppm, compared to 290 ppm 100 years ago, and it is likely to continue to increase over the next century. There is great uncertainty both about the relationship between carbon emissions (as projected by the models of the economies) and carbon concentrations and about the likely magnitude and timing of potential climatic change

Table 3.9. Projections of fuel use and carbon emissions according to four studies in 2020 (fuel in millions of tons of coal equivalent, carbon in billions of tons)

	Oil	Gas	Coal	Total fossil fuel	Carbon emissions from fossil fuels	Annual growth of world GDP
World Model OCF	6689	3952	5227	15868	9.0	2.8%
World Energy Conference						
Moderate growth	6013	3504	5814	15332	8.9[a]	3.0
Low growth	5363	2961	5650	12974	8.2[a]	2.0
Environmental Protection Agency[b]						
Slowly changing world (SCW)	—	—	—	12000	7.2	2.0
Rapidly changing world (RCW)	—	—	—	18000	10.3	3.6
SCW with "stabilizing policies"	—	—	—	9000	5.5	2.0
RCW with "stabilizing policies"	—	—	—	9000	5.5	3.6
Working Group on Global Energy Efficiency[c]						
Reference (moderate tech. change)	—	—	—	—	10.6	2.5
Efficiency	—	—	—	—	7.6	2.5

—: not available.

a. based on fuel use and IEA emission parameters.

b. Projections for 2025. Note that the figures for fossil fuel are only approximate as they are reported in charts but not tabulated.

c. WCGEE reported projected primary energy consumption only; also, fossil fuel use not distinguished from primary electricity.

Note: The World Energy Conference reports fuel use in tons of oil equivalent (toe); the conversion factor to tce is 1.4285. The EPA reports fuel use in exajoules; the conversion factor to tce is 34.12×10^6. WGGEE reports fuel use in quads; the conversion factor to tce is 36.00×10^6.

Source: World Model: Institute for Economic Analysis; WEC: Romain-Frisch, 1989; EPA: EPA, 1990; WGGEE: Levine, et al., 1991.

(EPA, 1989). Climate models have been used to investigate these relationships, but they need to rely on economic models to project future levels of emissions, which depend, in part, on future energy use.

Current research suggests that at least 50 percent of the carbon currently being released into the atmosphere remains there. The atmospheric concentration of carbon would continue to increase (to nearly 400 ppm by 2025 and more slowly thereafter, to nearly 500 ppm by 2100) even if future annual carbon emissions remain constant at today's rates. In fact, a 75 percent reduction in annual carbon emissions below their 1985 rate would be required to stabilize the current atmospheric carbon concentration (EPA, 1989). If annual carbon emissions double between 1985 and 2025, the concentration will clearly exceed 400 ppm by 2025 and will accelerate rapidly thereafter, reaching over three times the preindustrial concentration by the end of the twenty-first century. The corresponding increase in temperature from such concentrations is estimated at 1.2–3.5° C by 2025 and greater than 6° C by the end of the century (EPA, 1989).

Under the World Model Reference scenario, which assumes growth without technological changes, global emissions associated with projected energy use would be nearly three times as high in 2020 as in 1985. The results of the

OCF scenario showed that future emissions can be substantially reduced from what could be anticipated on the basis of today's technologies with no sacrifice of economic expansion in the world as a whole. However, carbon emissions continue to rise and by 2020 are indeed 75 percent higher than in 1985 (see Table 3.5).

The other studies show similar results. No carbon projections were made in the WEC study, but we have used their energy projections and the fuel-specific emission parameters developed for this study to estimate future carbon emissions. (Carbon emissions shown in Table 3.9 differ less between the two WEC scenarios than total fossil fuel use because of the greater reliance on coal in the Low Growth scenario.) The resulting projections, and those of the Efficiency Scenario of the WGGEE study, fall into the same range as the World Model projections.

In conclusion, the projections of fossil fuel use and carbon emissions made by the World Model system are of the same magnitude as those obtained in other studies. The World Model framework has the advantages of being comprehensive in its regional and sectoral coverage and fully integrated conceptually, ensuring that all the economic and emission results are compatible. Both the model and the data base are formulated in terms of detailed technical parameters, on a multisectoral and multiregional basis, that can be directly evaluated by technical experts and readily changed in order to explore the consequences of alternative scenarios.

Sulfur and Nitrogen Emissions

Estimates of past carbon emissions from all combustion sources combined are available at the country, regional, and global levels. In addition, projections for the future are readily made on the basis of projected fossil fuel use because the two are closely related. There are, however, few estimates of emissions of sulfur oxides or nitrogen oxides. Those estimates that have been made for the past are often not comprehensive with respect to combustion sources and are limited, in geographic coverage, mainly to Europe and North America. Furthermore, because the quantity of fuel use has a more complex relationship to the amount of sulfur and nitrogen emissions than in the case of carbon, few projections for the future—and none that we know of at the global level which also provides the level, with comprehensive sectoral and regional detail—have been made before this study. Estimates of these emissions, based on the technical parameters developed for this study, are compared with emissions reported in other sources (which were not used in developing the parameters) for the most recent year for which this is practical, 1980, to provide an indirect evaluation of our emission parameters.

Emissions of sulfur oxides and nitrogen oxides have been compiled for a number of regions for 1980 by the UN Statistical Commission with the European Economic Commission (UN/ECE) (1987) and by the UN Environmental Program with the World Health Organization (UN/WHO) (1988). These are shown, along with the World Model estimates for 1980, in Tables 3.10 and 3.11. Because both comparison studies relied on estimates from a wide variety of sources, the coverage of combustion sources is not, and cannot be expected to be, consistent. But the most important obstacle to using these figures (for comparison to World Model results) is that not all countries in any given region are included.

In order to compensate for the incomplete geographic coverage, the use of estimates for 1978 (rather than 1980) for some countries, and the incomplete coverage of sources of emissions, we constructed a "combined estimate," based on information from both the UN/ECE and the UN/WHO reports, for some regions. This combined estimate used the reported emissions for any country in a region included in either one, but not both, of these studies. For countries included in both studies, the higher estimate, or the estimate for the year closer to 1980, was used. This method was particularly useful for medium-income Western Europe and Eastern Europe, as only a few countries in each region were included in either comparison study.

Table 3.10. Estimates of anthropogenic sulfur oxide emissions by region in 1980 according to three sources (millions of tons of sulfur dioxide)

Region	UNEP/WHO	UN/ECE	Combined	World Model (OCF)
1 High-income North America	27.81	27.85		23.97
2 Newly industrializing Latin America	—	—		4.20
3 Other Latin America	—	—		1.00
4 High-income Western Europe	18.24	13.52	18.44	15.80
5 Medium-income Western Europe	4.46	3.92	5.45	6.40
6 Eastern Europe	12.57	8.83	14.07	25.70
7 Former Soviet Union	— 25.00[a]	12.80		23.80
8 Centrally planned Asia	14.21	—		13.66
9 Japan	1.64	1.26		1.60
10 Newly industrializing Asia	—	—		2.00
11 Low-income Asia	2.23	—		2.44
12 Major oil producers	0.20	—		0.84
13 Other Middle East and North Africa	0.29	—		0.73
14 Sub-Saharan Africa	—	—		0.33
15 Southern Africa	—	—		2.04
16 Oceania	1.48	—		1.47
World total	—	—		125.03

—: Not available.

a. Obtained from McCormick, 1985.

Notes: 1. The UNEP/WHO and UN/ECE estimates often do not cover all countries in each region. The coverage of activities is not uniform. In some countries, notably the United States, industrial emissions from sources other than combustion are included.

2. Three regions are covered by both sources, but with significant geographic gaps. In the "Combined" column we have aggregated the emissions for countries reported in only one of the sources and the higher of the two estimates, so as to include more economic activities, for countries included in both.

Source: Institute for Economic Analysis based on UN Environmental Program (UNEP) and World Health Organization (WHO), 1988, p.90; UN Statistical Commission and the Economic Commission for Europe (ECE), 1987, Table I–15.

Table 3.11. Estimates of anthropogenic nitrogen oxide emissions by region in 1980 according to three sources (millions of tons of nitrogen dioxide)

Region	UNEP/WHO	UN/ECE	Combined	World Model (OCF)
1 High-income North America	22.21	22.03		18.00
2 Newly industrializing Latin America	—	—		3.60
3 Other Latin America	—	—		1.20
4 High-income Western Europe	10.73	8.51	10.80	11.80
5 Medium-income Western Europe	1.40	1.09	1.53	2.35
6 Eastern Europe	—	2.96		5.00
7 Former Soviet Union	—	—		14.30
8 Centrally planned Asia	4.40	—		5.30
9 Japan	1.34	1.26		1.40
10 Newly industrializing Asia	—	—		1.30
11 Low-income Asia	—	—		1.39
12 Major oil producers	0.10	—		1.00
13 Other Middle East and North Africa	0.11	—		0.47
14 Sub-Saharan Africa	—	—		0.21
15 Southern Africa	—	—		0.71
16 Oceania	0.92	—		0.89
World total	—	—		69.00

—: not available.

Notes: 1. The UNEP/WHO and UN/ECE estimates often do not cover all countries in each region. The coverage of activities is not uniform. In some countries, notably the United States, industrial emissions from sources other than combustion are included.

2. Three regions are covered by both sources but with significant geographic gaps. In the "Combined" column we have aggregated the emissions for countries reported in only one of the sources and the higher of the two estimates, so as to include more economic activities, for countries included in both.

Source: Institute for Economic Analysis based on UN Statistical Commission and the Economic Commission for Europe (ECE), 1987, Table I–15, and UN Environmental Program (UNEP) and World Health Organization (WHO), 1988, p. 92.

Sulfur Oxides

Emissions of sulfur oxides according to the World Model and the comparison studies are shown in Table 3.10. In both comparison studies, emission sources for high-income North America include not only combustion but also industrial processes, which generated about 3.5 million tons of sulfur oxides in 1980. Taking this into account, the three estimates are very similar. Emissions from industrial processes are also included in the comparison studies' estimates for some OECD regions, accounting for their slightly higher totals.

There is a striking difference between the World Model and comparison sources for Eastern Europe: the World Model estimates Eastern European emissions at 25.70 million tons of sulfur dioxide while the comparison studies estimate at most 14.07 million tons. There is also considerable discrepancy in the emissions reported in Table 3.10 for the former Soviet Union. The UN/ECE reports 12.8 million tons, while McCormick (1985), purportedly using the same source documents, reports 25.0 million tons. The lower figure, 12.8 million tons, could have been obtained only under the unrealistic assumption that the average sulfur content of Soviet coal was less than 1 percent. Based on the technical literature, discussed in Chapter 4, we believe that the officially reported emissions for both these regions given in the comparison studies are too low.

The estimates of sulfur emissions for developing regions were reasonably comprehensive only for the two major coal-using regions, China (centrally planned Asia) and India (low-income Asia). The World Model figures correspond closely to these estimates.

Nitrogen Oxides

The UN/ECE and UN/WHO also provide estimates of emissions of nitrogen oxides (see Table 3.11), and many of the same caveats apply: geographic coverage is incomplete, and sources of emissions are not consistently covered. The problem is more severe in the case of nitrogen oxides, however, because direct measurement of these emissions is much more difficult. Sulfur emissions are generated by a relatively small number of sources, and the quantities emitted are governed by reasonably well-defined scientific principles; nitrogen oxides are generated by many diverse sources governed by a variety of mechanisms, often in highly variable circumstances (especially in the case of motor vehicles).

Emissions of nitrogen oxides, as calculated by the World Model, are lower than the estimates of the comparison studies for high-income North America, in part because the comparison studies include emissions from solid waste disposal and forest fires. World Model estimates are roughly the same for other OECD countries and somewhat higher for Eastern Europe. For other regions, even less information was presented in the comparison studies about nitrogen than about sulfur. Many countries were either entirely unaccounted for, or else only emissions from stationary source emissions were reported; this explains why the World Model estimates are generally higher.

Appendix 2: A Note about Results at Different Levels of Aggregation

According to the results reported in Chapter 3, the motor vehicle sector (XX17) will expand more rapidly than the population in all regions between 1990 and 2020. In fact, per capita production is more than three times higher in 2020 than in 1990 in the region containing most developing countries (see Table 3.7). Yet for the world as a whole, per capita production of motor vehicles grows only 14 percent faster than world population, a rate that is lower than that in any of the individual regions. This result may appear counterintuitive, and the purpose of this appendix is to show why it is true. To simplify the demonstration, let us assume that there is one region composed of two countries. We will show that per capita production of automobiles can grow in both countries and yet fall for the region as a whole.

Assume that a region is comprised of a small, rich country and a large, poor one. The volumes of automobile production and population are known for each country at two points in time. Let automobile production per capita in country r

at time t be $c_r^t = a_r^t / p_r^t$, where p is population and a is automobile production, and let the ratio for the region as a whole be $c^t = (a_1^t + a_2^t)/(p_1^t + p_2^t)$. Then the rates of change of automobile production per capita are $g_1 = c_1^2/c_1^1$, $g_2 = c_2^2/c_2^1$, and $g = c^2/c^1$.

Proposition. Assume that $g_1 > g_2$. There may be instances where $g > g_1$ or $g < g_2$.

Example. Take the case where

$a_1^1 = 20$	$a_1^2 = 30$	$a_2^1 = 1$	$a_2^2 = 3$	$a^1 = 21$	$a^2 = 33$
$p_1^1 = 200$	$p_1^2 = 200$	$p_2^1 = 1,000$	$p_2^2 = 2,000$	$p^1 = 1,200$	$p^2 = 2,200$
$c_1^1 = 0.100$	$c_1^2 = 0.150$	$c_2^1 = 0.001$	$c_2^2 = 0.0015$	$c^1 = 0.0175$	$c^2 = 0.0150$

It is easily seen that $g_1 = 1.500$, $g_2 = 1.500$, and $g = 0.857$.

Discussion. The region as a whole experiences a decline in auto production per capita, even though neither country does, because of the rapid growth in the share of population in the poor country where auto production is very small. The following expression, which is readily derived from the definition of g, shows that the low per capita production in the poor country in the second period is weighted by its increasing share of world population:

$$g = \frac{c_1^2 [p_1^2 / (p_1^2 + p_2^2)] + c_2^2 [p_2^2 / (p_1^2 + p_2^2)]}{c_1^1 [p_1^1 / (p_1^1 + p_2^1)] + c_2^1 [p_2^1 / (p_1^1 + p_2^1)]}$$

In the example,

$$\frac{0.150 \, (0.091) + 0.0015 \, (0.909)}{0.100 \, (0.167) + 0.001 \, (0.833)} = 0.857$$

II

CASE STUDIES

The chapters in Part II contain the ten case studies about the energy-intensive and material-intensive sectors that are the principal sources, directly and indirectly, of atmospheric emissions. The cases cover the relation of emissions to the combustion of fuel, electric power generation, industrial energy conservation, metal processing and fabrication, construction, cement, pulp and paper, chemicals, household energy conservation, and motor vehicle transportation. Each case study provides an overview of the status of one or more sectors in all parts of the world economy and describes the prospects for the future of these sectors. Each case study also contains the detailed information used to build the OCF scenario and the alternative scenarios.

An input-output case study methodology was developed to improve consistency among the case studies and to ensure a tight integration of each case study into the World Model and World Data Base. This methodology includes the following steps:

- Identify the relevant World Model sectors and determine the relevant units of analysis.
- Compile control totals for each region and use them to revise the variables and parameters for past years (i.e., 1980 and 1990), if necessary.
- Describe the technologies currently in use in each region and potential technological changes.
- Project parameters for the future on the basis of the technological changes anticipated for each region.
- Document the assumptions that have been made using a standard approach.

A more detailed discussion of the methodology is given in Appendix B.

4

Emissions

The profound, potentially long-lasting consequences of atmospheric pollution and the possible magnitude of the costs associated with controlling emissions demand careful physical and economic assessment of alternative strategies for reducing pollution. While the modeling of the physical emission processes is relatively well developed, the integration of the physical data with an economic model has often been identified as the weakest component of current environmental studies (EPA, 1990; Rind, Rosenzweig, and Rosenzweig, 1988).

In the past, many economic models constructed to address environmental issues have derived emission parameters for pollutants such as oxides of sulfur and nitrogen simply by dividing the reported levels of emissions of a sector by its reported sectoral output in a given year. While this approach, often used even in detailed technical studies, is adequate to replicate the level of emissions for historical periods, it is less useful as a basis for projections for the future because the fuel mix may change and because alternative technologies have different emission characteristics.

This chapter describes the development of parameters to represent emissions of carbon and oxides of sulfur and nitrogen that incorporate technical data about emission characteristics into the World Model. The section on each pollutant begins with a discussion of the technical factors characterizing emissions of the pollutant and identification of the specific data required for their representation within the framework of the World Model. While the parameters representing carbon emissions are relatively straightforward, the challenge of constructing fuel- and sector-specific emission parameters for sulfur and nitrogen for every region in the world required that guidelines be established to set priorities for data collection and to provide a basis for plausible assumptions where data were lacking. These guidelines are described and the estimated emission parameters used in this study are presented for the period 1980–2020.

Carbon Dioxide

The parameters governing the emission of carbon from the combustion of fossil fuels are well established in the technical literature (Keeling, 1973; Marland 1983; Marland and Rotty, 1984). Emission coefficients for carbon dioxide,

51

measured in metric tons of carbon per metric tce burned, are calculated as the product of the carbon content of the fuel and the amount of fuel oxidized. (There are currently no practical methods for removing carbon from the waste gas stream.) The two factors used to construct the carbon emission coefficients are discussed below, and the resulting coefficients are presented in Table 4.1.

Carbon Content of Fuels

The major categories of fossil fuels—oil, gas, and coal—are highly variable in terms of their energy and carbon content per unit of mass or volume. However, there is a very close correlation, based on the chemical and physical properties of the fuels, between the carbon and the energy contents of different grades within each fuel category. For example, the correlation for different grades of coal is close enough that it has been considered reasonable, for the calculation of carbon emissions, to use a single figure to represent the carbon content per ton for coal of all qualities. The same carbon-content parameter can be used for all regions and all years. These parameters are given in Table 4.1.

Oxidation of Fuel Carbon

Combustion of fuels is not always complete, and some portion of fuels is put to other uses in which oxidation may not take place at all, at least not without considerable delay. Incomplete combustion results largely in the formation of carbon monoxide, which is further oxidized to carbon dioxide within a relatively short period of time, so that all but about 1 percent of the carbon from the combustion of coal and gas can be assumed to become carbon dioxide within a year (Marland and Rotty, 1984). Oil is used in a number of applications in which the oxidation of carbon does not take place, such as asphalt and lubricants. This use of oil is represented by a lower oxidation parameter, 92 percent. These factors do not vary significantly among regions or over time, so the same values are used for all regions and years.

Table 4.1. Parameters governing the emission of carbon dioxide by type of fuel (metric tons of carbon per metric ton of coal equivalent)

	Carbon content	Percentage of fuel oxidized	Carbon emission coefficient
Oil	0.626	0.92	0.576
Gas	0.403	0.99	0.399
Coal	0.704	0.99	0.697

Note: These coefficients are used in all regions for all years.

Source: Institute for Economic Analysis, based on Keeling, 1973; Marland, 1983; Marland and Rotty, 1984.

Sulfur Oxides

The combustion of fossil fuels accounts for most of the emissions of sulfur oxides resulting from human activities. Uncontrolled emissions depend directly on the sulfur content of the fuel burned. Sulfur content can range in coal from less than 1 percent to over 7 percent by weight; in crude petroleum, from less than 1 percent to 4 percent (Smil, 1985; WEC, 1974).

Processing of fuels before combustion can reduce fuel sulfur significantly. Coal, which has the highest average sulfur content of the fossil fuels and, in addition, undergoes the least processing, is the largest source of sulfur oxides. Physical coal cleaning at the minehead, practiced to varying degrees in most developed regions, succeeds in removing only the inorganic sulfur, which accounts for 10–60 percent of the total fuel sulfur. Advanced chemical techniques for removing the remaining organic sulfur are still in the experimental stage and are prohibitively expensive. The refining of petroleum eliminates much of the sulfur: the most highly refined petroleum products, such as aviation gasoline, have virtually no sulfur, while the least refined products, such as Number 6 Fuel Oil used by electric utilities, may retain a large part of the fuel sulfur. Natural gas is always de-sulfured in processing; the end product contains negligible amounts of sulfur.

In the World Data Base, the parameters developed to represent the emission of sulfur per unit of fuel, in sulfur dioxide equivalents, are the product of the sulfur content of the fuel by weight (tons of sulfur per ton of fuel), the energy content of the fuel (physical amount of fuel per ton of coal equivalent), the conversion factor relating sulfur dioxide to fuel sulfur (tons of sulfur dioxide per ton of sulfur), and the proportion of sulfur not removed by pollution control equipment. Each of these factors is discussed and quantified below.

Sulfur Content of Fuels

The most important, and the most variable, factor governing sulfur emissions is the sulfur content of the fuel. No systematic, comprehensive information is available about the sulfur content of fuels worldwide, so priorities for data collection and use of rules of thumb for making estimates in the absence of data had to be established.

Data collection efforts focused on coal first, since it is the most important source of global sulfur emissions and it can be treated as a relatively homogeneous fuel, with respect to sulfur content, among coal-using sectors in a given region. However, there is considerable variation in the average sulfur content of coal in different regions. The variation in sulfur content of the different petroleum products requires that sectoral distinctions be made. Each sector uses a different mix of petroleum products, resulting in a different average sulfur content of petroleum. Because of the very low sulfur content of natural gas, it is not treated as a source of sulfur oxides.

Sulfur Content of Coal

The sulfur content of coal is determined by the geological conditions under which the coal was originally formed, and this may vary considerably both among and within regions. The average sulfur content of coal burned in each region depends on the quality of coal mined in that region, the imports of coal from other regions, and the extent of coal washing.

Given the difficulty of obtaining data about the sulfur content of coal used in every country, data collection efforts concentrated first on five World Model regions, which jointly accounted for more than 80 percent of the total coal consumed in 1980: high-income North America, centrally planned Asia, the former Soviet Union, Eastern Europe, and high-income Western Europe (see Table 4.2). Of the other eleven regions (which consumed the remaining 15 percent of total coal in 1980), five regions were minor coal consumers (each burned 1–5 percent of the total coal) and another six regions used insignificant amounts (each accounted for less than 1 percent of the total coal).

Generally, a single country, or several countries, dominate coal use in each region. In the absence of data for each country, the average sulfur content of coal for a region was represented by that of the dominant country or countries. Three of the five major coal-consuming regions are dominated by a single country: the United States accounted for 94 percent of the coal burned in high-income North America in 1980; China accounted for 91 percent of centrally planned Asia's coal consumption; and the former Soviet Union is a single-country region (see Table 4.3). The other two major coal-consuming regions are dominated by several countries: three countries (Germany, United Kingdom, and France) out of twenty accounted for 80 percent of the coal burned in high-income Western Europe in 1980, and three (Poland, the former German Democ-

Table 4.2. Consumption of coal by World Model region in 1980 (millions of metric tons of coal equivalent)

Region	Coal	Consumption
1 High-income North America	570.4	21.7%
7 Former Soviet Union	490.8	18.7
8 Centrally planned Asia	476.5	18.1
6 Eastern Europe	350.9	13.3
4 High-income Western Europe	336.3	12.8
11 Other Asia	102.4	3.9
9 Japan	80.5	3.1
15 Southern Africa	73.7	2.8
5 Medium-income Western Europe	53.0	2.0
16 Oceania	40.1	1.5
10 Newly industrializing Asia	25.6	1.0
2 Newly industrializing Latin America	17.8	0.7
3 Other Latin America	5.1	0.2
14 Sub-Saharan Africa	3.8	0.1
12 Major oil producers	1.8	0.1
13 Other middle-east and northern Africa	1.5	0.1
Total	2631.1	100.0

Source: Institute for Economic Analysis, based on United Nations, 1983.

Table 4.3. Consumption of coal by major countries in World Model regions in 1980 (millions of metric tons of coal equivalent)

1	High-income North America	570.4	100.0%
	United States	538.7	94.4
	Other countries[a] (3)	31.7	5.6
2	Newly industrializing Latin America	17.8	100.0%
	Brazil	8.4	46.8
	Mexico	5.8	32.4
	Other countries (3)	3.6	20.8
3	Low-income Latin America	5.1	100.0%
	Colombia	4.7	92.3
	Other countries (38)	0.4	7.7
4	High-income Western Europe	336.3	100.0%
	Germany, Federal Republic	116.7	34.7
	United Kingdom	101.6	30.2
	France	50.1	14.9
	Other countries (20)	67.7	20.2
5	Medium-income Western Europe	53.8	100.0%
	Spain	18.6	34.5
	Yugoslavia	19.6	36.4
	Turkey	10.4	19.3
	Other countries (6)	5.3	9.8
6	Eastern Europe	350.9	100.0%
	Poland	143.2	40.8
	German Democratic Republic	86.1	24.5
	Czechoslovakia	63.5	18.1
	Other countries (4)	58.2	16.6
7	Soviet Union	490.8	100.0%
8	Centrally planned Asia	476.5	100.0%
	China	432.2	90.7
	Other countries (2)	44.3	9.3
9	Japan	80.5	100.0%
10	Newly industrializing Asia	25.6	100.0%
	Korea	18.8	73.4
	Taiwan[b]	6	23.2
	Other countries (5)	0.8	5.4
11	Low-income Asia	102.4	100.0%
	India	95.1	92.9
	Other countries (15)	7.3	7.1
12	Major oil producers	1.7	100.0%
	Iran	0.9	54.8
	Algeria	0.6	34.7
	Other countries (10)	0.2	10.5
13	Other Middle East and North Africa	1.5	100.0%
	Egypt	0.7	46.2
	Morroco	0.6	42.0
	Other countries (14)	0.2	11.8
14	Sub-Saharan Africa	3.8	100.0%
	Zimbabwe	2.5	65.8
	Other countries (37)	1.3	34.2
15	Southern Africa	73.7	100.0%
	South Africa	73.7	100.0
16	Oceania	40.1	100.0%
	Australia	38.3	95.6
	Other countries[a] (2)	1.8	4.4

a. Including other small countries, territories, and possessions.
b. Coal consumption is estimated for taiwan from OECD statistics.
Note: The figures in parentheses are the number of other countries in the region.
Source: Institute for Economic Analysis, based on United Nations, 1983.

ratic Republic, and Czechoslovakia) out of seven accounted for 83 percent of the coal burned in Eastern Europe.

Data on the sulfur content of coal in these nine countries were used to form emission parameters for sulfur oxides for the five most important coal-burning regions. Where additional data were readily available for other countries in these regions, such as Canada and Western European countries, they were directly incorporated.

The five next most important coal-consuming regions also include one or several dominant countries: India dominates coal use in low-income Asia (93 percent of the region's total coal in 1980); Japan is a single-country region; southern Africa is the only coal consumer in that region; three out of nine countries dominate medium-income Europe (Spain, Yugoslavia, and Turkey account for 90 percent of the region's coal use); and Australia dominates Oceania (96 percent). A similar story can be told for the remaining six regions.

Data on the average sulfur content of coal used in each region in 1980 and 1990 (or more recently, where available) have been derived from published and unpublished sources and personal communications from energy agencies, environmental agencies, trade associations, and mining and other engineering organizations. The sources used for each region are shown in Table 4.4, and the

Table 4.4. Major sources for data on the sulfur content of fuels by World Model region

Region	Data source
All regions unless otherwise specified	Moller, 1984; Smil, 1985; World Energy Conference, 1974, 1978
High-income North America	Devitt et al. 1979; Hogan, 1989; U.S. DOE EIA, 1988; U.S. EPA, 1981, and 1989; Wald, 1990
Newly industrializing Latin America	Guzman et al., 1987
Low-income Latin America	U.S. Department of Commerce, ITD, 1989
High-income Western Europe	Cheshire and Robson, 1985; Ierland and Hutton, 1988; OCED, 1981a, 1982, 1985, 1988; UN ECE, 1987
Medium-income Western Europe	Ierland and Hutton, 1988; OCED, 1981a, 1982, 1985, 1988; UN ECE, 1987
Eastern Europe	Andersson, 1989; Bjorklund, 1989a, and 1989b; McCormick, 1985; Moldan and Schnoor, 1992; Paszynski, 1990; Scrieber, 1986; Thunberg, 1989; Vernon, 1990
Former Soviet Union	Dienes and Shabad, 1979; McCormick, 1985; Schnoor, personal communication, 1992; Vernon, 1990; Wilson, 1983
Centrally planned Asia	Dorian and Fridley, 1988; Smil, 1988; World Bank, 1985; Xia and Fong, 1990
Japan	OCED, 1981a, 1982, 1985 and 1988; UN ECE, 1987
Newly industrializing Asia	Foell and Green, n.d.; U.S. Department of Commerce, ITD, 1986, 1988, 1989
Low-income Asia	Foell and Green, n.d.; Meyers, 1983
Southern Africa	Meyers, 1983; U.S. Department of Commerce, 1990
Oceania	OCED, 1981a, 1982, 1985, 1988; OECD IEA, personal communication, 1989; UN ECE, 1987; U.S. Department of Commerce, ITD, 1989

Source: Institute for Economic Analysis.

parameters for 1980–2020 are reported in Table 4.5. The assumptions underlying the projections of parameters are discussed below.

Where there is extensive trade in coal and a history of rigorous enforcement of air pollution regulations, the data on sulfur content are fairly reliable and consistent among different sources. Regions meeting such criteria include high-income North America, low-income Latin America (Columbia is a major exporter of coal), high-income Western Europe, several countries in medium-income Western Europe, Japan, southern Africa, and Oceania. There is also close agreement among different sources about the sulfur content of coals used in low-income Asia, newly industrializing Asia, and centrally planned Asia. The other developing regions are not major coal users. In the absence of country-specific data, the world average sulfur content of 2 percent (Moller, 1984; Smil, 1985; WEC, 1974, 1978) is used for these regions.

Table 4.5. Parameters governing the emission of sulfur oxides from the combustion of coal by World Model region, 1980–2020

A. *Sulfur content, energy content, and conversion of fuel sulfur to sulfur dioxide, 1980*

	Percentage of sulfur by weight	Tons of coal per tce	SO_2/S t/t
1 High-income North America	1.38	1.256	1.92
2 Newly industrializing Latin America	2.00	1.051	1.95
3 Low-income Latin America	0.60	1.085	1.95
4 High-income Western Europe	1.08	1.451	1.87
5 Medium-income Western Europe	2.00	2.290	1.75
6 Eastern Europe	1.50	2.333	1.79
7 Former Soviet Union	1.50	1.358	1.88
8 Centrally planned Asia	1.00	1.401	1.95
9 Japan	1.00	0.998	1.95
10 Newly industrializing Asia	1.50	1.255	1.95
11 Low-income Asia	0.83	1.255	1.95
12 Major oil producers	2.00	1.000	1.95
13 North Africa and other Middle East	2.00	1.037	1.95
14 Sub-Saharan Africa	1.00	1.000	1.95
15 Southern Africa	1.00	1.467	1.95
16 Oceania	1.00	1.773	1.83

B. *Percentage sulfur by weight, 1990–2020 (all regions and parameters the same as for 1980, except for percentage of sulfur by weight in:)*

	1990	2000	2010	2020
1 High-income North America	1.30	1.15	1.15	1.15
4 High-income Western Europe	1.00	1.00	1.00	1.00
5 Medium-income Western Europe	2.00	1.75	1.53	1.34
6 Eastern Europe	1.50	1.31	1.15	1.00
7 Former Soviet Union	1.50	1.31	1.15	1.00
8 Centrally planned Asia	0.85	0.72	0.63	0.56
9 Japan	1.00	0.90	0.90	0.90
11 Low-income Asia	0.83	0.72	0.63	0.55
16 Oceania	0.52	0.52	0.52	0.52

Note: tce is tons of coal equivalent.

Source: Table 4.4; UN, ECE, 1983; U.S. EPA, 1985; and Institute for Economic Analysis estimates and projections.

Eastern Europe and the former Soviet Union are regions for which only limited information about coal sulfur content is available, and these estimates exhibit a considerable range of values. All researchers agree that Eastern Europe has, on average, the highest-sulfur coal in the world, and the former Soviet Union also has significant amounts of high-sulfur coal. This observation is at odds with officially reported levels of sulfur emissions, which imply a sulfur content of about 1 percent. Given the extensive firsthand data on sulfur content obtained from the sources listed for these regions, the implicit official estimate is suspect. The sulfur content assumed in this study for both regions, 1.5 percent, is lower than that of any of the sources cited but higher than the officially implied sulfur content.

With increasing environmental regulation, especially in developed regions, sulfur emissions from coal have declined in the last decade and will decline further in the future through the use of lower-sulfur coal and increased washing of coal. (Flue-gas desulfurization will also be used increasingly to reduce sulfur emissions. This is discussed in the next section.) Future plans to increase washing of coal, from a rate currently near zero to virtually 100 percent by 2020, will lower the sulfur content of coal by roughly 30 percent in Eastern Europe, the former Soviet Union, and the two developing regions that are major coal users, low-income Asia (mainly India) and centrally planned Asia (mainly China). The reduction of sulfur content in developed regions reflects the extent to which lower-sulfur coal is expected to be used to comply with future emission regulations.

The data required to calculate the regional sulfur emission parameters for coal are shown in panel A of Table 4.5. The average energy content of coal, calculated from data shown in United Nations (*Yearbook of Energy Statistics* 1983), is reported in column 2. The data that describe the chemical conversion of fuel sulfur to sulfur oxides, measured in sulfur dioxide equivalents, take into account the retention of some fuel sulfur in the ash. The conversion factor is lower for lignite (1.70) than for hard coal (1.95) because a higher amount of sulfur combines with impurities in lignite during combustion and is retained in the ash (EPA, 1985). A weighted average of the regional use of lignite and hard coal was used to calculate the regional conversion parameter.

The energy content of the fuels utilized and the factors governing the conversion of fuel sulfur to sulfur oxides are not likely to change substantially in the future. While the average energy content of coal has been steadily declining over the decades, this change has been slow. The conversion factor is likely to change only in regions that anticipate a large shift between lignite and hard coal and is unlikely to affect the sulfur emission parameters very much. For this study, future emission parameters are based on projected changes only in fuel sulfur content and pollution abatement. Other changes that affect a region's sulfur emissions, such as increased energy efficiency and substitution of natural gas for coal or oil, are represented directly in the model by sector-specific fuel inputs.

Sulfur Content of Oil

The sulfur content of oil, unlike that of coal, is sector specific in each region, reflecting the use of different mixes of petroleum products that may vary considerably in their sulfur content. Some sectors rely on characteristic product mixes; for example, electric utilities often use residual fuel oil, and transportation services use mainly gasoline or diesel fuel. Based on the relative similarity of the petroleum products used, the fifty World Model sectors were grouped into seven categories and the average sulfur content of oil was determined for each: agriculture, mining, industry, transportation, electric utilities, commercial sectors, and households. See Table 4.6 for the correspondence with World Model sectors. Systematic, comprehensive data are not readily available for the sulfur content of petroleum products used in each region; information was gathered and integrated from a wide range of sources (which were identified in Table 4.4). However, some of the most widely used petroleum products, such as gasoline, kerosene, and, to a lesser degree, diesel oil, have a fairly uniform sulfur

Table 4.6. Major energy-using groups of sectors: Major group and World Model sectors

Agriculture		Industry	
SE1	Livestock	XX3	Food processing
SE2	Oil crops	XX4	Petroleum refining
SE3	Grains	XX5	Metal processing
SE4	Root crops	XX6	Textiles and footwear
XX1	Other agriculture	XX7	Wood and cork
FS1	Fish	XX8	Furniture and fixtures
		XX9	Paper
Mining		XX10	Publishing
SE5	Copper	XX11	Rubber
SE6	Bauxite	XX12	Industrial chemicals
SE7	Nickel	XX13	Fertilizer
SE8	Zinc	XX14	Industrial chemicals
SE9	Lead	XX15	Fertilizer
SE10	Iron	XX16	Miscellaneous chemicals
SE11	Petroleum	XX17	Motor vehicles
SE12	Natural gas	XX18	Shipbuilding and other transportation equipment
SE13	Coal	XX19	Aircraft
XX2	Other resources	XX20	Metal products
		XX21	Machinery except electrical
Services		XX22	Electrical machinery
XX26	Construction	XX23	Scientific instruments
XX27	Trade	XX24	Miscellaneous manufacturing
XX29	Communications		
XX30	Other services	Transportation	
		XX28	Transportation services
Residential/government			
MA2	Household consumption	Electric utilities	
MA5	Government expenditure	XX25	Electric utilities

Source: Institute for Economic Analysis.

content throughout the world. The uncertainty about sulfur content is mostly limited to the heavier petroleum products, especially residual fuel oil.

Electric utilities and industry account for most of the sulfur emissions generated by the combustion of oil. A large amount of oil is used for transportation, most of which has a very low sulfur content; until recently, however, diesel fuel was fairly high in sulfur (e.g., 0.3 percent by weight in developed economies, 0.5–1.0 percent in some developing economies). The estimates of the sulfur content of oil by sector and region are given in Table 4.7.

The average sulfur content of oil used by electric utilities in a region is determined largely by its choice of fuel: residual fuel oil has a relatively high sulfur content (usually greater than 1 percent sulfur), while distillate oil is relatively low in sulfur. In the developed regions and in those developing regions that include large countries, such as low-income Asia (India) and newly industrializing Latin America (Brazil and Mexico), residual fuel oil dominates petroleum products used for thermal electric production because most electricity is produced in relatively large, modern plants. In some less developed regions with numerous small countries, such as sub-Saharan Africa, or in a large multi-island nation such as Indonesia, thermal electricity is often generated in small units (less than 100 MW), using distillate oil or diesel fuel, though the sulfur content is often higher than for the corresponding product in developed regions. The estimated sulfur content of oil used by electric utilities is given in the fifth column of Table 4.7. Where country-specific data were not available, electric utilities were assumed to use fuel oil (residual and distillate) with an average sulfur content of 2 percent, the known average for Western Europe at a time (1980) of virtually no emission controls.

The sulfur content of petroleum products used by industrial sectors also depends largely on the proportions of residual and distillate fuel oils consumed. Generally, smaller-scale facilities use distillate petroleum products (with about half of the sulfur content of residual fuel oil), and only the largest facilities use heavier petroleum products. In high-income North America, residual fuel oil provides about 70 percent of oil used in industry. In most other developed regions, the scale of operations is smaller and the proportion of residual fuel oil lower (50 percent). Production in developing regions usually takes place on a small scale relative to production in developed regions; consequently, developing regions use more light products in industrial and mining sectors than developed regions. Where detailed regional data were not available, regions were assumed to use half distillate and half residual fuel oil.

Use of oil in transportation, commercial, and residential sectors reflects both transportation and nontransportation use. The commercial and agricultural sectors use mainly distillate and diesel fuel oils and some gasoline. Petroleum products with negligible sulfur content, such as gasoline and kerosene, dominate household oil consumption; varying amounts of diesel oil are also used, depending on the region. Where no additional data were available to distinguish between diesel and other petroleum use in each of these sectors, it was assumed that agriculture, transportation, and other services used diesel oil, while the residential sector used gasoline, kerosene, and products with very little sulfur. In all developing regions except low-income Asia and centrally planned Asia, diesel oil is assumed to have a fairly high sulfur content: 0.75 percent compared to 0.30 percent in developed regions.

The other data needed to estimate sulfur emission parameters associated with oil use are the energy content of oil, the factor that represents the conversion of fuel sulfur to sulfur dioxide, and information about the extent of pollution abatement. Because the energy content of a ton of oil is much more uniform than that of a ton of coal, a single figure is used for all regions and sectors. Sulfur dioxide emissions per unit of fuel sulfur are also more uniform, at 1.90 tons of sulfur dioxide per ton of sulfur (indicated in the notes to Table 4.7).

With increasing environmental regulation, the sulfur content of oil has declined in the last decade, especially in Western Europe, in part due to the increased use of low-sulfur oils and partly due to increased processing of crude petroleum. Desulfurization of residual fuel oil during refining has already become more common in developed regions (reducing the average sulfur content of residual fuel oil in high-income Western Europe from 2 percent to 1 percent between 1980 and 1990), and the maximum sulfur content of diesel fuel will fall in the coming decade to 0.2 percent in developed regions.

Abatement of Sulfur Emissions

In 1980, the widespread use of flue-gas desulfurization for postcombustion abatement was limited mainly to electric utilities and industrial applications in Japan (see Table 4.8), with only a few installations in Western Europe and high-income North America. Since then, many developed countries have begun to install flue-gas desulfurization equipment that is capable of removing as much as 90 percent of the sulfur after combustion (see Table 4.4 for sources). In Japan and some countries of high-income Western Europe, installation will eventually reach 100 percent of electric utilities and large-scale industrial capacity. Funded by several Western European countries, Eastern Europe and the former Soviet Union are expected to install flue-gas desulfurization equipment as well. High-income North America will also install some blue-gas desulfurization equipment to meet regulations requiring stabilization of emissions by 2000.

Nitrogen Oxides

The anthropogenic emission of nitrogen oxides results primarily from the oxidation of nitrogen contained in fuels and in the atmosphere during combustion. Both the type of fuel and the combustion conditions, mainly the heat of combustion and the amount of air, are important in determining the amount of nitrogen oxides formed. Because of the dependence of emissions on complex and highly variable combustion conditions, the emission parameters for nitrogen are

Table 4.7. Parameters governing the emission of sulfur oxides from the combustion of oil by World Model region, 1980–2020

A. Sulfur content of oil by sector in 1980 (percentage by weight)

	Agriculture	Mining	Industry	Transport	Electric power	Commercial	Residential/government
1 High-income North America	0.30	0.88	0.88	0.08	1.00	0.30	0.035
2 Newly industrializing Latin America	0.75	1.50	1.50	0.75	2.00	0.75	0.035
3 Low-income Latin America	0.75	1.50	1.50	0.75	2.00	0.75	0.035
4 High-income Western Europe	0.30	1.50	1.50	0.17	2.00	0.30	0.035
5 Medium-income Western Europe	0.30	1.50	1.50	0.17	2.00	0.30	0.035
6 Eastern Europe	0.30	1.13	1.13	0.30	1.50	0.30	0.035
7 Former Soviet Union	0.30	1.13	1.13	0.30	1.50	0.30	0.035
8 Centrally planned Asia	0.30	0.30	0.30	0.30	0.80	0.30	0.035
9 Japan	0.30	0.50	0.50	0.17	0.80	0.30	0.035
10 Newly industrializing Asia	0.75	1.50	1.50	0.75	2.00	0.75	0.035
11 Low-income Asia	0.30	1.13	1.13	0.30	1.50	0.30	0.035
12 Major oil producers	0.75	1.50	1.50	0.75	2.00	0.75	0.035
13 North Africa and other Middle East	0.75	1.50	1.50	0.75	2.00	0.75	0.035
14 Sub-Saharan Africa	0.75	1.50	1.50	0.75	2.00	0.75	0.035
15 Southern Africa	0.30	1.13	1.13	0.17	1.50	0.30	0.035
16 Oceania	0.30	0.75	0.75	0.17	1.00	0.30	0.035

B. Sulfur content of oil by sector 1990–2020 (percentage by weight). All regions and sectors the same as 1980 except:

	Agri-culture	Mining	Industry	Transport	Electric power	Commercial	Residential/ government
1 High-income North America	0.20				0.78	0.20	0.030
4 High-income Western Europe	0.20	0.75	0.75	0.12	1.00	0.20	0.030
5 Medium-income Western Europe	0.20	0.75	0.75	0.12	1.00[a]	0.20	0.030
6 Eastern Europe	0.20			0.17		0.20	0.030
7 Former Soviet Union	0.20			0.17		0.20	0.030
9 Japan	0.20			0.12		0.20	0.030
10 Newly industrializing Asia	0.20	1.13	1.13	0.30	1.50	0.20	0.030
16 Oceania	0.20			0.12		0.20	0.030

a. Sulfur content is 1.25 percent in 1990, 1.00 percent in 2000–2020.

Notes: 1. Energy content of oil (tons of oil per tce of oil), all years, sectors, and regions: 0.71

2. Conversion of fuel sulfur to sulfur dioxide, all years, sectors, and regions: 1.90

Source: Table 4.4 and Institute for Economic Analysis estimates.

Table 4.8. Sulfur emissions abated in the electric power sector and industry, 1980–2020 (percentages)

	1980	1990	2000	2010	2020
A. Electric power					
1 High-income North America	0	20	30	30	30
4 High-income Western Europe	0	20	30	40	50
5 Medium-income Western Europe	0	0	10	15	25
6 Eastern Europe	0	0	10	15	25
7 Former Soviet Union	0	0	0	10	20
9 Japan	60	90	90	90	90
All other regions	0	0	0	0	0
B. Industry					
1 High-income North America	0	0	20	20	30
4 High-income Western Europe	0	10	20	20	20
5 Medium-income Western Europe	0	0	0	10	10
9 Japan	50	60	70	80	90
All other regions	0	0	0	0	0

Source: Table 4.4 and Institute for Economic Analysis estimates and projections.

potentially much more variable than those for sulfur. Nevertheless, a sector-specific and region-specific emission parameter for each fuel can be developed.

In 1980, 51 percent of anthropogenic emissions of nitrogen oxides in the United States resulted from stationary source fuel combustion, 44 percent from mobile sources (transportation), and the remaining 5 percent from industrial processes and other sources, like solid waste incineration and forest fires (EPA, 1983, Table 2-1). A roughly similar distribution of emissions by source occurs in other countries. Sectoral emission parameters used in the World Model (tons of nitrogen dioxide equivalent per tce) are calculated as the sum of the parameters for all types of combustion equipment associated with a fuel weighted by the distribution of equipment in a given sector and adjusted by the proportion of emissions from uncontrolled combustion that are removed by pollution control equipment.

The first step in developing sectoral emission parameters for a region was to identify the major technologies—combinations of fuel types and types of furnaces, boilers, or engines—used in each sector and the emission characteristics of each. The emission characteristics are associated with specific technologies and are assumed to be roughly the same for all regions using these technologies. Sectoral emission parameters will differ by region due to variations in the distribution of technologies in each region. The second step is to determine the distribution of the capacity of installed combustion technologies in each sector for a given region. Finally, the use of pollution control technologies, including both postcombustion equipment and modifications of the combustion process, must be taken into account. Emissions from stationary and mobile sources are addressed separately because the latter are determined by a more complicated set of conditions, including such factors as the altitude at which vehicles are operated and vehicle speed.

Nitrogen Emission Characteristics by Type of Combustion Equipment, Stationary Sources

Data on the emission characteristics of specific combustion equipment, distinguished by boiler capacity, firing mode, and fuel, have been compiled by the U.S. Environmental Protection Agency (EPA, 1983, 1985). These emission characteristics, reported in equivalent tons of nitrogen dioxide per weight or volume unit of fuel, cannot be incorporated directly into the World Data Base, in which fuel is measured in energy-equivalent units. The EPA emission characteristics were converted to tons of nitrogen dioxide per tce of fuel on the basis of the average energy content of fuels given in the source document. They are reported in Table 4.9 for the thirty-two boiler and fuel combinations responsible for stationary source emissions of nitrogen oxides in the United States.

Distribution of Stationary Source Combustion Equipment

Estimating the distribution of these technologies for every sector and every region is a challenging task. First, the major sources of stationary emissions of

Table 4.9. Stationary-source nitrogen oxide emission characteristics by type of boiler and fuel (tons of nitrogen dioxide equivalents per thousands of tons of coal equivalent of fuel)

Boiler type	Residual oil	Distillate oil	Natural gas	Coal Bituminous	Anthracite	Lignite
Boilers (>100 x 10^6 BTU/hr)						
Tangentially fired	4.094	—	7.677	8.495	—	8.154
Vertically fired	10.304	—	—	—	—	—
Front-wall fired	—	—	—	—	—	14.296
Other	6.550	—	15.353	11.907	10.747	12.248
Wet-bottom, pulverized coal	n.a.	n.a.	n.a.	19.243	10.747	—
Boilers						
(10–100 × 10^6 BTU/hr)	5.391	2.115	3.924	n.a.	n.a.	n.a.
(0.5–10 × 10^6 BTU/hr)	5.391	2.115	2.798	n.a.	n.a.	n.a.
(<0.5 × 10^6 BTU/hr)	na	1.945	2.798	n.a.	n.a.	n.a.
Boilers (crushed coal only, any capacity)						
Cyclone	n.a.	n.a.	n.a.	20.956	—	17.372
Spreader stoker	n.a.	n.a.	n.a.	7.918	—	6.141
Overfeed stoker	n.a.	n.a.	n.a.	5.427	—	—
Underfeed stoker	n.a.	n.a.	n.a.	4.300	—	—
All other stokers	n.a.	n.a.	n.a.	3.754	5.971	6.141
Hand-fired units	n.a.	n.a.	n.a.	1.707	1.808	—

a. Coal-burning units are pulverized coal, dry bottom, except where otherwise indicated.

—: not available.

n.a.: not applicable.

Source: EPA, 1985 and Institute for Economic Analysis.

nitrogen were identified. In the United States in 1980, electric utilities
accounted for nearly two-thirds of stationary source emissions, followed by
industrial fuel combustion (30 percent), with a small residual contribution
from the commercial/residential sector (EPA, 1983). The electric utilities dominate emissions, not only because of the large quantities of fuel they consume
but also because they usually burn fuel at higher temperatures than other sectors, a practice that results in the release of more nitrogen oxides per unit of
fuel. Since a similar distribution of emissions occurs in other developed countries, data collection focused initially on technologies used by the electric utilities sector.

Six regions dominate thermal electricity production, accounting for 87 percent of total production in 1980: high-income North America (33.3 percent), the
former Soviet Union (18.2 percent), high-income Western Europe (17.1 percent), Japan (7.0 percent), Eastern Europe (6.4 percent), and centrally planned
Asia (4.5 percent); see Table 4.10. Two of these six regions are single-country
regions—the former Soviet Union and Japan—and in two other regions, a single country dominates thermal electricity production: the United States produces 95 percent of thermal electricity in high-income North America, and
China produces 95 percent of thermal electricity in centrally planned Asia (see
Table 4.11). In the remaining regions, which account for 13 percent of thermal
electricity production, a few countries dominate in each region.

Fortunately, unpublished spreadsheets with information on every boiler for
every electric utility power plant in the United States and a census of boilers, in
terms of the boiler categories identified in Table 4.9 and the major groups of
sectors identified in Table 4.6, were made available by the United States Environmental Protection Agency for this study. These were used to estimate the

Table 4.10. Production of thermal electricity by World Model
region in 1980 (billions of kilowatt-hours)

Region	Production of thermal electricity	Percentage of total
1 High-income North America	1920.2	33.3
7 Former Soviet Union	1050.0	18.2
4 High-income Western Europe	987.2	17.1
9 Japan	401.8	7.0
6 Eastern Europe	371.4	6.4
8 Centrally planned Asia	256.6	4.5
5 Medium-income Western Europe	145.7	2.5
2 Newly industrializing Latin America	107.9	1.9
11 Low-income Asia	95.4	1.7
10 Newly industrializing Asia	89.8	1.6
13 Other Middle East and northern Africa	32.5	0.6
15 Southern Africa	89.3	1.6
16 Oceania	89.9	1.6
12 Major oil producers	84.5	1.5
13 Low-income Latin America	38.7	0.7
14 Sub-Saharan Africa	5.6	0.1
Total	5766.4	100.0

Source: United Nations, *Yearbook of Energy Statistics,* 1983.

distribution of technologies in the United States, and this distribution was assumed to represent the region of high-income North America.

Detailed information on the distribution of boilers is not readily available for other countries. However, the technical literature contains descriptions of the typical applications of the types of combustion equipment identified in Table 4.9, providing a basis for making plausible assumptions about the distribution of technologies where data are limited. The largest category of boilers ($> 100 \times 10^6$ BTU/hr) is used in virtually all electric power plants and large-scale industrial applications in developed countries.

Distillate oil is not often used in such large boilers. The intermediate categories of boilers ($0.5 - 100 \times 10^6$ BTU/hr) are often used in industrial applications and electric utilities in developing countries. The smallest category of boiler for each fuel ($< 0.5 \times 10^6$ BTU/hr, or hand-fired) is used in small commercial applications and households in all regions.

Table 4.11. Production of thermal electricity by major countries in World Model regions in 1980 (billions of kilowatt-hours)

1 High-income North America	1920.2	100.0%
United States	1820.5	94.8
Other countries[a] (3)	99.7	5.2
2 Newly industrializing Latin America	107.9	100.0%
Mexico	49.1	45.5
Argentina	22.2	26.6
Other countries (3)	26.9	27.9
3 Low-income Latin America	38.7	100.0%
Cuba	9.8	25.3
Colombia	6.2	16.0
Dominican republic	2.7	7.0
Other countries (37)	20.0	51.7
4 High-income Western Europe	987.2	100.0%
Germany, Federal Republic	306.4	31.0
United Kingdom	242.8	24.6
Italy	133.4	13.5
France	118.9	12.0
Other countries (19)	185.7	18.9
5 Medium-income Western Europe	145.7	100.0%
Spain	74.5	51.1
Yugoslavia	31.3	21.5
Other countries (6)	39.9	27.4
6 Eastern Europe	371.4	100.0%
Poland	118.6	31.9
German Democratic Republic	85.3	23.0
Czechoslovakia	63.5	17.1
Other countries (4)	104.0	28.0
7 Soviet Union	1050.0	100.0%
8 Centrally planned Asia	256.6	100.0%
China	242.4	95.0
Other countries (2)	14.2	5.0
9 Japan	401.8	100.0%

Table 4.11. (continued)

10 Newly industrializing Asia	89.8	100.0%
Korea	34.6	39.9
Thailand	13.8	15.9
Indonesia	12.9	14.9
Other countries (4)	28.5	29.3
11 Low-income Asia	95.4	100.0%
India	69.7	73.0
Other countries (15)	25.7	27.0
12 Major oil producers	84.5	100.0%
Saudi Arabia	18.9	22.4
Iran	16.8	19.9
Iraq	10.7	12.7
Kuwait	9.4	11.1
Algeria	6.9	8.2
Other countries (10)	21.8	25.7
13 Other Middle East and northern Africa	32.5	100.0%
Israel	12.5	38.5
Egypt	9.1	28.5
Other countries (14)	3.4	33.0
14 Sub-Saharan Africa[b]	5.6	100.0%
15 Southern Africa	89.3	100.0%
16 Oceania	89.9	100.0%
Australia	82.4	91.7
Other countries (2)	7.5	8.3

Note: The figures in parentheses are the number of other counties in the region.

a. Including territories and possessions.

b. No single country of the thirty-eight countries in this region produces more than 10 percent of the region's thermal electricity.

Source: Institute for Economic Analysis based on United Nations, *Yearbook of Energy Statistics,* 1983.

Additional information was pieced together from organizations such as government energy agencies, United Nations Industrial Development Organization (UNIDO) and other UN agencies, OECD's International Energy Agency, research organizations such as the Science Policy Research Unit of Sussex University, industry trade journals, and individual country monographs. (See Table 4.12 for a list of major sources.) Often these data reported primary fuel and boiler capacity but not firing mode. The distribution of technologies identified for each fuel and sector for the United States was initially assumed for other developed regions and, where the technical literature indicated, for developing regions. These parameters were then modified, if necessary, by the additional data on the average capacity rating of equipment for each region.

The availability of comprehensive data for the United States, which produced nearly one-third of the world's thermal electricity in 1980, guarantees that accurate emission parameters can be calculated for the region responsible for a large share of global nitrogen oxides and that estimates of emissions for other regions would at least be within a plausible range. For all but electric utilities and the largest industrial applications, firing mode is not a major factor and the variation of emission characteristics is not very large (see Table 4.9).

Table 4.12. Sources for data on stationary source combustion equipment and mobile source nitrogen emissions by World Model region

Region	Data source
All regions unless otherwise specified	Drake and Turpin, 1988; Ierland and Hutton, 1988; Smil, 1985; UNIDO, 1985a; U.S. EPA, 1983, 1985
Developing regions unless otherwise specified	Asian Development Bank, 1990; Jannsen and Milkop, 1987; Merrick 1984; Meyers, 1981; UN Division of Natural Resources and Energy, 1984; UNIDO, 1985a; World Bank, 1984a, and 1985
High-income North America	Devitt et al., 1979; Eskinazi, 1989; Hogan, 1989; Suprenant et al., 1976; U.S. DOE 1988; U.S. EPA, 1989
Newly industrializing Latin America	Guzman et al., 1987
High-income Western Europe	Chesire and Robson, 1985; OCED, 1982, 1983b, 1985a, 1985b; OECD IEA, 1988a, 1990; UN ECE, 1983, 1987
Medium-income Western Europe	OCED, 1982, 1983b, 1985a, 1985b; OECD IEA, 1988a, 1990; UN ECE, 1983, 1987
Former Soviet Union	Campbell, 1980; Wilson, 1983
Centrally planned Asia	Dorian and Fridley, 1988; Smil, 1988; World Bank, 1985.
Japan	Ando, 1989; OCED, 1982, 1983b, 1985a, 1985b; OECD IEA, 1988a, 1990; UN ECE, 1983, 1987
Sub-Saharan Africa	Bhagavan, 1985; Simoes, 1984
Low-income Asia	World Bank, 1984b.
Oceania	OECD, 1982, 1983b, 1985a, 1985b; OECD IEA, 1988, 1990; Trengove, 1986; UN ECE, 1983, 1987

Source: Institute for Economic Analysis.

Nitrogen Emission Characteristics by Type of Combustion Equipment from Mobile Sources

It is difficult to derive emission parameters for mobile sources from technical data because of the lack of information for many regions. Estimated mobile source emission coefficients were obtained for OECD countries from sources identified in Table 4.12. Typically, they specify emissions of nitrogen oxides per unit of fuel. Petroleum use in transportation is largely a mix of products, gasoline and diesel (with smaller amounts of aviation gasoline for air transport and residual and distillate fuel oils for shipping), with different emission characteristics. Emission coefficients reflect the extent of pollution controls and the relative use of diesel and gasoline. Developing regions, southern Africa, Eastern Europe, and the former Soviet Union are assumed to have the same emission parameters as Europe for uncontrolled combustion. Coal is used in transportation primarily for railroads, and the same nitrogen emission parameter is assumed for all regions.

Nitrogen Oxide Emission Parameters

The parameters governing nitrogen dioxide emissions per unit of fuel are reported in Table 4.13 by fuel and sectoral grouping (see Table 4.6) for all regions in 1980 (panel A), and those that are expected to change by 2020 are

Table 4.13. Parameters governing the emission of nitrogen oxides from the combustion of fuels by World Model region, 1980 and 2020 (tons of nitrogen dioxide equivalent per thousand tons of coal equivalent of fuel)

A. Parameters for 1980

	Agri-culture	Mining	Indus-try	Trans-port	Electric power	Commer-cial	Residential/government
Natural gas							
High-income North America, high-income Western Europe, former Soviet Union	2.74	3.84	3.84	n.a.	14.00	2.74	2.74
All other regions	2.74	3.84	3.84	n.a.	7.52	2.74	2.74
Coal							
High-income North America, high-income Western Europe, former Soviet Union	4.41	7.18	7.18	6.01	11.73	4.41	1.67
Low-income Latin America, North Africa and other Middle East, Sub-Saharan Africa	4.41	5.26	5.26	6.01	9.99	4.41	1.67
All other regions	4.41	7.18	7.18	6.01	9.99	4.41	1.67
Oil, stationary sources							
High-income North America, former Soviet Union	n.a.	4.61	4.61	n.a.	8.25	2.07	2.07[a]
High-income Western Europe, newly industrializing Latin America, low-income Latin America, low-income Asia, North Africa and other Middle East, Sub-Saharan Africa	n.a.	2.07	2.07	n.a.	8.25	2.07	2.07[a]
All other regions	n.a.	3.68	3.68	n.a.	4.01	2.07	2.07[a]
Oil, mobile sources							
High-income North America	33.71			15.83			7.63
Newly industrializing Latin America	33.71			36.64			20.30
Low-income Latin America	33.71			36.64			11.80
High-income Western Europe	33.71			30.78			7.93
Medium-income Western Europe	33.71			33.71			11.15
Eastern Europe	33.71			36.64			23.95
Former Soviet Union	33.71			36.64			14.23
Centrally planned Asia	33.71			36.64			8.39
Japan	33.71			19.05			7.63
Newly industrializing Asia	33.71			36.64			11.80
Low-income Asia	33.71			36.64			10.58
Major oil producers	33.71			33.71			16.66
North Africa and other Middle East	33.71			36.64			14.23
Sub-Saharan Africa	33.71			36.64			19.09
Southern Africa	33.71			33.71			20.30
Oceania	33.71			30.78			12.61

B. Parameters for 2020

	Transport	Electric power	Residential/ government
Natural gas (all regions and sectors the same as 1980 except:)			
High-income North America, high-income Western Europe, medium-income Western Europe		12.60	
Newly industrializing Latin America, centrally planned Asia, newly industrializing Asia, low-income Asia		10.76	
Coal (all regions and sectors the same as 1980 except:)			
High-income North America, high-income Western Europe, medium-income Western Europe		10.56	
Newly industrializing Latin America, centrally planned Asia, newly industrializing Asia, low-income Asia		10.86	
Oil, stationary sources *(all regions and sectors the same as 1980 except:)*			
High-income North America, high-income Western Europe, medium-income Western Europe		7.43	
Newly industrializing Latin America, centrally planned Asia, newly industrializing Asia, low-income Asia		6.13	
Oil, mobile sources *(all regions and sectors the same as 1980 except:)*			
High-income North America	13.46		6.04
High-income Western Europe	13.46		6.04
Medium-income Western Europe	19.05		6.90
Eastern Europe	30.78		14.61
Former Soviet Union	30.78		9.73
Japan	13.46		6.04
Oceania	19.05		10.76

a. Government sector only.

n.a.: not applicable.

Notes: 1. See Table 4.6 for definition of sectoral groupings.

2. Mobile source emissions are assumed only for agriculture, transportation services, and the residential sector (households) since all other sectors rely on transportation services.

3. Emissions per unit of fuel are assumed to remain unchanged after 1980 except in the case of electric power, among stationary sources, and transportation services and the residential sector, among mobile sources.

Source: Tables 4.9 and 4.10 and Institute for Economic Analysis projections.

indicated. Oil is subdivided into stationary and mobile sources, and its use in agriculture is assumed to be dominated by diesel-powered motor vehicles like tractors and trucks or other small motors with similar emission characteristics, such as irrigation pumps. Nitrogen emissions from household use of oil reflect transportation and other uses like heating, cooking, and lighting. These parameters were calculated as the average of the regional nitrogen emission coefficient for transportation and the emission coefficient for the smallest category of oil burner in Table 4.9, weighted by the shares of the two uses of oil by households given in Chapter 13.

While the emissions per unit of fuel in most sectors will not change significantly in the future, the diffusion of modern technologies in the developing regions and the extent of pollution abatement activities in the developed regions are expected to affect some nitrogen emission parameters. The most notable change will be the upgrading and modernization of capacity in developing regions as their economies grow and the scale of production increases, especially electricity production. In the two newly industrializing regions, as well as centrally planned Asia and low-income Asia, 50 percent of the equipment in place by 2020 can be expected to be comparable to the equipment used in developed economies in 1990, with the associated emission characteristics.

Pollution control measures have taken two basic forms: modification of existing combustion equipment to reduce the amount of nitrogen formed during combustion, such as low-nitrogen oxide burners and low-excess-air burners, and the use of add-on, postcombustion equipment to remove nitrogen from the waste gas stream. The former can reduce nitrogen emissions by 10–30 percent, depending on the modification. The latter can remove nearly 90 percent of nitrogen oxides but is very expensive. Much of the effort to control stationary source emissions in the developed regions will take the form of modifications to combustion equipment. In high-income North America, high-income Western Europe, and medium-income Western Europe, these modifications are assumed to be introduced in roughly one-half of electric power facilities by 2020, reducing the parameter by 10 percent (Table 4.13, panel B).

Currently, the United States has the strictest emission standards for motor vehicles. While there are no plans to increase the stringency of these standards significantly, a small decrease in the emission parameter (15 percent) is projected due to improvements in the efficiency of catalytic converters, their extension to all passenger vehicles and light trucks, and a small increase in the standard. In Europe, an attempt is currently being made to negotiate a protocol to reduce nitrogen emissions similar to that concluded for sulfur. By 2020, high-income Western Europe and Japan are expected to impose the new U.S. standard, represented by the same emission parameter; medium-income Western Europe and Oceania will achieve the reduction in emissions represented by the 1990 emission parameter for high-income North America; and Eastern Europe and the former Soviet Union, the 1990 medium-income Western Europe emission parameter. Emission parameters associated with motor vehicles are not expected to change significantly in the future for other regions.

Postcombustion Abatement of Nitrogen Emissions

Japan was the only country with a substantial postcombustion nitrogen abatement program in 1980 for stationary source emissions, which was assumed to remove 50 percent of the nitrogen emissions generated by its electric utilities. In 1980, most other developed countries had introduced only limited programs to reduce nitrogen emissions, mainly by phasing out combustion equipment with especially high nitrogen emissions such as cyclone furnaces. Nitrogen scrubbers remove most of the nitrogen but are expensive. A few European countries, such as Germany, also plan to introduce some nitrogen scrubbers in the future, but most countries have emphasized other methods of reducing nitrogen emissions. The abatement parameters are shown in Table 4.14.

Table 4.14. Percentage of nitrogen emissions subject to postcombustion abatement in the electric power sector and industry, 1980–2020

	1980	1990	2000	2010	2020
A. Electric power					
High-income Western Europe	0	0	5	7	10
Japan	50	50	50	50	50
All other regions	0	0	0	0	0
B. Industry					
Japan	0	10	15	20	25
All other regions	0	0	0	0	0

Source: Table 4.10 and Institute for Economic Analysis estimates and projections.

5

Electric Power Generation

The production and use of electricity are closely associated with industrialization and economic growth. Electricity is also closely associated with atmospheric pollution when it is generated through the combustion of fossil fuels. In this chapter, the regional distribution of electricity production is discussed, and control totals are developed for historical years. Changes made to improve the representation of production and use of electricity in the World Model are described. The most promising alternative technologies and improvements to conventional technologies for producing electricity are identified, and estimates of the relative capital and operating costs and fuel efficiencies of both conventional and alternative technologies are developed. These data are used for the construction of World Model parameters governing production of electricity for future years under the OCF scenario.

Regional Distribution of Production of Electricity

The share of the world's electricity produced in the developed regions fell between 1970 and 1987 (from 73 percent to 61 percent) while it rose in the rapidly growing, less developed economies (from 7 percent to 18 percent), especially in the newly industrializing economies of Asia and Latin America and in low-income Asia. These figures are shown in Table 5.1. Total worldwide production rose at a rate of over 5 percent annually between 1970 and 1980 but less rapidly from 1980 to 1987 (see Table 5.2) as fuel price increases led to significant reductions in the growth of demand for electricity in developed regions and slower economic growth in those developing regions that did not have the resources to adapt quickly to the changing energy situation. The production data in Table 5.2 provide control totals for World Model calculations of electricity output that are discussed in the next section.

Most electricity has been produced from the combustion of fossil fuels, predominantly coal, though the share of thermal electricity fell from 75 percent to 64 percent between 1970 and 1987, attributable mainly to the increase in nuclear power which provided less than 2 percent of the world's electricity in 1970 and 16 percent by 1987 (Tables 5.2 and 5.3). Hydroelectric power and other nonthermal renewables—mainly geothermal, solar, and wind—have provided the

Table 5.1. Shares of electricity produced by World Model region in 1970, 1980, and 1987 (percentage of kilowatt-hours)

	1970	1980	1987
High-income North America	37.4	33.3	30.6
Newly industrializing Latin America	2.4	3.5	4.1
Other Latin America	0.9	1.1	1.2
High-income Western Europe	21.3	19.1	17.5
Medium-income Western Europe	2.2	2.8	3.0
Eastern Europe	5.0	5.2	4.8
Former Soviet Union	15.0	15.8	16.0
Centrally planned Asia	na	4.2	5.4
Japan	9.5	7.5	6.7
Newly industrializing Asia	0.6	1.1	1.9
Low-income Asia	1.9	1.8	2.8
Major oil producers	0.4	0.8	1.7
North Africa and other Middle East	0.4	0.6	0.8
Sub-Saharan Africa	0.5	0.6	0.8
Southern Africa	1.0	1.2	1.2
Oceania	1.5	1.5	1.6
Total (excluding centrally planned Asia in 1970)	100.0	100.0	100.0

Source: Institute for Economic Analysis based on UN, *Yearbook of Energy Statistics,* 1984 and 1989.

remainder, 23 percent in 1970 and just under 20 percent in 1987. Almost all the nuclear power is generated in the developed regions, Eastern Europe, and the former Soviet Union, as is most of the hydroelectric power. However, hydroelectric power contributes a very high share of the electricity produced in the developing regions of Latin America, Africa, and Asia.

Table 5.2. Production of electricity by source in World Model regions in 1970, 1980, and 1987 (millions of kilowatt-hours)

	Thermal	Nuclear	Hydro-electric[a]	Other	Total
1970					
High-income North America	1,413.8	22.8	407.9		1,844.5
Newly industrializing Latin America	51.1	0.0	64.9		116.0
Other Latin America	27.9	0.0	16.8		44.7
High-income Western Europe	723.2	43.3	286.1		1052.6
Medium-income Western Europe	53.8	0.9	54.2		108.9
Eastern Europe	234.7	0.5	12.2		247.4
Soviet Union	613.1	3.5	124.4		741.0
Centrally planned Asia	n.a.	n.a.	n.a.		n.a.
Japan	382.4	11.0	76.8		470.2
Newly industrializing Asia	21.9	0.0	5.5		27.4
Low-income Asia	55.8	0.0	39.1		94.9
Major oil producers	15.4	0.0	4.2		19.6
North Africa and Middle East	13.8	0.0	7.8		21.6
Sub-Saharan Africa	5.4	0.0	17.3		22.7
Southern Africa	51.1	0.0	0.1		51.2
Oceania	49.1	0.0	23.0		72.1
Total (excluding centrally planned Asia)	3,712.5	82.0	1,140.3		4,934.8

Case Studies

Table 5.2. (continued)

	Thermal	Nuclear	Hydro-electric[a]	Other	Total
1980					
High-income North America	1,902.0	287.0	528.7	5.1	2,722.8
Newly industrializing Latin America	101.3	2.3	180.3	0.9	284.8
Other Latin America	53.5	0.0	34.1	0.4	88.0
High-income Western Europe	997.3	200.3	365.7	2.6	1565.9
Medium-income WesternEurope	143.6	5.4	82.5	0.0	231.5
Eastern Europe	375.8	21.5	26.2	0.0	423.5
Soviet Union	1,055.0	60.0	180.0	0.0	1,295.0
Centrally planned Asia	262.4	0.0	78.8	0.0	341.2
Japan	435.8	83.2	92.1	0.9	612.0
Newly industrializing Asia	77.6	3.5	9.6	0.0	90.7
Low-income Asia	88.1	3.2	55.6	0.0	146.9
Major oil producers	59.1	0.0	7.0	0.0	66.1
North Africa and Middle East	32.1	0.0	16.7	0.0	48.8
Sub-Saharan Africa	6.0	0.0	41.6	0.0	47.6
Southern Africa	93.1	0.0	2.7	0.0	95.8
Oceania	87.1	0.0	34.2	1.2	122.5
Total	5,769.8	666.4	1,735.8	11.1	8,183.1
1987					
High-income North America	2,064.8	532.6	571.0	14.5	3,182.9
Newly industrializing Latin America	155.7	7.5	262.2	4.3	429.7
Other Latin America	59.0	0.0	59.8	1.1	119.9
High-income Western Europe	840.5	593.0	376.5	3.4	1,813.4
Medium-income Western Europe	177.0	45.8	84.9	3.5	311.2
Eastern Europe	409.8	56.8	29.4	0.0	496.0
Soviet Union	1,258.1	187.0	219.8	0.0	1,664.9
Centrally planned Asia	424.9	0.0	131.1	0.0	556.0
Japan	423.5	189.8	84.1	1.6	699.0
Newly industrializing Asia	136.9	39.3	21.6	0.2	198.0
Low-income Asia	195.3	5.9	84.0	4.5	289.7
Major oil producers	169.9	0.0	9.5	0.0	179.4
North Africa and Middle East	70.7	0.0	11.3	0.0	82.0
Sub-Saharan Africa	45.1	0.0	33.5	0.0	78.6
Southern Africa	117.8	3.9	0.8	0.0	122.5
Oceania	127.9	0.0	34.2	2.0	164.1
Total	6,676.9	1,661.6	2,013.7	35.1	1,0387.3

a. Includes other types, mainly geothermal.

Note: Data for centrally planned Asia were not available for 1970.

Source: Institute for Economic Analysis based on UN, *Yearbook of Energy Statistics,* 1984 and 1989.

Representation of Electricity in the World Model

Electricity is represented in the World Model as the output of sector XX25, measured in value terms in constant, base year U.S. prices. Interregional trade of electricity is not currently represented and is in most cases negligible. Two kinds of improvements, discussed below, were made to the representation of electricity in the World Model: a shift from a net to a gross measure of output and a revision of the input coefficients for electricity to other sectors.

In the World Model, electricity production was represented net of own use,

Table 5.3. Shares of electricity produced by source in World Model regions in 1970, 1980, and 1987 (percentages)

	Thermal	Nuclear	Hydro-electric[a]	Other	Total
1970					
High-income North America	76.6	1.2	22.1		100.0
Newly industrializing Latin America	44.1	0.0	55.9		100.0
Other Latin America	62.4	0.0	37.6		100.0
High-income Western Europe	68.7	4.1	27.2		100.0
Medium-income Western Europe	49.4	0.8	49.8		100.0
Eastern Europe	94.9	0.2	4.9		100.0
Soviet Union	82.7	0.5	16.8		100.0
Centrally planned Asia	n.a.	n.a.	n.a.		n.a.
Japan	81.3	2.3	16.3		100.0
Newly industrializing Asia	79.9	0.0	20.1		100.0
Low-income Asia	58.8	0.0	41.2		100.0
Major oil producers	78.6	0.0	21.4		100.0
North Africa and Middle East	63.9	0.0	36.1		100.0
Sub-Saharan Africa	23.8	0.0	76.2		100.0
Southern Africa	99.8	0.0	0.2		100.0
Oceania	68.1	0.0	31.9		100.0
Total (excluding centrally planned Asia)	75.2	1.7	23.1		100.0
1980					
High-income North America	69.9	10.5	19.4	0.2	100.0
Newly industrializing Latin America	35.6	0.8	63.3	0.3	100.0
Other Latin America	60.8	0.0	38.8	0.5	100.0
High-income Western Europe	63.7	12.8	23.4	0.2	100.0
Medium-income Western Europe	62.0	2.3	35.6	0.0	100.0
Eastern Europe	88.7	5.1	6.2	0.0	100.0
Soviet Union	81.5	4.6	13.9	0.0	100.0
Centrally planned Asia	76.9	0.0	23.1	0.0	100.0
Japan	71.2	13.6	15.0	0.1	100.0
Newly industrializing Asia	85.6	3.9	10.6	0.0	100.0
Low-income Asia	60.0	2.2	37.8	0.0	100.0
Major oil producers	89.4	0.0	10.6	0.0	100.0
North Africa and Middle East	65.8	0.0	34.2	0.0	100.0
Sub-Saharan Africa	12.6	0.0	87.4	0.0	100.0
Southern Africa	97.2	0.0	2.8	0.0	100.0
Oceania	71.1	0.0	27.9	1.0	100.0
Total	70.5	8.1	21.2	0.1	100.0
1987					
High-income North America	64.9	16.7	17.9	0.5	100.0
Newly industrializing Latin America	36.2	1.7	61.0	1.0	100.0
Other Latin America	49.2	0.0	49.9	0.9	100.0
High-income Western Europe	46.3	32.7	20.8	0.2	100.0
Medium-income Western Europe	56.9	14.7	27.3	1.1	100.0
Eastern Europe	82.6	11.5	5.9	0.0	100.0
Soviet Union	75.6	11.2	13.2	0.0	100.0
Centrally planned Asia	76.4	0.0	23.6	0.0	100.0
Japan	60.6	27.2	12.0	0.2	100.0
Newly industrializing Asia	69.1	19.8	10.9	0.1	100.0
Low-income Asia	67.4	2.0	29.0	1.6	100.0
Major oil producers	94.7	0.0	5.3	0.0	100.0
North Africa and Middle East	86.2	0.0	13.8	0.0	100.0
Sub-Saharan Africa	57.4	0.0	42.6	0.0	100.0

78   *Case Studies*

Table 5.3. (continued)

	Thermal	Nuclear	Hydro-electric[a]	Other	Total
Southern Africa	96.2	3.2	0.7	0.0	100.0
Oceania	77.9	0.0	20.8	1.2	100.0
Total	64.3	16.0	19.4	0.3	100.0

a. Includes other types, mainly geothermal.

Note: Data for centrally planned Asia were not available for 1970.

Source: Institute for Economic Analysis based on Table 5.2.

distribution, and transmission losses, while most statistical sources report gross output. It is advantageous to include these explicitly in the World Data Base since own use and losses constitute major potential sources of efficiency gains, especially in developing regions, where losses are currently as high as 30 percent or more of gross production.

Because data about own use and losses are not systematically reported and are often incomplete, a simple rule of thumb was used for the historical period, 1970–90. In industrial, market economies about 10 percent of gross electricity output is used within the plant or is lost in transmission and distribution. The newly industrializing economies and the formerly socialist economies have had higher losses, estimated at 15 percent through 1990. The developing countries experience the greatest losses, assumed to average 20 percent through 1990. Assumptions about losses in future years will be addressed in the section about projections under the OCF scenario.

Electricity outputs were recomputed after the change to a gross production basis and converted to physical units using the base year U.S. price per kilowatt-hour of electricity. These results were compared with the control totals in Table 5.2. For years after 1970, revisions were necessary because the original data base did not take account of the significant conservation efforts in developed regions resulting from fuel price increases in the 1970s or the rapid expansion of the use of electricity in developing regions, especially centrally planned Asia and newly industrializing Latin America and Asia.

The inputs of electricity to specific sectors were revised for 1980 and 1990 by scaling the original coefficients for 1980 and 1990 by the control totals for electricity production in 1980 and 1987. Data for 1987, increased slightly to account for economic growth, were used for 1990.

Production Technology

Electricity generation in all World Model regions is dominated by public or private utilities relying on conventional thermal, nuclear, and hydroelectric technologies. A number of alternatives for meeting future requirements for electricity are possible: alternative electric generation technologies including the refurbishment of aging plants to extend their useful lifetime (plant betterment), load management, promotion of greater energy conservation, increasing use of small-scale power production from sources outside the utility industry, and the use of renewables.

New technologies not currently widely used, but likely to have an impact on the electricity-generating capacity after 2000, are listed in Table 5.4, along with their major advantages and disadvantages, followed by a comparison of the costs of conventional and alternative technologies in Table 5.5. Certain technologies, such as solar satellites and nuclear fusion, are not discussed because they are not considered promising at this time. While the reported costs of alternative technologies are those given in the main reference for this section (OTA, 1990), other sources were consulted as well, notably, EPRI (1988), Fulkerson et al. (1990), Jack Fawcett Associates (1987), and Johansson et al. (1990).

Table 5.4. Alternative technologies for production of electricty

Technology	Advantages	Disadvantages
Solar photovoltaics and thermal	Energy source is free, renewable,widely available, and has no emissions. Installation has short lead time, wide variation in installation sizes.	Supply is intermittent, requiring development of energy storage technologies. Technology is capital and land intensive and sensitive to exposure to the elements. Land requirements make remote locations likely, increasing the difficulty of maintenance.
Fluidized-bed combustion, atmospheric and pressurized (AFBC and PFBC)	Greater fuel efficiency and flexibility, lower emissions of sulfur and nitrogen oxides, less solid waste, and available in small sizes relative to conventional pulverized coal plants. PFBC is more compact and offers greater fuel efficiency.	Neither form of FBC has been able to produce successfully on a scale needed by electric utilities (100–200 MWe). PFBC faces serious technical obstacles and has not yet had a successful demonstration. Potentially long lead times because of the complexity of this new technology.
Integrated gasificationt/combined cycle (IGCC)	High fuel efficiency, low emisions of sulfur and nitrogen oxides. Requires less land and water than conventional combustion systems. Much less solid waste generated than conventional coal or AFBC plants. Can be installed modularly.	Potentially long lead times (ten years) because it is a new, complex technology.
Geothermal	Energy source is free, renewable, and has no emissions.	Limited availability. Exploration and development is expensive. Much of the available geothermal heat is relatively low in temperature (150–250°F), requiring special equipment to exploit it.
Wind	Energy source is free, renewable, and has no emissions.	Limited opportunities, land intensive, excessively noisy.
Fuel cells	Short lead times, wide variation in installation sizes, easily recovered waste heat, fuel flexibility, ability to operate unattended, expected to use natural gas, which will minimize emissions.	Uncertain reliability and lifetime.

Source: Institute for Economic Analysis based on OTA, 1990.

Table 5.5. Relative capital, fuel, and operating costs expected for the mid-1990s for conventional and alternative electricity technologies

	Capital costs (1983 $US/kW)	Operations and maintenance (1983 $US/kWh)	Fuel conversion Efficiency
Coal	1260–1580[a]	0.0057[b]	35%
Natural gas	777[b]	0.0045[b]	37
Solar			
Flat plate	1,000–11,000	0.004–0.028	n.a.
Concentrator	1,000–8,000	0.004–0.023	n.a.
Solar thermal	2,000–3,000	0.015–0.023	n.a.
AFBC	1,260–1,580	0.077	35
IGCC	1,200–1,350	0.006–0.012	35–40
Geothermal	1,500–2,000	0.010–0.015	n.a.
Wind	900–1,200	0.006–0.014	n.a.
Fuel cells			
small	950–3,000	0.004–0.012	36–40
large	700–3,000	0.004–0.012	40–44

a. From U.S. Congress, OTA (1990).

b. For mid-1980s.

Notes: 1. Costs and performance of conventional coal and natural gas plants represent the average for new 800-MW plants, including all equipment needed to comply with environmental regulations, including flue gas scrubbers for the coal plant. Costs in (Jack Fawcett Associates, 1987) were in 1982 U.S. dollars and were converted to 1983 U.S. dollars using information from OTA, 1990, p. 320.

2. Costs and performance of alternative technologies correspond to commercial or demonstration installations, which vary in size.

Source: Institute for Economic Analysis. Based, for conventional technologies, on Jack Fawcett Associates, 1987, pp. 101–5. Alternative technologies based on OTA, 1990, pp. 316–17.

The estimates of capital and operating costs from different sources were all similar for conventional technologies; cost estimates for alternative technologies varied, though not by a great deal. OTA figures are reported because they appear to represent the most balanced and comprehensive analysis.

All the technologies listed in Table 5.4 can provide base load, as well as intermediate and peak load, capacity. The most important drawback of these technologies is their cost relative to that of conventional combustion systems. The range of both capital and operating costs is large for most alternative technologies. While the lower bound is generally competitive with conventional coal combustion technology (but not with natural gas technology, which has low capital costs), the upper bound is usually much higher. Operating costs for AFBC are more than ten times higher than for conventional coal technology.

The costs of the new technologies are expected to fall steeply if greater demand during the 1990s allows for mass production. Even as costs come down, however, there may be considerable resistance among the utilities to invest heavily in complex, new technologies. Most of these new technologies will be implemented in smaller industrial applications in the 1990s, with prospects for providing a significant share of electricity only after 2000 (Romain-Frisch, 1989).

Plans for installing capacity must be made years in advance, and uncertainty over demand growth, along with complex environmental regulations that new plants must meet in the developed regions, have made the traditionally conservative utility industry even more wary of commitment to new, large-scale installations. Consequently, the replacement of conventional by alternative technologies is likely to be further delayed as utilities have come to rely increasingly on methods to increase the supply of electricity without building new capacity: plant betterment, load management, energy conservation, and increased use of small-scale power production from nonutility sources.

In order to avoid replacing large portions of their capacity or building on new sites, which would require lengthy regulatory reviews, utilities are now investing in *plant betterment,* a process of rehabilitating aging facilities to extend their lifetime. Plant betterment involves some relatively low-cost or even costless adjustments, such as revising procedures for startup and operation, as well as more costly replacement and upgrading of selected components.

Load management involves providing economic incentives to encourage demand during off-peak periods and discourage demand during peak periods. This shift of demand allows the utility to meet higher overall electricity demands without adding to capacity and allows greater utilization of the more efficient base load capacity.

Promotion of energy conservation is an extremely attractive method of increasing the effective supply of electricity. The greatest potential reduction in fuel use by electric utilities will be obtained not from changes in the generation of electricity, but from the reduction of electricity end use through conservation and the introduction of new technologies in other sectors. This subject is discussed in Chapters 6 and 12.

Modern utilities are connected through grids that allow the transfer of electricity from a surplus to a deficit area. Increasingly, small-scale, nonutility producers are connecting to the grid and providing electricity. Typically, this surplus electricity is produced by industrial cogeneration systems. While fuel and electricity were relatively cheap, cogeneration systems were not attractive. However, in the past twenty years, high energy prices have made cogeneration cost effective. U.S. federal law now enables industries to sell excess, self-generated electricity to the utility grid at prices close to the true cost of other alternative sources. This legislation has provided the security needed to ensure investment in cogeneration.

Projections Under the OCF Scenario

The representation of alternative fuel mix and alternative technologies in the World Model requires assumptions about the relative shares of fuels used to generate electricity, improvements in thermal conversion efficiency, the electricity sector's own use of electricity, and the use of add-on pollution control equipment. The changes, and the corresponding World Model parameters, are shown in Table 5.6. After an overview of trends and of the major factors affecting future energy use, each of these parameters is discussed.

Given the long lead times required to bring new capacity on-line, plans for

Table 5.6. Projected changes in the production of electricity, 2000–2020, under the OCF scenario

Parameters	Reasons for change
SE11, SE12, SE13 (fossil fuels) inputs to XX25 (electricity)	Fuel mix change, improved conversion efficiency
XX25 input to XX25	Decreased own use and losses
XX16 (limestone) input to XX25	Pollution control measures
Capital output ratio for XX25	Increased capital required for improved conversion efficiency, decreased own use and losses, pollution control measures

Source: Institute for Econornic Analysis.

2000, by and large, have already been determined for most regions. The alternative technologies discussed in the preceding section are not likely to contribute significantly to the production of electricity until the beginning of the next century (OECD, International Energy Agency [IEA], 1990); (OTA, 1990; Romain-Frisch, 1989). The situation after 2000 is highly uncertain and will be heavily influenced by the development of an international agreement on carbon dioxide emissions, the future of nuclear power, and the success of exploration for natural gas.

While there is a serious commitment to curbing emissions of carbon, there has been little parallel development of methods to achieve these reductions. Some countries have proposed a carbon tax, which would presumably spur greater energy conservation efforts or make the cost of alternative technologies competitive with those of fossil fuel technologies. However, the details about the means to achieve this ambitious objective are rarely specified. Unfortunately, alternative power technologies, especially solar power, have suffered from lack of funding for the research and development that might be able to bring down their costs, as well as from the fall in oil prices of the late 1980s (Romain-Frisch, 1989).

The ability to reduce carbon emissions significantly will depend in part on the future of nuclear power, which currently provides 16 percent of the world's electricity. Many of the operating licenses of nuclear plants in the developed regions expire about 2010. Renewal of licenses for aging plants in North America and Western Europe (except France) will meet stiff opposition. This makes the expansion of nuclear power unlikely in most countries and has resulted, for example, in the replacement of nuclear plants in the former East Germany by oil-fired plants. The continued operation of nuclear plants throughout Eastern Europe and the former Soviet Union is in question. Japan has planned to stabilize carbon emissions in part by expanding its nuclear generating capacity from about 30 percent to 60 percent of all electricity by 2020. However, public opposition makes this expansion extremely unlikely; even additions to nuclear capacity currently planned for 2000 are being questioned. Sweden has plans to decommission all of its nuclear power plants, which currently provide about two-thirds of its electricity, by 2010, but it is unclear how this capacity will be replaced without increasing carbon emissions.

Natural gas, with a carbon content only 60 percent of that of coal per unit of energy, could provide a means to stabilize carbon emissions. However, it is estimated that current proven reserves would be 85–90 percent exhausted by 2020 if the current rate of use is even slightly increased with moderate world economic growth (2 percent annually) (Romain-Frisch, 1989). While it is likely that estimates of reserves will increase in the future, currently there is less exploration for natural gas than for oil, and natural gas is still flared at oil wells in some countries. The infrastructure for transportation of natural gas is more complicated than that required for oil, and an integrated system for world trade of natural gas comparable to that of oil would need to be developed.

The massive changeover from coal to natural gas, which could possibly stabilize global carbon emissions, would require the collaboration of the world's major coal users: China, the former Soviet Union, the United States, Australia, India, and South Africa. The relatively poor countries, China and India, are likely to increase their use of natural gas but cannot afford to abandon their plentiful, inexpensive coal, especially as economic growth puts pressure on their limited oil resources. The former Soviet Union and the United States may increase use of natural gas, particularly as environmental regulations make coal less attractive, but they are constrained by resource availability. The importance for the former Soviet Union of the export earnings generated by natural gas will limit expansion of its domestic use. Australia and South Africa are also unlikely to replace much coal by natural gas. Under current conditions, substantial replacement of coal by gas is considered highly unlikely (Romain-Frisch, 1989).

Specific assumptions about thermal conversion efficiencies, own use of electricity, and the fuel mix for generating electricity in the future are discussed below.

Technology and Thermal Conversion Efficiencies

Thermal conversion efficiencies average about 35–36 percent in most developed regions, but they are considerably lower in developing regions (Flavin, 1986; World Bank, 1984a;). (Data for calculating thermal efficiency for developing regions, such as those of the OECD IEA [1988b] and the UN [1988], are not complete and, in some cases, not reliable.) Developing regions have the potential to improve conversion efficiencies without substantial cost increases through better utilization of current technology. Many new technologies that have potentially higher conversion efficiencies are not yet commercially proven. Given the long lead time needed to bring a new electric power plant on-line and the long lifetime of a thermal power plant (over thirty years with plant betterment), an increase in average thermal efficiency will occur slowly in the developed regions.

Under the OCF scenario, a 5 percent improvement in conversion efficiency is assumed for the developed regions, bringing the average efficiency up to 37–38 percent by 2000. Additional increases of 5 percent for each decade after 2000 will increase the average efficiency to about 40 percent, the current conversion efficiency of an integrated gasification combined cycle plant (Table 5.5). Improvements in conversion efficiency for groups of regions are summarized in Table 5.7.

In developed regions, these changes result in part from improvement of existing and new conventional technologies, especially the increased use of natural gas technologies (Williams and Larson, 1989) and in part from the gradual introduction of some of the alternative technologies, such as fluidized-bed combustion and fuel cells, discussed in the previous section. The improvement of existing technology through plant betterment, load management, and the use of nonutility electricity will increase the capital requirements. The use of scrubbers on coal-fired and oil-fired plants, which meet sulfur emission standards by means other than reducing the sulfur content of fuel, increases the capital requirements for a plant by roughly 10 percent (EPRI, 1987, 1988; OECD IEA, 1989; Williams and Larson, 1989). It is estimated that scrubbers will be used on less than one-third of coal-fired capacity in the United States (about 17 percent of total projected capacity for 2000, less in future years) and on 50 percent or more of the coal- and oil-fired plants in some countries of Western Europe. The use of low–nitrogen oxide burners or other equipment to reduce nitrogen emissions does not significantly increase the capital requirements (except for scrubbers, which are not expected to be widely used except for current installations in Japan). The increase in average capital requirements after 1990 due to the use of scrubbers is expected to be low, in the range of 1.5 percent to 3 percent. The net increase in capital requirements for improving performance is expected to be small, rising by 15 percent between 1990 and 2020: capital costs for natural gas plants are considerably lower than for conventional coal- or oil-fired plants (see Table 5.5), offsetting the relatively higher capital costs of advanced technologies. (This is a conservative assumption, overestimating the costs, since the costs of advanced technologies are most likely to decline over the next twenty years relative to those of conventional technologies.)

In developing regions, Eastern Europe, and the former Soviet Union, the average conversion efficiency will be brought up to the current level of the developed regions by 2020; this can be achieved by improvements in existing capacity and the use of modern conventional technologies for expansion of capacity. While many of these improvements can be achieved without significant additional costs (e.g., through better startup procedures), some of them will probably require replacement of important parts of the electricity generating

Table 5.7. Improvements in thermal conversion efficiency and increases in capital to output ratios in electric power generation, 2000–2020 (percentage change in coefficient from previous decade, conversion efficiency in percentage)

	Fuel inputs		Capital output ratio		Conversion efficiency	
	2000	2010 and 2020	2000	2010 and 2020	1990	2020
Developed market economies	–5%	–5%	5%	5%	35–36%	40%
Eastern Europe and former Soviet Union	–10	–7.5	10	7.5	< 30	36
Newly industrializing and other developing economies	–10	–7.5	5	7.5	<30	36

Source: Institute for Economic Analysis.

system, including upgrading the transmission and distribution system, which is expected to raise the capital requirements 20–25 percent between 1990 and 2020. The higher capital costs for Eastern Europe and the former Soviet Union, between 1990 and 2000 reflect accelerated replacement of inefficient equipment and installation of emission controls that are not expected to be installed in significant quantities in developing regions.

In Eastern Europe, the former USSR, and the developing regions, efficiency is assumed to increase more rapidly than in the developed regions between 1990 and 2000 and at the same rate as for the developed regions thereafter.

Own Use of Electricity and Pollution Control Equipment

In industrial, market economies, about 10 percent of gross electricity output is used for operations within the plant or is lost in transmission and distribution. Barring an unexpected technological breakthrough, such as the commercial use of superconductors, this loss will not be greatly reduced in future years. In fact, the use of energy-using pollution control devices, like scrubbers on coal plants, will increase the use of electricity by the electricity sector. However, this increase, about 10 percent in the electricity already used to operate the plant (about 3 percent of total production [Moore, 1991]), is quite small. Furthermore, in developed regions where these devices are likely to be installed, introduction of offsetting energy conservation measures is anticipated, such as adjustable-speed drives that can reduce electricity requirements by 20–50 percent (Moore, 1991). The overall effect will be to reduce the own use of electricity from 10 percent to about 9 percent between 1990 and 2020 in developing regions (see Table 5.8).

The newly industrializing economies and the formerly socialist economies are assumed to reduce their losses to 10 percent by the year 2000 and to 9 percent by 2020. The developing regions will gradually reduce their losses to 15 percent by 2000 and to 10 percent by 2020.

Additional inputs affected by the pollution control policies that are expected for the developing regions, Eastern Europe, and the former Soviet Union include the use of chemicals, in particular limestone, for the capture of fuel sulfur and increased capital inputs (already discussed). The use of limestone is represented by an increase in the input of glass and clay products (XX16) into

Table 5.8. Inputs of electricity to electricity generation, 1980–2020 (kWh/kWh)

	1980 and 1990	2000 and 2010	2020
Developed economies	0.100	0.095	0.090
Newly industrializing economies	0.150	0.100	0.090
Eastern Europe and former Soviet Union	0.150	0.100	0.090
Developing economies	0.200	0.150	0.100

Source: Institute for Economic Analysis.

electricity. An estimate by Jack Fawcett Associates (1987) of that input as a proportion of intermediate inputs (0.00340 dollars per dollar of output in 1970 U.S. prices) is multiplied by the share of coal-fired and oil-fired electric capacity assumed to use flue gas desulfurization and fluidized-bed combustion in each region. This produces very small input coefficients for 2020, ranging from 0.00034 (in medium-income Western Europe) to 0.00126 (in Japan).

Fuel Mix

Despite concerns about global warming and commitments to reduce carbon emissions, virtually all OECD countries except Japan are planning to increase the share of electricity generated by fossil fuels between 1988 and 2005. This is seen in Table 5.9, which shows capacity in 1988 and planned capacity in 2005. An increase in the share of electricity provided by natural gas for North America and Western Europe is intended to replace oil, nuclear power, or other (renewable) sources of electricity, whose shares are expected to fall, rather than coal. High-income Western Europe will maintain its 1988 share of coal-fired capacity, and medium-income Western Europe plans a significant expansion of coal use. The use of natural gas will decline in Japan and Oceania, where an increase is planned for coal-fired plants.

For the developed regions in 2000, initial estimates of fuel input coefficients (SE11, SE12, and SE13 inputs to XX25) were obtained as the product of the 1990 coefficients and the ratio of the 2005 to the 1988 shares of capacity. (While the coefficients reflect use, not capacity, there is a close enough correspondence to make the use of capacity acceptable for this purpose.)

An increase in the share of electricity produced by the combustion of fossil fuels is also planned in low-income Asia and newly industrializing Asia,

Table 5.9. Capacity for electricity generation by source in developed market economies, 1988–2005 (percentages)

Region	Coal	Oil	Gas	Nuclear	Hydro-electric[a]	Total
1988						
High-income North America	52	5	8	19	16	100
High-income Western Europe	31	8	6	32	22	100
Medium-income Western Europe	37	9	2	26	24	100
Japan	15	28	18	26	14	100
Oceania	78	2	9	0	11	100
2005						
High-income North America	49	4	15	14	19	100
High-income Western Europe	31	8	12	28	20	100
Medium-income Western Europe	49	10	6	15	21	100
Japan	18	14	16	38	14	100
Oceania	83	1	7	0	9	100

a. Includes geothermal and others.

Source: Institute for Economic Analysis based on OECD, IEA, 1990.

though no details about individual fuels are available for many countries (see Table 5.10). Fuel input coefficients for 2000 were developed in two steps for these regions: first, all fuel inputs were adjusted by the ratio of thermal capacity in 2000 to 1990; then the fuel mix for 2000 was adjusted to reflect the expected decline in the use of oil and a small increase in the use of gas and coal. Information about the capacity likely to be in place in 2025 was obtained for India, Indonesia, and Korea (Sathaye and Goldman, 1991). For India, a decline in the nuclear and hydroelectric share of capacity from 37 percent in 1985 to 34 percent in 2025 is balanced by an increase in the share of natural gas, while the share of coal is projected to remain constant. (The share of oil is near zero in all years.) Since India produces nearly three-quarters of the region's electricity (see Chapter 4), developments in this country are largely indicative of trends for the region.

Korea and Indonesia account for only somewhat more than half of the electricity produced in newly industrializing Asia, so the extrapolation of trends in these countries to the rest of the region must be done with care. The major changes in these two countries are the increase in the use of natural gas (which accounted for 2 percent of electricity produced in 1985 and 17 percent in 2025), a decline in the use of oil, and an expansion of nuclear power from 25 percent to 36 percent. The increasing share of natural gas to replace oil in Korea and Indonesia is assumed to be representative of the entire region. The replacement of oil by nuclear power is expected to proceed more slowly throughout the region, with the share of nuclear power increasing by 5 percent and the share of oil decreasing by 5 percent between 2000 and 2020.

Projections for centrally planned Asia are based on data obtained on China (see Table 5.11). The combined share of nuclear and hydroelectric power is projected to increase from 20 percent in 1985 to 32–39 percent in 2025 (Sathaye and Goldman, 1991). However, other experts on energy use in China find these plans for rapid expansion of nuclear and hydroelectric capacity "extremely ambitious, and none has a high chance of being fully realized" (Smil, 1988,

Table 5.10. Capacity for electricity generation by source in low-income Asia and newly industrializing Asia, 1987 and 2000 (percentages)

	Thermal	Nuclear	Hydro-electric[a]	Total
1987				
Low-income Asia	65.4	1.9	32.7	100.0
Newly industrializing Asia	75.2	10.5	13.3	100.0
2000				
Low-income Asia	68.5	1.5	29.9	100.0
Newly industrializing Asia	78.2	8.7	13.2	100.0

a. Includes geothermal and others.

Notes: Data on planned capacity are available for India, Pakistan, Bangladesh, and the Philippines for low-income Asia. Data on planned capacity for Korea (newly industrializing Asia) did not include details about the type of capacity: the share of nuclear and hydroelectric capacity is assumed to increase slightly after from 1990. Detail about fuels used for thermal generation was also not provided.

Source: Institute for Economic Analysis based for 1987 on UN, 1984, 1989; based for 2000 on Asian Development Bank, 1990.

Table 5.11. Capacity for electricity generation by source in China and centrally planned Asia, 1985 and 2025 (percentages)

	1985	2025 High	2025 Low	2020 centrally planned Asia
Coal	65	67	58	65
Oil	15	1	1	1
Gas	0	1	2	6
Nuclear and geothermal	0	7	9	3
Hydroelectric	20	25	30	25
Total	100	100	100	100

Source: Sathaye and Goldman, 1991, and IEA projections.

p. 72). The assumptions made for centrally planned Asia in the OCF scenario (last column of Table 5.11) reflect the general trends reported by Sathaye and Goldman (1991), tempered by the practical concerns expressed by other experts on China, which indicate a somewhat greater use of fossil fuels and a more slowly growing nuclear capacity.

Between 1990 and 2020, the fuel mix for other regions (except the major oil producers and North Africa/other Middle East) has been adjusted to reflect a slightly decreasing use of oil and, for the former Soviet Union, an increase in the use of gas and coal. Under the OCF scenario, the share of electricity produced with fossil fuels is expected to remain constant after 2000, except in centrally planned Asia and newly industrializing Asia, because the use of nonthermal technologies—nuclear, hydroelectric, and other renewables—is unlikely to expand rapidly enough to reduce significantly the share of electricity produced from fossil fuels. We assume that public opposition in Japan to further expansion of nuclear power after 2000 prevents the announced increase in the share of nuclear electricity. Though the share of fossil fuels is projected to increase slightly in India, a constant share is assumed for the region as a whole. These assumptions are in line with projections made for the WEC by Romain-Frisch (1989).

Under the OCF scenario, the share of electricity generated from natural gas is assumed to increase, largely in response to environmental concerns, replacing 15 percent of the coal- or oil-fired capacity in the regions indicated in Table 5.12 between 2000 and 2020. This assumes a reversal throughout most of Western Europe of policies which have discouraged the use of gas for electricity and, therefore, have impeded the financing necessary to expand natural gas extraction and trade in the developing world.

Alternative Scenario Assumptions

Two scenarios were formulated about nonfossil-fuel electricity generation: one based on increased use of nuclear and hydroelectric power (OCF/HN) and another based on solar power (OCF/S). The estimated capital costs for nuclear and hydroelectric plants are estimated from data provided by the Electric Power Research Institute (EPRI, 1988). Current nuclear power plants incur

Table 5.12. Fuel switching in the electric power industry by World Model region, 2020

	Substitution of natural gas for:	
15 percent of coal-fired capacity	15 percent of oil-fired capacity	7.5 percent oil-fired and 7.5 percent coal-fired capacity
High-income North America	Newly industrializing Asia	High-income Western Europe
Japan	Newly industrializing Latin America	Former Soviet Union
Oceania	Low-income Latin America	Centrally planned Asia
Medium-income Western Europe	Major oil producers	
Eastern Europe	North Africa and other Middle East	
Southern Africa	Sub-Saharan Africa	

a. Six percent of oil-fired capacity only.

Source: Institute for Economic Analysis.

roughly twice the capital costs of conventional technologies they displace. Estimates for costs of hydroelectric power plants vary enormously when the cost of a dam must be accounted for. Without a dam, construction costs for hydroelectric plants can be as much as those for conventional fossil-fuel plants. For this scenario, the cost of constructing a dam was assumed to be equal to all other construction costs for a hydroelectric plant; this falls toward the high end of cost estimates for a dam.

As a conservative estimate,* we assume that the construction of both nuclear and hydroelectric plants requires twice as much capital per unit of capacity as a conventional fossil-fuel plant, while the operating costs are naturally lower due to savings on fuel. A more detailed nuclear/hydroelectric scenario would account for the full costs of these technologies; for example, one should keep track of the nuclear waste generated and the amount of land inundated in the construction of dams for hydroelectric plants. Table 5.13 shows the nuclear and hydroelectric capacities assumed in each region under the OCF/HN scenario: we consider this the maximum feasible rate of installation of this capacity by 2020.

A cost breakthrough in solar technology, making it competitive with conventional technology, is assumed under the OCF/S scenario. Consequently, we assume no additional capital requirements per unit of output for solar power plants above those of conventional technology. The OCF/S scenario assumes the same shares of nuclear and hydroelectric power as the OCF scenario. The capacity provided by solar technology is equal to that furnished by additional nuclear and hydroelectric power under the OCF/HN scenario.

---

* Current nuclear power technology requires, on average, twice the capital of conventional technology. New nuclear technology is expected to have the same capital costs as conventional technology.

Table 5.13. Percentage of electricity generated by nuclear and hydroelectric plants in World Model regions in 1987 and in 2020 under alternative scenarios

	Nuclear			Hydroelectric			Total			
	1987	2020, OCF	2020, OCF/HN	1987	2020, OCF	2020, OCF/HN	1987	2020, OCF	2020, OCF/HN	2020, OCF/s
High-income North America	16.7	12.3	20.0	18.4	21.9	25.0	35.1	34.2	45.0	11.0
Newly industrializing Latin America	1.7	1.7	4.0	62.0	62.0	70.0	63.7	63.7	74.0	10.3
Low-income Latin America	0.0	0.0	0	50.8	50.8	65.0	50.8	50.8	65.0	15.0
High-income Western Europe	32.7	28.6	35.0	21.0	19.1	20.0	53.7	47.7	55.0	7.3
Medium-income Western Europe	14.7	8.5	15.0	28.4	24.8	30.0	43.1	33.3	45.0	11.7
Eastern Europe	11.5	11.5	10.0	5.9	5.9	10.0	17.4	17.4	20.0	2.6
Former Soviet Union	11.2	11.2	10.0	13.2	13.2	25.0	24.4	24.4	35.0	10.6
Centrally planned Asia	0.0	3.0	9.0	23.6	25.0	30.0	23.6	28.0	39.0	11.0
Japan	27.2	39.8	63.0	12.2	12.2	12.0	39.4	52.0	75.0	23.0
Newly industrializing Asia	19.8	16.2	28.0	11.0	10.8	12.0	30.8	27.0	40.0	13.0
Low-income Asia	2.0	1.6	4.0	30.6	28.0	35.0	32.6	29.6	39.0	9.4
Major oil producers	0.0	0.0	0	5.3	5.3	6.0	5.3	5.3	6.0	0.7
North Africa and Middle East	0.0	0.0	0	13.8	13.8	14.0	14.0	13.8	13.8	0.0
Sub-Saharan Africa	0.0	0.0	0	42.6	42.6	55.0	42.6	42.6	55.0	12.4
Southern Africa	3.2	3.2	5.0	0.7	0.7	2.0	3.9	3.9	7.0	3.0
Oceania	0.0	0.0	0	22.0	18.0	25.0	22.0	18.0	25.0	7.0

a. Share of electricity produced by solar power under the DCF/s scenario OCF/s.

Note: See text for description of the alternative scenarios: HN (hydro and nuclear) and s (solar).

Source: for 1987: UN, 1989; for 2020, Institute for Economic Analysis projections.

6

Industrial Energy Conservation

One of the most attractive ways to increase the effective energy supply is through energy conservation. Energy conservation measures are usually relatively inexpensive and can be implemented quickly compared to the replacement of existing capacity with new, more energy-efficient equipment. This chapter describes the kinds of obstacles that in the past prevented the full implementation of these measures. Conservation measures are then discussed in some detail, and the investment and energy savings that can be envisaged for the next several decades are quantified for specific industries defined in terms of World Model sectors. World Model parameter projections under the OCF scenario are described by region and decade.

Obstacles to Conservation

While many conservation measures were introduced in the industrial, market economies after the oil price increases of the 1970s, industry in the formerly socialist and developing countries has been slow to adopt such measures except in some of the newly industrializing countries. Even in the industrial countries, additional conservation measures can be taken, especially in the United States, where relatively low energy prices have slowed their adoption compared to Western Europe and Japan.

There are both technical and institutional barriers that will have to be overcome in order for these measures to be implemented in developing countries. For example, some highly efficient electrical equipment cannot tolerate the fluctuations in voltage often found in developing countries (OTA, 1991). Some measures, such as cogeneration or dry cement production, may be less cost effective for the small-scale operations that dominate much of the manufacturing in developing countries. In addition, these cottage industries are plagued by a less reliable supply of electricity, poorer-quality equipment and materials, and less access to the financial resources needed to introduce some of these measures.

Even large-scale operations in developing countries, such as electricity generation, are susceptible to many types of inefficiency. For example, the construction of power plants has often been financed, at least in part, by different foreign sources. Each plant is generally designed by a team representing the funding source and uses equipment produced in the sponsor country, making it difficult or impossible for the receiving country to centralize operations like maintenance and repair or training of technical personnel. Nonetheless, as these economies develop, the average plant size is expected to increase and the transportation infrastructure will improve, making possible the cost-effective introduction of more conservation measures.

Energy pricing policies are also responsible, in part, for the inefficient use of energy in developing countries (Munasinghe, 1986; World Bank, 1983). Many factors are considered when choosing a particular technology or type of equipment, only one of which is energy efficiency. Some of these other factors, such as durability, the ability to operate above rated capacity, and the ability to use fuel that varies in quality, may dictate a choice of technology that is not optimal from an energy-efficiency perspective. Low energy prices ensure that energy efficiency will not be given a high priority in decisions about technology.

Many of the technical barriers to the cost-effective introduction of energy conservation measures experienced by developing countries are not present in Eastern Europe and the former Soviet Union. However, the policy commitment to low energy prices in these regions has resulted in technological decisions that assign a low priority to energy efficiency. Institutional changes needed to provide incentives to implement these measures, including energy price reform, are now underway (Jaczewski, 1991; Volfberg, 1991).

In the developed market economies there is still considerable room for conservation measures, particularly the more sophisticated ones, such as the introduction of adjustable-speed drives and an increase in cogeneration, as well as simpler ones, such as improved lighting and waste heat recovery. A number of institutional changes, such as favorable tax treatment for energy conservation and facilitating the connection of firms with excess electricity from cogeneration to the main electrical grid, would spur further improvements in energy efficiency. Specific conservation measures are described below.

Energy Conservation Measures and Reductions in Energy Use

There are several categories of industrial energy conservation measures, ranging from virtually costless housekeeping to more costly investment in additional equipment for cogeneration. These measures are identified in Table 6.1, where they are presented in order of increasing cost and complexity. The table and the following discussion are based primarily on a synthesis of country and industry studies undertaken for developing countries by the World Bank (Gamba, Caplin, and Mulckhuyse, 1986) and Lin (1991) and for developed countries by Fickett, Clark, and Lovins (1988), Geller (1989), Howarth and Schipper (1991), Johansson, Bodlund, and Williams (1989), and Ross and Steinmeyer (1990).

Housekeeping measures include checking for small leaks; replacing worn belts, damaged insulation, and bad bearings; and cleaning dirty heating surfaces and lamps in a regular, timely fashion. These procedures can be carried

Table 6.1. Industrial energy conservation measures

1. Housekeeping: measures to reduce energy use at little cost that can be undertaken by current personnel, such as shutting off standby furnaces, continuous operations (rather than shutting down and starting up, which waste energy), regular tune-ups and calibration of instruments to improve combustion efficiency
2. Waste heat recovery: the capture and reuse of heat currently treated as an unwanted by-product
3. Combustion and steam system improvements: efficiency in steam boiler systems can be improved through housekeeping, waste heat recovery, and use of specialized equipment that improves operational efficiency
4. Electric system improvements: retrofit with variable-speed drive motors and more efficient lighting, load management, installation of high-efficiency motors and transformers
5. Process modification: generalizations about process modifications are specific to the kind of process and to the age and design of the plant
6. Cogeneration: any form of joint production of electrical/mechanical energy and useful thermal energy

Source: Institute for Economic Analysis based on Gamba, Caplin, and Mulckhuyse, 1986, pp. 25–34.

out during regular maintenance and require no additional investment. Other measures, such as regular tune-ups and calibration of instrumentation, as well as checking that the rating of the insulation is matched to the heat generated along distribution lines, are more complicated but virtually costless and not difficult to implement.

Waste heat recovery is a significant and very cheap source of energy savings, provided that there is a use for the heat and that it can be delivered in adequate quantities. Both high- and medium-temperature waste heat, typically obtained from metal processing, incinerators, and cement kilns, can be used to drive a steam turbogenerator. Low-temperature waste heat (<230° C) from process steam condensate, refrigeration condensers, and cooling water from high-temperature process equipment, can be used for various processes. For example, hot exhaust gas from brickfiring kilns can be used to dry wet bricks before firing.

Combustion and steam system improvements include measures such as the use of preheated air, turbolators, recuperation of heat from blowdown, return of clean condensates, cleaning of contaminated condensates for use as boiler feed water, and monitoring of steam traps. In a factory with low, continuous steam requirements, one large boiler can be replaced by several smaller ones, which would then be run at full capacity, with excess capacity shut down until needed.

The efficiency of electrical systems can be improved by converting lighting systems to more efficient fluorescent and high-intensity discharge lamps, rescheduling operations to reduce peak load, installing automatic controls, replacing oversized electric motors, installing capacitors, and using synchronous motors and variable-speed drives that match speed to power demand.

Process modifications can require substantial changes and need to be evaluated on a case-by-case basis to determine if they are cost effective relative to the construction of a new plant. For example, the conversion of a wet-process cement plant (capacity, 1,500 tons/day) to a modern dry-process plant (capacity, 2,700 tons/day) would cost $50 to $60 million (1983 prices), while a new plant might cost $220 to $280 million. Processes can often be modified through changes in process conditions, such as drying at lower temperatures or using catalysts to permit chemical reactions at lower temperatures. Evaporation and distillation, among the most energy-intensive processes in the chemical, food, and petroleum industries, can be modified by installing reflux level controls, lowering temperatures, adding distillation trays, and installing steam jet pumps in multieffect distillation.

Cogeneration, the joint production of electrical or mechanical energy and thermal energy, results in higher overall energy efficiencies than those obtained by producing power and heat through separate processes, typically reducing energy requirements by 10–30 percent. Efficient cogeneration can entail substantial costs and may require a completely different plant design and layout. However, retrofitting is possible and has not yet been carried out in some industries, such as petroleum refining, where the potential energy savings are great.

The potential for sector-level energy conservation in developing countries is quantified in Table 6.2 as a percentage reduction of energy input requirements attributable to specific combinations of measures. The World Bank study (on which the table is based) identified eight sectors for detailed treatment because they are estimated to account for more than 70 percent of industrial energy use in developing countries.

Relatively simple, inexpensive measures and the associated energy savings are identified in panel A of Table 6.2. These are mainly housekeeping measures and minor combustion and steam system improvements requiring, at most, one-time installation or replacement of minor equipment. The World Bank study estimated the payback period for the cost of implementing these measures at one to two years. While this method of cost evaluation is sensitive to assumptions about energy prices, it still offers a rough indication that the cost is quite low.

In panel B of Table 6.2, the more extensive changes needed for additional gains in energy efficiency, with an estimated payback period of three to four and a half years, are identified for the same sectors. While the World Bank studies focused on developing countries, similar industrial conditions with the potential for energy savings exist in Eastern Europe and the former Soviet Union.

In the developed regions, a great deal can still be done to improve energy efficiency. Some of the additional measures are similar to those identified by the World Bank, such as the use of adjustable-speed drives and energy-efficient lighting fixtures. Adjustable speed drives, estimated to reduce motor drive energy requirements by 20 percent (Lamarre, 1990), have yet to be widely used in developed regions (Geller, 1989).

Other conservation measures are more complicated, such as the use of automated lighting systems and high-efficiency elevators. Improved heating and cooling systems, greater insulation, and integrated design of heating, ventilation, and cooling systems are of greater concern for the developed regions, which use more energy for space conditioning than the developing regions. The development of small-scale, packaged cogeneration systems for commercial applications is expected to become more widely used as well (Chandler, Geller, and Ledbetter, 1988; Douglas, 1988).

Table 6.2. Energy-saving measures and related energy savings in developing countries

A. Short-term, low-cost measures

Sector	Examples of processor product	Potential energy savings (percentages)	Examples of major energy-saving measures
XX3 Food processing	Raw cane sugar	16–18	Improve boiler combustion efficiency,
	Cane sugar refining	16–18	steam systems and insulation, evaporator
	Edible oils	8–10	management.
XX4 Petroleum	Refining	7–12	Improve combustion controls, increase steam condensate return.
XX5 Metal processing	Raw steel finishing	5–7	Improve combustion controls and insulation.
	Hall-Heroult aluminum smelting	2–4	Improve combustion controls in remelting furnaces, insulation and power factors.
XX6 Textiles	Finishing	12–15	Improve boiler combustion and steam distribution efficiency.
XX9 Pulp and paper	Integrated chemical	12–14	Improve boiler and steam system, recondition insulation.
XX13 Fertilizer	Ammonia	2–5	Insulate primary reformer, housekeeping measures.
XX15 Cement	Dry and wet processes	10–20	Improve combustion, insulation, and housekeeping.
XX16 Glass and clay products	Flat and containers	10–12	Improve combustion controls and insulation.
	Bricks	10–15	Improve flue gas recirculation, combustion controls, and kiln insulation. Replace burner.
All other industrial and extractive sectors		5–10	Improve combustion, insulation, operation scheduling, maintenance.

B. Long-term measures

Sector	Examples of processor product	Potential energy savings (percentages)	Examples of major energy-saving measures
Xx3 Food processing	Raw cane sugar	up to 85	Increase use of waste-heat recovery, improve evaporators.
	Cane sugar refining	15–30	
	Edible oils	12–15	
XX4 Petroleum	Refining	15–25	Recover waste heat, replace inefficient equipment.
XX5 Metal processing	Raw steel finishing	5–10	Recover waste heat, replace inefficient equipment.
	Hall-Heroult aluminum smelting	5–10	Install process controls, increase waste-heat recovery and recycling.

Table 6.2. (continued)

B. Long-term measures

Sector	Examples of processor product	Potential energy savings (percentages)	Examples of major energy-saving measures
XX6 Textiles	Finishing	15–17	Install waste-heat recovery equipment, replace old boilers, improve water and liquor systems.
XX9 Pulp and paper	Integrated chemical Other	14–16 10–15	Increase use of waste fuels, black liquor, cogeneration, and waste-heat recovery from dryers.
XX13 Fertilizer	Ammonia	20–25	Recover waste heat in reformer, recover hydrogen and carbon monoxide, and replace compressors.
XX15 Cement	Dry and wet processes	10–30	Convert from wet to dry process. Install high-efficiency heat systems and process controls.
XX16 Glass and clay products	Flat glass and containers	15–20	Install efficient recuperators and waste-heat boilers, increase boosting.
	Bricks	15–20	Increase stack gas recuperation, rebuild kiln.
All other industrial and extractive sectors		5–10	Improve combustion, insulation, operation scheduling, maintenance.

Note: measures identified in panel A include mainly housekeeping and minor modifications.

Source: Institute for Economic Analysis based on Gamba, Caplin, and Mulckhuyse, 1986, Table 13, pp. 40–41.

Projections Under the OCF Scenario

The World Model sectors potentially affected by these measures include all the manufacturing and service sectors, XX1–XX30 (except for transportation, XX28, and electric power, XX25, which are treated separately), plus mining, SE5–SE13. Energy inputs (oil, SE11; natural gas, SE12; coal, SE13; and electric power, XX25) per unit of output to these sectors will be reduced by the introduction of conservation measures. In addition, the displacement of fossil fuel use by the use of purchased electricity will be addressed.

All the energy conservation measures identified above will be implemented in developing regions, Eastern Europe, and the former Soviet Union over the period 1990–2020 under the OCF scenario. Energy coefficients for 1980 and 1990 are assumed to have taken into account past energy conservation efforts (since they have been scaled to match regional control totals). The World Bank study identified opportunities for additional conservation in the mid-1980s, few of which were actually implemented by 1990, in part because of the relative decline in oil prices. Except in those sectors covered by case studies for which new technologies have been projected under the OCF scenario, new capacity is assumed to be similar to existing capacity, but more efficient because of the introduction of conservation measures.

Under the OCF scenario, the technical and institutional barriers to improving energy efficiency, especially in the developing regions, Eastern Europe, and the former Soviet Union, will be substantially reduced over the period 1990–2020. This assumption has been made by others for Eastern Europe (Jaczewski, 1991), the former Soviet Union (Volfberg, 1991), and the newly industrializing regions (Gamba et al., 1986) but is problematic for some of the other regions. In particular, there are doubts that China will significantly change its energy policies (Ledic, 1991); the incentives for some oil-rich economies to introduce stringent energy-efficiency measures are not strong; and the availability of resources in Sub-Saharan Africa to implement even these inexpensive measures is questionable (OTA, 1990). Nevertheless, the OCF scenario reflects the optimistic view that these measures will be introduced.

We have been conservative in our projections of energy savings by assuming that new capacity put in place is no more energy efficient than existing capacity with new conservation measures (except in those sectors covered by other case studies for which new technologies have been projected). In addition, if different energy savings were identified for different processes within a single sector, the lower energy savings estimate was used.

Table 6.3 identifies the energy savings assumed under the OCF scenario. By the year 2000, all the housekeeping measures are assumed to have been adopted in developing regions, Eastern Europe, and the former Soviet Union, reducing the energy coefficients from their 1990 values, for the sectors identified in Table 6.2, by the upper bounds of potential gains in energy efficiency given in panel A. By 2010, some retrofitting is assumed to have taken place in these regions to the extent that the lower bounds of potential gains in energy efficiency shown in panel B of Table 6.2 are achieved. By the year 2020, all possible retrofitting of existing capacity is assumed to have occurred; energy coefficients are reduced by the upper bounds given in panel B of Table 6.2.

Information about region- and sector-specific conservation measures was not available for developed regions. To reflect the expected continuation of energy conservation practices in the developed regions, a further rate of reduction of energy inputs of about 20 percent is applied to the industrial sectors in developed regions for the period 1990–2020 (see Table 6.3, panel B).

For the first round of savings between 1990 and 2000, the measures have been identified as virtually costless by the World Bank study. Additional reductions of energy inputs are achieved by the installation of some additional equipment, electrical and electronic machinery, instrumentation, and other machinery at an estimated cost amounting to roughly 0.10 – 0.15 percent of annual investment by developing regions in the World Model in 1990. In order to represent these costs, the investment requirements for each region were increased by 0.25 percent in each year after 1990. This investment requirement is higher than that estimated by the World Bank and reflects a conservative view about the costs that may be incurred to increase energy conservation.

In the past, economic growth has been accompanied by the apparent displacement of direct use of fossil fuels in production by purchased electricity. In developing countries, this trend is expected to continue as electricity supplies

Table 6.3. Projections of energy savings due to industrial energy
conservation under the ocf scenario, 2000–2020 (percentage
reduction in energy input coefficients from previous decade)

Sector	2000	2010	2020
A. Developing regions, Eastern Europe and former Soviet Union			
XX3 Food processing	10	12	3
XX4 Petroleum refining	12	15	10
XX5 Metal processing	4	5	8
XX6 Textiles	15	15	2
XX9 Pulp and paper	14	10	5
XX13 Fertilizer	5	20	5
XX15 Cement	20	10	20
XX16 Glass and clay products	12	15	5
All other industrial, extractive, and service sectors	10	5	5
B. Developed regions			
All industrial, extractive, and service sectors	10	5	5

Notes: 1. The energy savings estimated for all other industrial and extractive sectors in
Table 6.2 was assumed for service sectors.

2. Where the process or product identified in Table 6.2 does not account for all or most of a
sector's production, the potential energy savings for the process or product is assumed to
be representative of the energy savings potential of the sector as a whole.

Source: Institute for Economic Analysis based on sources in Table 6.2.

become more reliable. Projections of the displacement of fossil fuels by electricity in industrial and commercial applications in developing countries are based on rough estimates from a series of country studies conducted by Lawrence Berkeley Laboratories (Sathaye and Goldman, 1991). Most developing regions are projected to displace 20 percent of fossil fuel use by electricity between 1990 and 2020 (30 percent is displaced in centrally planned Asia and newly industrializing Asia). In each region, the dominant fuel or fuels in industry and commercial applications is affected (see Table 6.4). (No sectoral detail was available, so the same rate of displacement was applied to all relevant sectors.) These adjustments to fossil fuel and electricity coefficients were made after coefficients were adjusted to represent energy conservation.

Table 6.4. Projection of the displacement of fossil fuel inputs by
purchased electricity under the ocf scenario, 1990–2020
(percentages)

	Oil	Gas	Coal
Centrally planned Asia	0	0	30
Newly industrializing Asia	15	0	15
Low-income Asia	10	0	10
Low-income Latin America, North Africa other Middle East, Sub-Saharan Africa	20	0	0
Newly industrializing Latin America, major oil producers	10	10	0
All other regions	0	0	0

Source: Institute for Economic Analysis estimates based on Kahane, 1989;
Sathaye and Goldman, 1991; and personal communication with industrial
energy experts.

In the developed regions, further displacement of fossil fuel use by purchased electricity is likely to be minimal, according to cross-country evaluations of a number of specific technologies in different sectors (Boyd and Ross, 1989; Kahane, 1986, 1989; Norgaard, 1989; Williams, 1989; and personal communications with industrial energy experts). There is potential for increased displacement in processing industries which is described in detail in (Schurr, Burwell, Devine, and Sonenblum, 1990). There are, however, compensating factors like the priority accorded by electric utilities to conservation and the likelihood of increased reliance on industrial cogeneration (which is accounted for as a purchase of fuels not of electricity). For these reasons, no further displacement of fossil fuels by purchased electricity is projected for the future in developed regions under the OCF scenario.

7

Processing and Fabrication of Metals

Representation of Metals in the World Model

The World Model explicitly tracks the extraction of six nonfuel metallic ores: copper (SE5), bauxite (aluminum) (SE6), nickel (SE7), zinc (SE8), lead (SE9) and iron ore (SE10). There is a single sector for primary processing of metals (XX5). To retain detail about the mix of metals in refined metals, the metal fabricating sectors purchase their refined metal inputs in two parts, the ore directly from the mining sectors (SE5–10) and the services for transforming ore to semi-manufactured inputs from the refining sector (XX5). The metal extraction, processing, and principal metal fabricating sectors are shown in Table 7.1.

The World Model directly tracks only virgin metal from ore, and the consumption of metal by the metal fabricating sectors is represented in terms of the metal content of ores. The consumption of scrap metal, of great importance because it can substitute for virgin metals from ore, is taken into account indirectly. Estimates and projections of the share of scrap consumption are an integral part of the data preparation. All estimated input coefficients are reported

Table 7.1. Metal extraction, processing and principal fabricating sectors

		Unit
Extraction		
SE5	Copper	millions of metric tons
SE6	Bauxite	millions of metric tons
SE7	Nickel	thousands of metric tons
SE8	Zinc	millions of metric tons
SE9	Lead	millions of metric tons
SE10	Iron	millions of metric tons
XX2	Residual resources	billions of dollars in 1970 U.S. prices
Processing		
XX5	Primary metal processing	billions of dollars in 1970 U.S. prices
Fabrication		
XX17	Motor vehicles	billions of dollars in 1970 U.S. prices
XX18	Shipbuilding	billions of dollars in 1970 U.S. prices
XX19	Aircraft industry	billions of dollars in 1970 U.S. prices
XX20	Metal products	billions of dollars in 1970 U.S. prices
XX21	Machinery	billions of dollars in 1970 U.S. prices
XX22	Electrical machinery	billions of dollars in 1970 U.S. prices

in this chapter on a gross basis (including consumption of scrap metal) to facilitate comparisons and to reflect the technical and economic conditions in the fabricating sectors, and the share of scrap in consumption is reported separately. The coefficients actually used in the World Model, however, are net of scrap.

Regional Distribution of Production and Use of Metals

Demand for metals in developed market economies has leveled off in the last two decades. In the United States, for instance, despite annual GDP growth of almost 3 percent between 1975 and 1985, crude steel demand fell by 13 percent over the decade, primary aluminum and copper demand increased by only 4 percent and 10 percent, respectively, and for most other metals there was a substantial decrease in demand. The energy price shocks were responsible for increasing the cost of metal processsing, thus promoting a substitution away from metals. In developed market economies, there has also been increased efficiency in the use of materials, substitution of cheaper materials or materials with more desirable characteristics for traditional materials, saturation of demand for bulk materials, and shifts in consumer preferences at higher income levels to goods and services that incorporate less materials (Herman, Ardekani, and Ausubel, 1989; Williams, Larson, and Ross, 1987).

Growth in infrastructure and construction activities has slowed substantially in developed economies, and today demand for materials for infrastructure (railroads, roads, factories) is mainly for replacement. The situation is similar for consumer durables, such as household appliances and cars, and for capital goods. The number of cars per capita is growing slowly, and the material input per car has fallen substantially. New technologies often economize materials in capital goods, and the shift toward service sectors is typically capital-saving.

The situation is different, of course, in developing countries. Beyond a subsistence income level, there is rapid growth in cars, household appliances, and material-intensive production of consumer and durable goods, as well as expansion of infrastructure.

Primary metal processing is very energy intensive, and the increase in the world price of fossil fuels, especially oil, has had a major impact on the relative costs of production in different geographic regions. While most developed regions have already exploited the most accessible energy sources and are dependent on imports of fossil fuels, several developing regions have large untapped reserves of hydropower, natural gas, and low-cost coal. The development of these reserves is often inexpensive, but a lack of nearby markets involves steep transportation costs. The indirect export of energy through its use in mineral processing often yields a higher return.

Most metal-processing technology is capital intensive and exhibits increasing returns up to a large scale of operations. Adding capacity to an existing plant is typically far cheaper than constructing a greenfield plant of the same size. Several of the developing regions, however, have well-established refining industries and can, to a large extent, draw on existing infrastructure and knowledge in the addition of new capacity. Proximity to their rapidly growing domestic markets reduces transportation costs and provides information about the markets.

There has been rapid development of metal processing industries in newly industrializing Asia, with its very efficient, low-cost labor force; newly industrializing Latin America, with its large reserves of ore, actual and potential hydroelectric power, and natural gas; centrally planned Asia (China), with large reserves of coal and some of the metals; the oil-rich countries, with their low-cost natural gas that often is not easily transported to market; and low-income Asia (India), with substanial coal and mineral reserves. Most of these regions have large domestic or regional markets for processed metals and relatively modern industry (Brown and McKern; 1987; Meunier and de Bruyn Kops, 1984; Strout, 1985).

We foresee a steadily increasing role for developing countries in primary processing, even though the situation will vary substantially among regions and for different metals, depending on reserves of ores and energy, production technology for the different metals, level of industrial development, regional infrastructure, and demand patterns. There will be increasing use of refined metals in developing countries with metal and energy reserves and increasing self-sufficiency in their provision. There will also be a significant expansion in exports of processed metals. Increases in refining can be anticipated even in developing economies that are dependent on imports for the production process.

Three developing regions—Sub-Saharan Africa, other Middle East and North Africa, and low-income Latin America—are in a different situation. These regions do not have large domestic markets; furthermore, the infrastructure and the basic refining industries are not well established, making expansion expensive. In addition, like some of the other regions, they have significant foreign debt, high capital charges, and a history of problems in reaching and maintaining high levels of capacity utilization. These difficulties will not easily be overcome despite large resources of various minerals.

The processing of metals has been subject to steady progress in energy efficiency, and the share of recycled materials, which can require substantially lower energy inputs than the use of virgin materials, is growing. (See discussion in Chapter 6.) The increased importance of scrap recycling (and secondary production using exclusively recycled materials) will substantially lengthen the economic life of the world's ore deposits.

There will be a continuing shift away from fossil fuels, especially oil, to hydroelectric power and gas in the mineral processing industry. Much of this substitution will take place through relocation to regions with cheaper and potentially more environmentally sound energy sources.

All of these developments can be expected to slow the growth of global pollution below what it might otherwise have been. However, pollution generated in developing countries, from both production and consumption, could rise sharply compared to current levels, in the absence of concerted efforts to contain it.

Use of Metals by the Metal-Fabricating Sectors in 1980 and 1987

The input coefficients for metals to the principal metal-fabricating sectors were estimated for 1980 and 1990, and projections were prepared for future years. The reestimation of the historical coefficients enabled us to make explicit assumptions about the parameters governing recycling as a basis for projecting the future coefficients for the OCF scenario.

Coefficients for past years were derived from accounting data by separately estimating the numerator (metal consumption by a given sector in a particular region) and the denominator (corresponding sectoral output). For most countries and regions, there are no readily available statistics for the consumption of metals by sector. The metal input coefficients were calculated for the United States, for which these data are available for 1980 and 1987, and the coefficients for other regions were derived from them.

Control totals are easily assembled for metals since they are relatively uniform and measured in physical units. The sources for metal inputs to the United States fabricating sectors are *Mineral Commodity Profiles* (U.S. Department of Interior, Bureau of Mines, 1983) and various editions of the *Minerals Yearbook,* published by the same agency. The outputs of the metal-fabricating sectors (measured in constant U.S. prices) have been obtained from unpublished national accounting data supplied by the U.S. Department of Labor.

Except for lead, metal inputs for 1980 were taken from *Mineral Commodity Profiles* because it reports in greater detail than the *Yearbook* and it identifies sectors by SIC code. For lead, the *Yearbook* was used because it provided more detail.

In some cases, the information in the *Commodity Profiles* was more aggregate than the World Model sectoral scheme. This was the case for transportation equipment, for which disaggregation to the three World Model sectors is reported only for nickel. For the other four metals, use was distributed according to the value of output of the using sectors. In a few other cases, inputs also had to be disaggregated, but these estimates should not influence the order of magnitude of the coefficients in any of the major metal-consuming sectors. As in the original World Model, inputs of metal to construction are charged through the metal products sector.

Finally, the estimated coefficients have been scaled so that calculated consumption is equal to apparent consumption (metal production less net exports), as reported in the *Minerals Yearbook.* The resulting coefficients are reported in Table 7.2.

The 1987 coefficients were constructed in the same way as the 1980 coefficients; changes relative to the 1980 coefficients are shown in Table 7.3. For lead inputs, the *Minerals Yearbook* was used directly. For copper and aluminum, the *Yearbook* time series data have been adjusted to take advantage of the detail in the 1980 input table in the *Commodity Profiles.* For zinc the *Yearbook* provides the shares of metal inputs to the different sectors. Another approach was used for steel and nickel: the 1980 coefficients were scaled so that projected consumption (the sum of coefficients times output) added up to actual 1987 consumption.

Table 7.2. Gross metal input coefficients to World Model sectors in the United States in 1980 (millions of metric tons of metal per billion 1970 U.S. dollars' worth of output; nickel in thousands of metric tons)

		Copper	Aluminum	Nickel	Zinc	Lead	Steel
XX4	Petroleum refining	0	0	0	0	0.0056	0
XX5	Primary metal processing	0	0	0	0	0	0
XX6	Textiles, apparel	0	0	0	0	0	0
XX7	Wood and cork	0	0	0	0	0	0
XX8	Furniture, fixtures	0	0	0	0	0	0
XX9	Paper	0	0	0	0	0	0
XX10	Printing	0	0	0	0	0.0003	0
XX11	Rubber	0	0	0	0.0044	0	0
XX12	Industrial chemicals	0	0.0196	0.4973	0	0	0
XX13	Fertilizer	0	0	0.4983	0	0	0
XX14	Finished chemical products	0	0	0.4923	0.0019	0.0008	0
XX15	Cement	0	0	0	0	0	0
XX16	Glass	0	0.0187	0	0	0.0026	0
XX17	Motor vehicles	0.0018	0.0108	0.3887	0.0022	0.0006	0.3666
XX18	Shipbuilding	0.0018	0.0107	0.8687	0.0021	0.0002	0.3627
XX19	Aircraft	0.0017	0.0105	1.0197	0.0022	0.0002	0.3656
XX20	Metal products	0.0097	0.0547	0.7872	0.0108	0.0024	0.9996
XX21	Machinery	0.0035	0.0060	0.2079	0.0010	0	0.1823
XX22	Electric machinery	0.0176	0.0101	0.5899	0.0022	0.0096	0.2089
XX23	Scientific instruments	0	0	0	0	0	0
XX24	Miscellaneous manufacturing	0	0	0	0	0	0
XX25	Electricity, water	0	0	0	0	0	0
XX26	Construction	0	0	0	0	0	0
XX27	Trade	0	0	0	0	0	0
XX28	Transport	0	0	0	0	0	0
XX29	Communication	0	0	0	0	0	0
XX30	Services	0	0	0	0	0	0

Note: This table has been transposed for convenience of presentation. Each column of the table represents a row of input coefficients.

Source: Institute for Economic Analysis based on U.S. Department of the Interior, Bureau of Mines, *Minerals Yearbook*, various years; U.S. Department of the Interior, Bureau of Mines, *Mineral Commodity Profiles*, 1983; U.S. Department of Labor, 1990.

One important reason for constructing the U.S. coefficients for both 1980 and 1987 was to examine the major changes in the input structures and identify trends that might continue into the projection period. These changes, evident in Table 7.3, are discussed below.

The input coefficients for deliveries of metal-refining services (margins) to the metal-fabricating sectors were also estimated for the United States. These coefficients are calculated by summing the metal input coefficients to a sector, each weighted by the processing "margin" for that metal. (The latter is measured as the price of refined metal less the value of the ore and is based on data from the *Minerals Yearbook* and the *Commodity Yearbook*.) These coefficients are reported in Table 7.4.

The gross metal input coefficients for the fabricating sectors in the sixteen World Model regions are derived from the 1980 and 1987 U.S. coefficients in the following way: apparent regional consumption according to control totals (see

Table 7.3. Gross metal input coefficients for the United States in 1987 relative to 1980

	Copper	Aluminum	Nickel	Zinc	Lead	Steel
XX 4 Petroleum refining					0.17	
XX 5 Primary metal processing						
XX 6 Textiles, apparel						
XX 7 Wood and cork						
XX 8 Furniture, fixtures						
XX 9 Paper						
XX10 Printing					0.03	
XX11 Rubber				0.46		
XX12 Industrial chemicals		1.21	0.82			
XX13 Fertilizer			0.82			
XX14 Finished chemical products			0.82	0.63	0.68	
XX15 Cement						
XX16 Glass		1.16			0.89	
XX17 Motor vehicle	0.69	1.05	0.82	1.29	0.57	0.83
XX18 Shipbuilding	0.67	1.06	0.82	1.32	0.97	0.83
XX19 Aircraft	0.70	1.08	0.82	1.27	0.59	0.83
XX20 Metal products	1.09	1.19	0.82	1.13	0.72	0.83
XX21 Machinery	0.60	0.72	0.82	1.50	0.17	0.83
XX22 Electrical machinery	0.79	0.74	0.82	0.67	1.14	0.83
XX23 Scientific instruments						
XX24 Miscellaneous manufacturing						
XX25 Electricity, water						
XX26 Construction						
XX27 Trade						
XX28 Transport						
XX29 Communication						
XX30 Services						

Note: Entries correspond to the 1987 coefficient divided by the 1980 coefficient. Blanks correpond to zero coefficients in 1980.

Source: Institute for Economic Analysis based on Table 7.2 and sources cited there.

Table 7.4. Input coefficients for metal refining margins (XX5) in the United States in 1980 and 1987 ($/$, 1970 U.S. prices)

A. 1980		B. 1987	
XX4 Petroleum refining	0.0016	XX4 Petroleum refining	0.0003
XX10 Printing	0.0001	XX10 Printing	0.0000
XX11 Rubber	0.0012	XX11 Rubber	0.0005
XX12 Industrial chemicals	0.0101	XX12 Industrial chemicals	0.0121
XX14 Finished chemical products	0.0008	XX14 Finished chemical products	0.0005
XX16 Glass	0.0102	XX16 Glass	0.0116
XX17 Motor vehicles	0.0577	XX17 Motor vehicles	0.0489
XX18 Shipbuilding	0.0570	XX18 Shipbuilding	0.0483
XX19 Aircraft	0.0572	XX19 Aircraft	0.0484
XX20 Metal products	0.1765	XX20 Metal products	0.1600
XX21 Machinery	0.0316	XX21 Machinery	0.0253
XX22 Electric machinery	0.0549	XX22 Electric machinery	0.0453

Note: The coefficients measure the value of metal refining services delivered by metal processing (XX5) per dollar of output of the fabricating sectors. These figures comprise a row of the input matrix.

Source: Sources cited in Table 7.2 and Institute for Economic Analysis estimates.

Case Studies

Table 7.5) was divided by apparent consumption calculated by the World Model for all regions, using the U.S. metal input coefficients for fabricating sectors. The coefficients for each region were then scaled so that the two measures of consumption matched, on the assumption that differences in the use of each metal among regions affect all sectors using that metal similarly. The scale factor by metal and region in 1980, and the change in coefficients by metal and region between 1980 and 1987, are reported in Table 7.6. Metal-processing margins were then calculated using the method described earlier.

Table 7.5. Apparent consumption of metals in World Model regions in 1980 and 1987 (thousands of tons of metal content, except iron, millions of tons of metal content)

	Copper	Bauxite	Nickel	Zinc	Lead	Iron
A. 1980						
1 High-income North America	2027	6141	156	960	1178	134
2 Newly industrializing Latin America	364	763	16	315	212	30
3 Low-income Latin America	60	122	1	67	35	5
4 High-income Western Europe	2120	4483	199	1748	1592	122
5 Medium-income Western Europe	411	683	11	183	251	22
6 Eastern Europe	340	604	39	282	315	61
7 Soviet Union	115	1308	132	977	745	154
8 Centrally planned Asia	283	426	19	227	185	52
9 Japan	1649	2845	126	752	303	77
10 Newly industrializing Asia	117	313	114	238	66	17
11 Low-income Asia	143	362	11	132	51	10
12 Major oil producers	35	189	0	17	19	10
13 North Africa and other Middle East	10	157	0	16	28	4
14 Sub-Saharan Africa	27	148	1	92	11	4
15 Southern Africa	32	94	4	89	21	7
16 Oceania	227	330	5	153	76	7
World	8960	18969	734	6247	5087	717
B. 1987						
1 High-income North America	2052	7105	136	1224	1292	119
2 Newly industrializing Latin America	577	869	17	393	245	31
3 Low-income Latin America	46	41	1	72	43	5
4 High-income Western Europe	1614	4623	207	1862	1310	103
5 Medium-income Western Europe	430	556	17	289	255	24
6 Eastern Europe	706	476	41	319	308	56
7 Soviet Union	1094	2150	121	1086	775	170
8 Centrally planned Asia	392	547	22	684	351	79
9 Japan	1558	2608	138	747	283	73
10 Newly industrializing Asia	615	628	23	271	142	26
11 Low-income Asia	114	273	18	92	27	117
12 Major oil producers	82	316	0	27	23	14
13 North Africa and other Middle East	18	97	0	27	51	3
14 Sub-Saharan Africa	42	195	1	88	6	3
15 Southern Africa	55	131	8	116	26	7
16 Oceania	333	542	3	163	103	7
World	9727	21155	752	7462	5238	734

Note: Apparent consumption is calculated as domestic production of refined and semimanufactured metal less net exports.

Source: Institute for Economic Analysis based on UN COMTRADE data base; UN (1989); U.S. Department of Interior, Bureau of Mines (various years); UNCTAD (various years), and Institute for Economic Analysis calculations.

Table 7.6. Gross metal input coefficients in World Model regions relative to U.S. coefficients in 1980 and 1987

	Copper	Aluminum	Nickel	Zinc	Lead	Steel
A. 1980						
High-income North America	0.71	0.74	0.64	0.61	0.85	0.84
Newly industrializing Latin America	1.31	1.04	0.70	2.47	1.54	2.45
Low-income Latin America	2.65	0.95	0.37	3.40	5.87	2.21
High-income Western Europe	1.13	0.84	1.29	1.77	1.78	1.27
Medium-income Western Europe	2.33	1.41	0.84	2.15	2.95	2.68
Eastern Europe	0.59	0.38	0.80	0.97	1.15	2.11
Soviet Union	1.43	0.57	2.04	2.34	1.94	3.79
Japan	1.62	1.21	1.80	1.69	0.63	1.68
Centrally planned Asia	1.38	0.64	0.84	2.08	2.53	4.43
Newly industrializing Asia	0.86	0.90	1.38	3.93	0.93	3.10
Low-income Asia	1.08	0.82	1.03	1.80	1.07	1.31
Major oil producers	1.34	1.21	0.08	0.65	0.46	3.96
North Africa and other Middle East	0.29	1.01	0.07	0.63	2.36	1.57
Sub-Saharan Africa	2.94	3.02	0.68	12.23	5.77	5.09
Southern Africa	2.13	1.30	2.10	7.44	2.63	6.36
Oceania	2.83	1.27	0.69	3.24	1.86	1.60
B. 1987 relative to 1980						
High-income North America	0.67	0.86	0.64	0.94	0.68	0.67
Newly industrializing Latin America	1.73	1.06	0.94	1.17	1.15	0.96
Low-income Latin America	0.47	0.27	0.38	0.81	0.41	0.87
High-income Western Europe	0.62	0.81	0.81	0.83	0.55	0.68
Medium-income Western Europe	1.03	0.60	1.09	1.17	0.90	0.82
Eastern Europe	1.45	0.55	0.77	0.76	0.66	0.63
Soviet Union	0.57	1.05	0.58	0.68	0.59	0.68
Japan	0.51	0.56	0.65	0.59	0.43	0.59
Centrally planned Asia	0.66	0.63	0.56	1.46	0.65	0.82
Newly industrializing Asia	2.49	0.92	0.79	0.50	0.92	0.65
Low-income Asia	0.41	0.49	0.90	0.44	0.20	1.13
Major oil producers	2.24	1.35	0.64	1.41	1.53	1.18
North Africa and other Middle East	1.40	0.46	0.39	1.33	0.87	0.69
Sub-Saharan Africa	0.55	0.88	0.49	0.62	0.08	0.58
Southern Africa	1.47	1.13	1.41	1.05	1.02	0.75
Oceania	1.20	1.24	0.54	0.78	1.06	0.73

Note: Entries correspond to the coefficient for the given region divided by the U.S. coefficient.

Source: Institute for Economic Analysis. See text for derivation.

Changes in Metal Use in the United States and Other Developed Economies in the 1980s

The metal-processing sectors with both the highest metal input coefficients and the highest total metal inputs are the three sectors producing transportation equipment (XX17-XX19) and the sectors producing metal products (XX20), machinery (XX21), and electrical machinery (XX22). This is seen in Tables 7.2, 7.3, and 7.4, which are the principal focus of discussion in this section.

There was a sharp decline in the United States—and in the other rich, developed economies—in gross input coefficients for most metals in most sectors in the 1980s. While the average input coefficients for aluminum and zinc increased by 5 percent and 1 percent, respectively, between 1980 and 1987, the intensity of lead consumption (measured by input coefficients weighted by the share of outputs of using sectors) declined 8 percent and that of steel, nickel, and copper by more than 15 percent.

Copper

Copper has high electrical and thermal conductivity and is nonmagnetic, making it useful for a variety of electrical applications. It is estimated that approximately 70 percent of copper consumption in the United States is for electrical or electronic uses. A large part of this use is outside the electrical machinery sector, such as in electrical equipment in cars and wiring. Copper also has a variety of other uses in plumbing and heating, air conditioning, refrigerators, roof and wall cladding, marine transportation and other transportation, ordnance, chemicals, and other areas.

In 1983, 50 percent of the direct use of copper in Western Europe, the United States, and Japan was for electrical and electronic equipment; general engineering accounted for 16–20 percent, transportation equipment for 8–15 percent, construction for 8–17 percent, and domestic uses for 7–8 percent (OECD, 1983a). Copper has been competing with aluminum, stainless steel, plastics, and minor metals. The most important new competitors are fiber optics and possibly superconductors.

At present, copper is being replaced by optical fibers in telecommunication appllictions in the OECD countries. In 1985, 10 percent had been displaced. This increased to 32 percent in 1989, and the share might reach 70 percent by 1995 (UNIDO, *Industry and Development Global Report*, 1990). Fiber optics have a clear advantage over copper in the long distance network, but copper might be able to retain its position in the local feeder and distribution loop. This market is, however, saturated in the developed countries due to the high level of telephone ownership. Copper demand for cables, electricity-generating equipment, electrical installations, and motors has also leveled off.

Aluminum

Aluminum is a main competitor for copper, especially in wiring and car radiators, where it now holds one-third of the market. Use of aluminum reduces weight and increases mileage since aluminum has a specific gravity that is one-third that of copper.

Demand in OECD countries accounted for two-thirds of the world's primary aluminum production in 1980. Annual growth in OECD demand fell from nearly 12 percent in the early 1960s to roughly 5 percent in the early 1970s, to less than zero between 1976 and 1981, and well below 2 percent between 1980 and 1987. Demand in developing countries has continued to grow at a high rate— over 9 percent a year between 1976 and 1981, when their share of world demand reached 11 percent, five times the share twenty-five years earlier. With the exception of China, the demand in developing countries continued to grow rapidly between 1980 and 1987, at a rate of almost 8 percent per year (UNIDO, 1985c).

Due to its low weight, high strength-to-weight ratio, electrical conductivity, and corrosion resistance, aluminum is competing successfully with an array of different materials. Aluminum consumption increased by almost 19 percent in the United States between 1980 and 1987. The highest intensity of aluminum use is in metal products (XX20), which includes among its outputs construction materials, containers, and packaging, and in transportation equipment. Together, construction, packaging, and transportation equipment accounted for 56 percent of the direct use of aluminum in OECD Europe and almost 70 percent in Japan and the United States in 1980. The major new competitor of aluminum in these markets is plastics.

In the beverage can market, aluminum has replaced tin cans and competes with glass and plastic, and half of the aluminum is recycled. In the United States, most aluminum cans are recycled, and 28 percent of the end use of aluminum in 1980 was in packaging compared to 10 percent in OECD Europe and 6 percent in Japan.

In the United States, where the beverage can market is saturated, the weight of the cans has been declining. In the rest of the OECD area there may still be substantial growth, depending on governmental regulations regarding glass and plastic bottles, which still dominate but are more difficult to recycle than aluminum. An expanded market for cans will have a smaller influence on the demand for primary aluminum since it will be accompanied by an increase in recycling.

Light weight, strength, and corrosion resistance, together with the possibility of prefabrication of construction parts, has made aluminum a widely used construction material for non-weight-bearing structures, replacing steel. In Japan 33 percent of end use was in this sector compared to about 20 percent in the United States and in OECD Europe.

Aluminum has been used to replace ferrous materials to improve the mileage of motorized transportation equipment: 1 kg of aluminum substitutes for 2.7 kg of ferrous metals. In OECD Europe 7 percent of end use was in this sector compared to 26 percent in Japan and 19 percent in the United States. Ninety percent of aluminum used in auto manufacturing in developed countries has been recycled. In electrical uses, aluminum competes with copper; in various types of machinery, iron is its most important competitor. In many uses, plastics, both traditional and new high-strength ones, are important competitors.

Steel

The most important properties of steel are its high strength and its comparatively low cost. Traditional carbon steel is being displaced by high-strength steel alloys (which require less steel for the same strength), by other metals like aluminum, and by various other materials. The most dramatic example of this displacement is in the automotive industry.

Between 1978 and 1988, the content of high-strength steel in the typical U.S. car increased from 60 to 105 kg, while other iron and steel inputs declined from 1139 to 896 kg. The aluminum content increased from 51 to 68 kg, and plastics and plastic composites increased from 82 to 101 kg.

In spite of the strong decline in the steel input coefficients seen in Table 7.3, however, overall steel consumption declined less than 3 percent.

Nickel

Nickel has experienced a pattern of change similar to that of steel since it is an important material in steel alloys. It is estimated that of U.S. primary nickel consumption in 1987, 42 percent was used in stainless and heat-resisting steel, 14 percent in superalloys, and 17 percent in other nonferrous alloys.

Due to the large use of nickel-alloyed steel (superalloys) in the aircraft industry, this sector has the greatest nickel consumption. Nickel and steel compete with various materials and with other alloying materials.

Lead

Lead is used primarily for the production of batteries in the United States. It also has important nonmetal uses that are rapidly declining in the United States. As late as 1980, more than 10 percent of lead consumption took the form of gasoline additives. Especially during the 1980s, this use sharply declined, and the lead input coefficient into petroleum refining in 1987 was less than 20 percent of the 1980 coefficient. The phasing out of leaded paints due to environmental regulation is the major reason for the decline in the lead input coefficient to chemicals. The most rapidly declining input coefficient has been in publishing, where the use of lead was almost completely eliminated by modern technology during the 1980s.

Zinc

Because of its high resistance to corrosion, the most important uses of zinc as a metal are for surface treatment and alloying. In 1980 almost half of slab zinc consumption was used for galvanizing, more than 30 percent for zinc base die-casting alloys, and 12 percent for brass products. Between 1980 and 1987 the consumption of zinc for galvanizing and for brass and bronze increased by more than 40 percent, while the consumption of zinc base alloys showed a small decline. Due to their high specific weight, almost as high as that of iron, zinc die-castings in a typical American car declined from 14 to 8 kg between 1978 and 1984.

Differences in Metal Use Among Regions

The metal input coefficients for World Model regions derived from the U.S. coefficients, shown in Table 7.6, are subject to many possible errors. These include errors in estimating total consumption of the various metals in the different regions, the estimated level of intermediate deliveries from the fabricating sectors, and final demand for fabricated goods as estimated or computed by the model. One example is evident in Table 7.6, where the North American coefficients are considerably lower than the ones for the United States; the relative magnitudes, however, seem to be realistic for all regions, including North America.

It is pertinent to compare actual world consumption of metals in 1980 with the hypothetical consumption, assuming U.S. input structures (calculated by the World Model using U.S. coefficients for all regions). One finds that for all metals except aluminum, the U.S. coefficients would result in lower material use. For steel the level would be 40 percent lower, for lead 23 percent, for zinc 31 percent, for nickel 7 percent, and for copper 8 percent, while for aluminum it would be 23 percent higher. Clearly, the rest of the world uses metals (except aluminum) more intensively than the United States and this fact is reflected in the regional coefficients.

Several conclusions can be drawn from the ratios in Table 7.6. The fabricating sectors in regions other than North America are more steel intensive than those of the United States, and the substitution of aluminum or nickel-alloyed steel for ordinary steel is much more advanced in developed than developing countries. The formerly centrally planned economies are, on average, very steel intensive and have a fairly high use of nickel compared to steel, but they have low aluminum input coefficients.

The relative size of the input coefficients in the two largest developed market economy regions outside North America—high-income Western Europe and Japan—are very much in line with the estimated U.S. levels in 1980, and the developments between 1980 and 1987 are quite similar. Compared to the steel input coefficients, the aluminum ones are somewhat lower, while the nickel ones are somewhat higher than those of the United States. We see from Table 7.6 that during the 1980s, both nickel and aluminum coefficients increased relative to steel coefficients in high-income Western Europe, while in Japan this was the case only for nickel (probably because of well-known problems in the Japanese aluminum industry). As in the United States, lead and copper coefficients declined the most in high-income Western Europe and Japan, while the zinc coefficients increased relative to most of the other metal input coefficients.

Of the three remaining developed market economy regions, the most developed one, Oceania, has a metal input coefficient structure similar to those of the United States, high-income Western Europe, and Japan in 1980, while southern Africa and medium-income Western Europe are relatively more steel intensive. As in the other developed market economies, the steel input coefficients declined more than most other coefficients.

The newly industrializing regions of Asia and Latin America are more steel intensive than all the developed market economies, and other developing regions are on average also relatively more steel intensive than the United States. The most striking difference from the developed market economies is the very low nickel coefficients and, to a lesser extent, the low aluminum and copper coefficients. With few exceptions, the nickel and aluminum coefficients declined further relative to the steel coefficients during the 1980s.

The formerly centrally planned economies are very steel intensive compared to the United States, while their aluminum intensity is very low: the ratio of their aluminum-to-steel coefficients is only 15–20 percent of that for the United States. While the former Soviet Union and Eastern Europe have a nickel-to-steel input ratio equal to the lowest of the developed market economies, China's is even lower, quite similar to that of the other developing regions. The copper, lead, and zinc coefficients are all of the same order of magnitude. Like most other developing countries, China became relatively more steel intensive during the 1980s, while the former Soviet Union succeeded in substituting aluminum for other metal inputs.

Virgin Metal Use in World Model Regions

Gross metal inputs per unit of output must be multiplied by the estimated shares of virgin metals in consumption to arrive at the input coefficients for virgin metal that are used by the World Model. The shares of virgin metals are shown in Tables 7.7 and 7.8.

The consumption of virgin metals in the fabricating sectors in a region has been estimated as the region's production of ore (by metal content) plus the metal content of net imports of metal products ranging from ore to semimanufactured goods. (This approximation errs by counting imported secondary metal, still extremely small for most regions, as primary.)

Ore production by region is reported in the annual UN *Industrial Statistics Yearbook*. Net exports of ore and unrefined metal products were estimated by subtracting the ore content of a region's primary refined production from its total ore production. Primary production estimates are from the *Yearbook*; minor scaling was necessary so that the regional figures add up to total world ore production.

For iron and steel there is no clear concept of primary production: pig iron includes a small percentage of impurities, and with the exception of production of directly reduced iron, scrap is used in varying degrees throughout the steel-making process. As an estimate for primary production of iron and steel, the sum of pig iron and directly reduced iron was used (after being scaled down by a small percentage so that the regional total matches total world ore production). For refined and semimanufactured products, the main sources of information on exports and imports have been the UN COMTRADE data base and the *Commodity Yearbook* (UNCTAD, annual).

Tables 7.7 and 7.8 show that the share of virgin zinc, which is used as alloying and coating material, is higher than for other metals; this is due to greater

Table 7.7. Share of virgin metal in metal consumption by metal and region in 1980

	Copper	Aluminum	Nickel	Zinc	Lead	Steel
High-income North America	0.73	0.75	0.76	0.97	0.43	0.71
Newly industrializing Latin America	0.83	0.91	1.00	0.94	0.67	0.80
Low-income Latin America	1.00	1.00	1.00	1.00	1.00	0.84
High-income Western Europe	0.84	0.78	0.76	0.81	0.61	0.72
Medium-income Western Europe	0.89	0.90	0.90	0.97	0.83	0.60
Eastern Europe	0.96	1.00	0.90	1.00	1.00	0.63
Soviet Union	0.91	0.87	0.90	0.92	0.70	0.80
Japan	0.95	0.72	0.76	0.95	0.95	0.79
Centrally planned Asia	0.93	1.00	1.00	1.00	0.81	1.00
Newly industrializing Asia	1.00	1.00	1.00	1.00	1.00	0.80
Low-income Asia	0.99	1.00	1.00	1.00	1.00	0.98
Major oil producers	1.00	1.00	1.00	1.00	0.89	0.99
North Africa and other Middle East	1.00	1.00	1.00	1.00	1.00	0.71
Sub-Saharan Africa	1.00	1.00	1.00	1.00	1.00	0.86
Southern Africa	1.00	1.00	1.00	1.00	1.00	0.90
Oceania	0.91	0.88	1.00	0.97	0.58	1.00
World total	0.86	0.81	0.82	0.92	0.66	0.77

Note: The shares for nickel are Institute for Economic Analysis estimates.

Source: Institute for Economic Analysis based on sources cited in Table 7.5.

difficulties in scrap recovery. At the other extreme, lead, used mainly in batteries that are relatively easy to recover, has the lowest share.

The main factors influencing the share of virgin metals in metal consumption in the different regions are

- scrap availability compared to consumption,
- the relative processing costs of scrap and virgin metals, and
- the possibility of cost-effective scrap collection.

Table 7.8. Share of virgin metals in metal consumption by metal and region in 1987

	Copper	Aluminum	Nickel	Zinc	Lead	Steel
High-income North America	0.79	0.71	0.76	0.94	0.43	0.69
Newly industrializing Latin America	0.92	0.93	1.00	0.98	0.68	0.97
Low-income Latin America	1.00	1.00	1.00	1.00	1.00	0.70
High-income Western Europe	0.77	0.76	0.76	0.79	0.50	0.68
Medium-income Western Europe	0.93	0.87	0.90	0.96	0.82	0.53
Eastern Europe	0.99	0.88	0.90	1.00	1.00	0.52
Soviet Union	0.87	0.72	0.90	0.90	0.65	0.77
Japan	0.96	0.60	0.76	0.97	0.98	0.71
Centrally planned Asia	0.91	1.00	1.00	1.00	0.89	0.98
Newly industrializing Asia	1.00	1.00	1.00	1.00	1.00	0.64
Low-income Asia	0.99	1.00	1.00	1.00	1.00	0.91
Major oil producers	1.00	1.00	1.00	1.00	0.96	0.95
North Africa and other Middle East	1.00	1.00	1.00	1.00	1.00	0.69
Sub-Saharan Africa	1.00	1.00	1.00	1.00	1.00	0.99
Southern Africa	1.00	1.00	1.00	1.00	1.00	0.97
Oceania	0.92	0.93	1.00	0.97	0.82	0.92
World total	0.87	0.76	0.82	0.92	0.65	0.73

Note: The shares for nickel are Institute for Economic Analysis estimates.

Source: Institute for Economic Analysis based on sources cited in Table 7.5.

Increased energy prices, the slowdown in the growth of metal demand compared to earlier periods, and pressure for recycling for environmental reasons have resulted in lowering the share of virgin ores in fabricated metals, mainly in the rich, developed regions. Scrap processing is less energy intensive than processing of virgin metals, and the reduced growth of demand has increased the relative availability of old scrap.

Developing countries use on average a very high proportion of virgin metals in their metal consumption. The growth of metal consumption is rapid compared to developed countries, so there is far less old scrap, making scrap collection and processing costly. To a large extent, discarded items are directly transformed into useful items.

Between 1980 and 1987, world steel consumption increased only slightly, and the share of virgin metals declined (from 77 percent to 73 percent). Copper and zinc consumption grew more than 2 percent annually, with a virtually unchanged share of virgin metals. Aluminum consumption grew at the same rate, and its share of virgin metals decreased by 6 percent. The energy requirements for processing aluminum scrap are only 5–10 percent of those needed to process virgin metal compared to around 50 percent for steel (Eketorp, 1989; OECD, 1989).

Projections Under the OCF Scenario

Metal input coefficients for the future have been projected by adjusting the 1990 coefficients on the basis of likely future technological changes and material substitutions. As pointed out earlier in this chapter, the stage of development, region specific factors, and the use of scrap contribute to a large variation in the regional coefficients. Different rates of change in coefficients can be expected for different regions in the future.

The World Model regions have been divided into four groups for the purpose of making projections:

1. Developed
   North America
   Western Europe
   Oceania
   Southern Africa
   Japan

2. Newly industrializing
   Newly industrializing Asia
   Newly industrializing Latin America

3. Other developing
   Other Latin America
   North Africa and other Middle East
   Sub-Saharan Africa
   Low-income Asia

Centrally planned Asia
Major oil producers

4. Formerly centrally planned
   Eastern Europe
   Former Soviet Union

The projections of metal input coefficients are based on the following assumptions:

- Present technological and economic trends will continue.
- Real prices of fossil fuels will increase slowly.

Metal processing margins were adjusted to reflect changes in gross metal inputs projected for the future.

The Developed Regions

For the developed regions, it is assumed that:

1. The trend toward lower input coefficients for materials will continue due to substitution between products in the same sector, improved production processes, material-saving design, and innovative use of traditional materials.
2. New materials such as engineering plastics and optical fibers will to an increasing degree substitute for all metals.
3. Intermetal substitution will continue to be an important factor. Plain carbon steel will increasingly be replaced by high-strength specialty steel requiring less metal, and aluminum will continue replacing other metals.
4. The decline in metal coefficients in future years will be slower than the decline in the 1980s since the latter decline was partly attributable to the sharp increase in the prices of fossil fuels.

It is assumed that copper will experience the largest percentage decline. In communications, especially long distance, optical fibers in the future will take over the role of copper. It is also likely that copper will experience greater competition from other materials such as aluminum for wiring and auto batteries, plastics for plumbing, and various materials for architectural and structural uses. Improvements in design and increased use of alloyed copper will also work in the same direction.

The trend toward higher quality and high-strength specialty steels is also assumed to continue, reducing the required amount of steel per unit of output. Steel is expected to maintain a strong position within its main use areas such as construction, transportation equipment, and machinery but will continue to lose ground to aluminum for non-weight-bearing structures and in transportation and to cement in some areas such as construction of bridges.

It is assumed that nickel, used mainly as a steel-alloying material, will follow the developments of steel, while zinc, used mainly in surface treatment to protect steel from corrosion, will decline more slowly.

The aluminum coefficients are assumed to increase slowly. Aluminum will substitute for steel and to some extent for copper but may be displaced by plastics in some uses.

It is assumed that the drive toward unleaded gasoline will continue and that lead will be phased out in paints but retain its position in its main use, batteries.

The Developing Regions

The advanced developing regions can be expected to have access and know-how to utilize the same types of technologies as the developed regions; the technological gap between them will narrow over the next few decades. The steel coefficients will decline most rapidly, due to the increasing production and consumption of alloyed and special steels such as nickel-alloyed steel, which at present is low, and due also to substitution possibilities that have already been exploited in the developed market economies.

For other developing regions, it is assumed that the input structures will move toward the present input structures of the developed regions and that in some areas—for instance, cable communication, where optical fibers will be used instead of copper—these countries will be able to adopt the most advanced technology.

Eastern Europe and the former Soviet Union

For the formerly centrally planned economies, it is assumed that there will be a major shift from very steel-intensive industrialization strategies with a focus on heavy industry toward patterns of metal use more typical of the production of consumer goods. It is also assumed that the technological gap between the developed market economies and these regions will diminish and that there will be increasing incentives to avoid wasting materials. It is projected that the steel coefficients will decline rapidly, while the input coefficients for aluminum will increase more rapidly than in most other regions.

One important factor in the reduction of steel coefficients both in developing countries and in the former centrally planned economies is the continued growth in the share of continuous casting, reducing crude steel requirements relative to inputs of finished steel in the metal-fabricating sectors.

Projections about changes in future gross metal input coefficients in all regions, based on the preceding analysis, are given in Table 7.9.

The Share of Virgin Metals

Even though the assumed increase in energy prices makes recycling more profitable relative to the use of virgin metals, the share of virgin metals is expected to continue to decline relatively slowly. A large proportion of metals is used for

Table 7.9. Changes in gross metal input coefficients under the ocf scenario, 1990–2020 (average annual rate of change) (percentages)

	Copper	Aluminum	Nickel	Zinc	Lead	Steel
High-income North America	−1.50	0.50	−1.00	−0.50	−0.50	−1.00
Newly industrializing Latin America	−1.50	0.50	−0.50	−1.00	−1.00	−2.00
Low-income Latin America	−1.00	1.50	0.50	−1.00	−1.00	−2.00
High-income Western Europe	−1.50	1.00	−1.00	−0.50	−0.50	−1.00
Medium-income Western Europe	−1.50	0.50	−0.50	−0.50	−0.50	−2.00
Eastern Europe	−1.50	1.50	−0.50	−0.50	−0.50	−2.00
Former Soviet Union	−1.50	1.00	−1.00	−1.00	−1.00	−2.50
Japan	−1.50	0.50	−1.00	−0.50	−0.50	−1.00
Centrally planned Asia	−1.50	1.00	−0.50	−1.00	−1.00	−2.75
Newly industrializing Asia	−1.50	1.00	−0.50	−1.00	−0.50	−2.00
Low-income Asia	−0.50	1.50	−0.50	0.00	0.00	−1.50
Major-oil producers	−1.50	0.00	3.00	0.00	−0.50	−2.75
North Africa and other Middle East	−0.50	1.00	4.00	0.00	−0.50	−1.00
Sub-Saharan Africa	−1.50	0.00	0.00	−1.00	0.00	−2.00
Southern Africa	−1.50	0.50	−0.50	−0.50	−0.50	−1.00
Oceania	−1.50	0.50	−0.50	−0.50	−0.50	−1.00

Source: Institute for Economic Analysis projections.

construction and infrastructure, and much of this is difficult to recover due in part to a very long life cycle. The increasing use of composite materials and of alloys, often complex ones incorporating an array of different metals, also reduces the potential for recycling.

We anticipate that the share of virgin metals in total metal consumption will continue to decline in the future at an annual rate of 0.5 percent for all regions and all metals. Corresponding decreases in energy requirements were quantified in Chapter 6. In the developed regions, the availability of scrap will increase due to slow demand growth. In the developing regions, the increased level of scrap production will make scrap more available and its collection more profitable.

International Trade in Metals

Export shares for metals had been computed, along with those for all other sectors, using the UN COMTRADE data base. However, these data are measured in values only, and it was now possible to compute new export and import shares, in tons of metal content, using the same definitions and classifications as for consumption and production of these materials. Net export shares and net import shares are shown in Tables 7.10 and 7.11 for 1980 and 1987. (*Net* in this context means that each region is treated as either an exporting or an importing region. Therefore, any given region is either a net exporter or a net importer but not both.) Net exporters were assigned export shares equal to the values given in Table 7.10 for 1980 and in Table 7.11 for 1990. For those regions identified in the tables as net importers, apparent production (calculated as use minus net imports) is treated as an exogenous variable and the export share is set to zero. The 1987 shares were assumed for 1990 and for all subsequent years.

Table 7.10. Regional distribution of world trade in metals in 1980 (percentages)

	Copper	Aluminum	Nickel	Zinc	Lead	Steel
A. Exports						
High-income North America	11.7	0.0	11.7	18.4	23.5	0.0
Newly industrializing Latin America	26.3	3.6	0.0	3.9	4.5	45.4
Low-income Latin America	8.0	30.6	16.8	28.6	13.4	0.1
High-income Western Europe	0.0	0.0	0.0	0.0	0.0	0.0
Medium-income Western Europe	0.0	4.3	0.8	10.0	2.3	0.0
Eastern Europe	4.4	0.0	0.0	0.6	0.0	0.0
Soviet Union	0.0	0.0	6.0	0.0	0.0	4.7
Japan	0.0	0.0	0.0	0.0	0.0	0.0
Centrally planned Asia	0.0	0.0	0.0	5.0	10.6	4.0
Newly industrializing Asia	0.0	0.3	6.2	0.0	0.0	0.0
Low-income Asia	5.3	0.0	3.8	0.0	0.0	8.3
Major oil producers	0.0	0.0	0.0	1.4	0.0	0.0
North Africa and other Middle East	0.0	0.0	0.0	0.3	7.8	1.8
Sub-Saharan Africa	33.6	21.5	8.4	5.0	0.4	4.7
Southern Africa	5.9	0.0	6.1	1.6	8.9	5.0
Oceania	5.0	39.7	40.3	25.2	28.7	26.2
World total	100.0	100.0	100.0	100.0	100.0	100.0
B. Imports						
High-income North America	0.0	41.7	0.0	0.0	0.0	10.7
Newly industrializing Latin America	0.0	0.0	2.8	0.0	0.0	0.0
Low-income Latin America	0.0	0.0	0.0	0.0	0.0	0.0
High-income Western Europe	46.7	30.9	52.8	42.4	56.6	27.8
Medium-income Western Europe	5.3	0.0	0.0	0.0	0.0	3.1
Eastern Europe	0.0	0.6	7.4	0.0	11.0	18.5
Soviet Union	1.1	0.2	0.0	7.6	7.8	0.0
Japan	42.7	19.8	34.7	32.7	19.2	29.5
Centrally planned Asia	2.3	1.8	2.2	0.0	0.0	0.0
Newly industrialized Asia	0.8	0.0	0.0	11.9	3.6	6.4
Low-income Asia	0.0	0.7	0.0	5.4	1.6	0.0
Major oil producers	0.9	1.8	0.1	0.0	0.2	4.0
North Africa and other Middle East	0.1	1.5	0.1	0.0	0.0	0.0
Sub-Saharan Africa	0.0	0.0	0.0	0.0	0.0	0.0
Southern Africa	0.0	0.9	0.0	0.0	0.0	0.0
Oceania	0.0	0.0	0.0	0.0	0.0	0.0
World total	100.0	100.0	100.0	100.0	100.0	100.0

Note: Trade in each region is computed net; that is, it is considered either an exporting or an importing region.

Source: Institute for Economic Analysis based on UN COMTRADE data base; UN, 1989; U.S. Department of the Interior, Bureau of Mines, various years, *Minerals Yearbook*; UN, Economic Commission for Europe, various years; UN Conference on Trade and Development, various years; and Institute for Economic Analysis calculations.

Net exports of processed metal (XX5) are represented as a weighted sum of net exports of the component metals. The weights represent the ratio of processed to crude metal exports for a given metal, region, and time period. These weights have not been revised at this time.

118

Table 7.11. Regional distribution of world trade in metals in 1987 (percentages)

	Copper	Aluminum	Nickel	Zinc	Lead	Steel
A. Exports						
High-income North America	11.5	0.0	15.2	17.1	15.7	0.0
Newly industrializing Latin America	33.6	4.1	0.0	3.3	5.1	43.0
Low-income Latin America	10.7	16.8	15.0	33.0	18.9	0.1
High-income Western Europe	0.0	0.0	0.0	0.0	0.0	0.0
Medium-income Western Europe	0.0	4.9	0.0	8.1	1.0	0.0
Eastern Europe	0.0	1.6	0.0	0.0	0.0	0.0
Soviet Union	1.8	0.0	17.0	0.0	0.0	3.8
Centrally planned Asia	0.0	0.0	0.8	0.0	5.1	1.8
Japan	0.0	0.0	0.0	0.0	0.0	0.0
Newly industrializing Asia	0.0	0.0	5.2	0.0	0.0	0.0
Low-income Asia	4.5	1.7	0.0	0.0	2.6	9.2
Major-oil producers	0.0	0.0	0.0	1.0	0.2	0.0
North Africa and other Middle East	0.0	0.0	0.0	0.0	2.3	2.6
Sub-Saharan Africa	29.6	24.8	6.9	3.2	0.6	3.0
Southern Africa	4.6	0.0	6.8	2.1	9.8	3.3
Oceania	3.7	46.2	33.3	32.2	38.7	33.4
World total	100.0	100.0	100.0	100.0	100.0	100.0
B. Imports						
High-income North America	0.0	43.0	0.0	0.0	0.0	15.3
Newly industrializing Latin America	0.0	0.0	1.0	0.0	0.0	0.0
Low-income Latin America	0.0	0.0	0.0	0.0	0.0	0.0
High-income Western Europe	30.9	28.5	51.3	41.3	45.9	26.4
Medium-income Western Europe	5.2	0.0	2.0	0.0	0.0	2.9
Eastern Europe	4.3	0.0	7.5	3.7	13.0	14.5
Soviet Union	0.0	5.1	0.0	9.3	6.0	0.0
Japan	42.7	13.7	35.8	31.2	24.6	27.4
Centrally planned Asia	1.2	1.2	0.0	1.9	0.0	0.0
Newly industrializing Asia	14.6	3.8	0.0	10.4	10.6	8.3
Low-income Asia	0.0	0.0	2.3	1.6	0.0	0.0
Major-oil producers	1.0	2.7	0.1	0.0	0.0	5.1
North Africa and other Middle East	0.2	0.8	0.1	0.6	0.0	0.0
Sub-Saharan Africa	0.0	0.0	0.0	0.0	0.0	0.0
Southern Africa	0.0	1.1	0.0	0.0	0.0	0.0
Oceania	0.0	0.0	0.0	0.0	0.0	0.0
World total	100.0	100.0	100.0	100.0	100.0	100.0

Note: Trade in each region is computed net; that is, it is considered either an exporting or an importing region.

Source: Institute for Economic Analysis based on UN COMTRADE data base; UN, 1989; U.S. Department of the Interior, Bureau of Mines (various years), *Minerals Yearbook*; UN, Economic Commission for Europe, various years; UN Conference on Trade and Development, various years; and Institute for Economic Analysis calculations.

8

Construction

The Role of the Construction Industry

The construction industry plays a major role in development, as it provides buildings, roads, bridges, power plants, ports, dams, water systems, and other infrastructure. Typically, construction accounts for 40–70 percent of gross fixed capital formation in developing countries.* In most developed market economies the share is 50–60 percent (UN, 1991a).

Construction activities account for 3–8 percent of GDP in most developing countries. The newly industrializing countries and the oil-rich regions tend to have the highest shares. For developed market economies the share is around 5 percent; Japan was exceptional, with almost 10 percent of GDP devoted to construction in the late 1980s. Construction accounted for more than 10 percent of net material product in the former Soviet Union and most of Eastern Europe (UN, 1991b).

The construction industry is material intensive, and inputs of metallic and nonmetallic minerals, wood, and chemicals account for more than 30 percent (by value) of all inputs to the sector. It is estimated by the United Nations Industrial Development Organization (UNIDO, 1985d) that of domestic production of nonmetallic minerals (ISIC 369,362) such as lime, cement, clay, glass, bricks, and so on in developing regions, 62–86 percent end up in the construction industry. For developed regions, the share varies between 50 percent and 67 percent.

About one-third of the total use of primary metals (ISIC 371,372) in most developed and developing regions is for construction. For finished metals (ISIC 381) the share is around 40 percent for most developed regions and ranges from 22 percent to 60 percent for developing regions. For wood products (ISIC 331,122), typical shares for developed and developing countries range between one-third and one-half, and most regions use about one-half of chemical products (ISIC 35) such as pitch, tar, bitumen, paints, plastics, and glue in construction. For minimally processed products, such as stone, sand, gravel, asphalt, and dolomite (ISIC 29), the share in developed regions is approximately one-

* The single most important source for this chapter is the United Nations Industrial Development Organization's study of the building materials industry in developing countries (UNIDO, 1985c and 1985d).

half, while for most developing regions it is 60–85 percent, reaching 96 percent in Sub-Saharan Africa.

The construction sector itself is not very energy intensive, but indirectly it is a major consumer of energy. Because of the large size and material intensity of construction activities, the evolution of this sector is of crucial importance for development and for the use of energy and materials in both developed and developing regions.

The rapid growth of the construction sector in the developing countries has precipitated both a strong expansion of the material-processing sectors and an increase in imports of materials. During the 1970s, imports of building materials to developing countries grew at a rate twice that for total industrial imports, and the share of developing countries in world imports of building materials increased from 24 percent in 1970 to 35 percent in 1980. Measured in current dollars, the net imports of building materials to developing countries increased from $3 billion in 1970 to almost $30 billion in 1980 and $35 billion in 1982. The rapid increase in the trade deficit for building materials has contributed substantially to the balance of payment problems of developing countries.

Exports of building materials from developed to developing countries are mainly in capital- and skill- intensive products: in 1980 54 percent by value was metals, 33 percent was equipment, and the remainder consisted of wood, mineral products, glass, and paints. By contrast, developing countries' exports of building materials to developed countries was very resource- and labor-intensive: 74 percent of these exports consisted of wood products with a low level of processing, 17 percent was metals, and 7 percent was equipment.

The rapid growth of imports of building materials to developing countries has increased the trade among developing countries. The share of imported building materials from other developing countries increased from 13 percent in 1970 to 17 percent in 1980. Importantly, this trade was far more capital intensive than were developing countries' exports of building materials to developed countries. The share of metal products was 30 percent and that of equipment was 15 percent. While trade among developing countries amounted to only 40 percent of developing countries' exports of building materials to developed countries in 1970, by 1980 it had reached 80 percent. The developing countries themselves play an increasingly important role as export markets for each other, especially for more capital-intensive and processed materials.

Subsectors of Construction

Construction activities involve the erection of infrastructure and engineering projects, as well as residential and nonresidential buildings. Repair and maintenance on current account are usually distinguished from new construction and capital repair. Subsectors of construction and the sectors producing the main material inputs are identified in Table 8.1, which also shows that most construction is absorbed as investment in plant (including housing investment) or direct-

Table 8.1. Principal subsectors, material inuts, and purchasing sectors for construction (XX26)

Subsectors	Material inputs	Purchasing sectors
Construction of residential buildings	SE5 Copper SE6 Bauxite SE10 Iron XX2 Residual resources	IN2 Plant investment MA5 Government expenditures
Construction of nonresidential buildings	XX5 Primary metal processing XX7 Wood products XX14 Finished chemicals XX15 Cement	
Engineering construction	XX16 Glass, stone, clay and concrete products XX20 Metal products	
Repair and maintenance	XX21 Machinery XX22 Electrical machinery	

Note: The three first subsectors include new construction and capital repair (e.g., restorations and conversions). The fourth subsector is repair and maintenance on current account.

Source: Institute for Economic Analysis.

ly by the government. Table 8.2 shows the relative intensity of use of different materials in the subsectors of the construction industry.

The shares of engineering, residential, and nonresidential building construction (both new and repair) in overall construction in selected countries in most World Model regions are provided in Table 8.3. On average, the developing countries have substantially higher shares of engineering construction than the developed countries. Typically, at very low levels of development, the infrastructure/engineering share is as much as half of the total, declining to less than 30 percent in higher-income economies. At subsequent stages of development, the share of residential construction increases from 28 percent in economies with per capita GDP (in 1979 U.S. dollars) of $200 to nearly 40 percent as per capita GDP rises to $2,000. The nonresidential share is similar to the residential share at the lowest incomes, but it climbs more slowly and reaches the residential share in societies with incomes of $10,000 per capita.

Table 8.2. Intensity of material use in subsectors of the construction sector

	Residental	Nonresidental	Engineering	Repair and maintenance
SE5–SE10 Metals	−	+	+	−
XX2 Residual resources	−	−	+	+
XX7 Wood products	+	−	−	−
XX14 Finished chemicals	−	−	−	+
XX15 Cement	+	+	−	−
XX16 Glass, stone, clay, and concrete products	+	+	−	−

Note: (+) indicates above-average intensity in the use of the material; (−) indicates below-average intensity.

Source: Institute for Economic Analysis based on UNIDO, 1985c; U.S. Department of Commerce, BEA, 1991; U.S. Department of Labor, BLS, 1980.

Table 8.3. Shares of construction subsectors in total new plus repair construction in selected countries in 1985 (percentages)

Region	Country	Residential	Nonresidential	Engineering
High-income North America	U.S.	45	34	21
Newly industrializing Latin America	Brazil (1980)	35	18	47
	Mexico	14	15	72
Low-income Latin America	Panama	38	33	29
High-income Western Europe	France	40	34	26
	Italy	36	36	29
	Netherlands	51	30	19
Medium-income Western Europe	Portugal	47	21	32
	Yugoslavia	35	37	29
	Turkey (1982)	26	47	27
Japan	Japan	32	29	40
Newly industrializing Asia	Malaysia	27	33	39
	Singapore	53	33	14
	Thailand	31	26	43
Low-income Asia	India	37	19	44
	Pakistan	23	39	39
Major oil producers	Libya	27	25	48
	Nigeria (1980)		60	
North Africa and other Middle East	Syria	33	16	51
	Tunisia	22	32	47
Sub-Saharan Africa	Tanzania	30	27	43
	Zimbabwe	54		
Southern Africa	South Africa	28	33	39

Source: Institute for Economic Analysis based on UN, *Construction Statistics Yearbook,* 1988 and 1975.

This pattern suggests that in the future there will continue to be substantial changes in the input structure of the construction industry as economies develop. Typically, engineering construction is very metal intensive, while nonresidential building construction is less metal intensive but more cement intensive on average.

Residential construction uses less metal and cement than nonresidential construction but more wood, paints, and other chemicals. Detailed data are available on the material inputs to construction in the United States in 1973. They show that public utility construction was almost three times as metal-intensive as residential construction, while nonresidential construction was almost twice as metal intensive (see Table 8.4).

New residential building construction in the United States relies heavily on wood. Input from sawmills and planing mills, millwork, plywood, and other wood products together accounted for 14 percent of the value of all inputs to this sector compared to only 2.4 percent for new, nonresidential buildings. The very high share of wood in residential building construction in the United States is due to the increasingly high share of one-family dwellings in new residential construction, which increased (in value) from 60 percent in 1973 to almost 82 percent by 1988 (U.S. Dept. of Labor, 1990), or from 13 percent in 1970 to 20 percent in 1988 of total construction. During the same period, the median size of new, one-family dwellings increased by 50 percent (*New York Times,* 1991).

Table 8.4. Material inputs to subsectors of construction in the United States in 1973 (direct requirements per unit of output, 1972 producers' prices)

	Residential	Nonresidential	Public utility	Highway construction	Other new construction	Repair and maintenance
Wood products	0.141	0.024	0.033	0.012	0.050	0.018
Finished chemicals	0.015	0.014	0.007	0.011	0.014	0.036
Paints	0.007	0.005	0.002	0.008	0.005	0.033
Plastic products	0.008	0.008	0.004	0.001	0.005	0.003
Other chemicals	0.000	0.001	0.001	0.002	0.004	0.000
Stone and clay mining and quarrying	0.002	0.003	0.005	0.043	0.012	0.010
Stone, clay, glass, and concrete products	0.075	0.089	0.061	0.093	0.065	0.031
Glass	0.001	0.005	0.001	0.000	0.001	0.004
Cement and concrete	0.054	0.058	0.040	0.089	0.052	0.013
Stone and clay products	0.020	0.025	0.020	0.005	0.012	0.014
Metals	0.094	0.161	0.266	0.098	0.160	0.080
Primary ferrous metals	0.006	0.008	0.060	0.028	0.052	0.012
Primary nonferrous metals	0.016	0.018	0.076	0.001	0.012	0.008
Heating apparatus and plumbing fixtures	0.018	0.011	0.001	0.000	0.003	0.012
Fabricated structural metals	0.043	0.106	0.100	0.064	0.077	0.034
Other fabricated metal products	0.011	0.017	0.029	0.005	0.016	0.015

Source: U.S. Department of labor, BLS, 1980.

The relative intensity of use of the most important materials among segments of construction is very similar in other countries. For example, material inputs to three types of construction projects in Kenya are shown in Table 8.5. Engineering projects are the most metal-intensive activities, followed by nonresidential building construction. Residential buildings are the most wood intensive, followed by nonresidential buildings, and, as in the United States, nonresidential building construction is very cement and concrete intensive. Residential building construction stands out as requiring more chemical products (paints) than other new construction.

In early phases of development, the share of metals and cement among building materials is high due to the predominance of engineering and infrastructure projects and nonresidential building construction. Urbanization is accompanied by increased use of cement and other mineral products that predominate in urban residential buildings. In developing countries the cost of roofs might be as high as 50 percent of total construction costs in simple dwellings, and some of the cheapest and simplest technologies for roof construction are cement intensive. With increased prosperity and better access to public and private transportation, suburbanization and the share of wood-intensive, one-family dwellings increase.

Both the design and the material input mix of engineering projects are very

Table 8.5. Material inputs to three types of construction projects in Kenya (inputs per unit of output in local prices of the late 1970s)

Type of input	Residential building	Nonresidential building	Engineering projects
Sand	0.046	0.064	0.030
Aggregate	0.056	0.052	0.099
Cement	0.100	0.134	0.030
Hydrated lime			0.024
Concrete products	0.060	0.038	0.028
Hardcore fillings	0.015	0.009	
Wood products	0.089	0.030	0.004
Steel products	0.030	0.179	0.229
Hardware and windows	0.045	0.029	0.030[a]
Paints	0.082	0.022	
Glass	0.010	0.013	
Floor tiles	0.052	0.017	
Roofing materials	0.041	0.023	
Plumbing and sanitary fixtures	0.078	0.050	
Electric installations	0.052	0.021	
Explosives			0.030
Fuels, bitumen, and lubricants			0.024
Total of above (all materials)	0.756	0.680	0.527
Other inputs	0.244	0.320	0.473
Total	1.000	1.000	1.000

a. Includes paints.

Source: Institute for Economic Analysis based on UNIDO, 1985c. The table in the UNIDO report is based on United Nations Centre for Human Settlements, Nairobi, Kenya: "Role and Contribution of the Construction Industry to Socio-economic Growth of Developing Countries," Cambridge, MA: CMT Inc., November 1980 (revised April 1982), IV–44.

similar in developed and developing countries, and there is limited room for substitution among materials. This is not the case, however, for residential construction. The inputs for constructing residences depend on factors like climate, local availability of building materials, especially wood, the income levels of the potential residents, and shares of one-family versus multifamily dwellings.

Maintenance and Repair Construction

As the stock of durable structures increases and grows older, the need for maintenance and repair increases. In the United States, for instance, the share of maintenance and repair construction increased from 24 percent of the value of total construction activities in 1970 to 33 percent in 1988. Most of the developed economies have experienced a similar trend and typically have substantially higher shares of current maintenance and repair than the developing countries (see Table 8.6).

Officially reported shares of maintenance construction in many countries may be underestimated because a great deal of maintenance and repair construction is likely to be accomplished informally. In many developing countries, construction projects, including the construction of new dwellings, may go unreported, leading to underestimation of dwelling construction and the size of the total construction sector.

The increasing relative importance of repair and maintenance activities clearly exerts a strong downward pressure on most material input coefficients for the construction sector as a whole. Input requirements for cement and concrete per unit of repair and maintenance activities were 0.013 (dollars per dol-

Table 8.6. Share of repair and maintenance in total construction for selected countries (percentages)

Region	Country	1970	1985
High-income North America	Canada	18	15
Low-income Latin America	Cuba		20
High-income Western Europe	France	12	40
	Italy	11	18
	Netherlands	27	41
	Norway	18	20
	Switzerland	4	5
	United Kingdom	28	46
Medium-income Western Europe	Portugal	5	8
	Yugoslavia	5	8
Eastern Europe	Czechoslovakia	16	17
Newly industrializing Asia	Hong Kong		22
	Malaysia	6	3
Low-income Asia	India	17	18
North Africa and other Middle East	Tunisia	15	12
Sub-Saharan Africa	Ghana	14	9
	Zambia	9	10

Source: Institute for Economic Analysis based on UN, *Construction Statistics Yearbook*, 1988 and 1979.

lar) in the United States in 1973, less than one-third of the input, by value, for other types of construction. For fabricated structural metals the input coefficient was 0.034, and for wood, 0.018. By contrast, maintenance requires large volumes of chemicals. For paints and allied products, the input coefficient for maintenance was 0.033 compared with 0.007 for new residential construction.

The most recent official input-output table for the U.S. economy depicts the same overall picture as the more disaggregated coefficients presented for 1973 despite changes in relative prices (including energy prices) and substitution among materials; this can be seen in Table 8.7.

Input Coefficients

Construction receives inputs from a wide array of sectors. In the following discussion, we shall concentrate on the major inputs of material- and energy-intensive products: cement and other nonmetallic minerals, metals, wood, and chemicals.

Cement

In the original World Model, a substantial share of cement production was charged to the stone, glass, clay, and concrete products sector (XX16) for the production of ready-mixed and prefabricated concrete. In the United States most cement is purchased by this sector for subsequent resale as concrete to construction, but there is little information about the extent to which this is true

Table 8.7. Inputs to different types of construction in the United States in 1982 (input per unit of output, in current producers' prices)

	New construction	Repair and maintenance
Wood products	0.043	0.023
Finished chemicals	0.012	0.030
Paints	0.005	0.015
Plastic products[a]	0.007	0.015
Stone and clay mining and quarrying	0.004	0.010
Glass, stone, clay, and concrete products	0.054	0.038
Glass	0.001	0.001
Other[b]	0.053	0.036
Metals	0.116	0.089
Primary ferrous metals	0.025	0.011
Primary nonferrous metals	0.011	0.008
Heating, plumbing, and fabricated structural metals	0.060	0.049
Other fabricated metal products	0.019	0.022
Value added	0.439	0.551

a. Includes rubber.

b. Includes cement.

Source: U.S. Department of Commerce, BEA, 1991.

in other regions. Because almost all cement ends up in construction, we have decided to charge cement production directly to construction. While the production of cement (the subject of Chapter 9) is very energy intensive, the production of concrete from cement requires no energy.

The cement input coefficients to construction for 1970, 1980, and 1990 have been revised on the basis of control totals for apparent consumption (domestic production plus net imports). Data on production for each region, measured in physical units (millions of tons), were obtained from the UN *Industrial Statistics Yearbook*. Data on imports and exports were obtained from the UN's COMTRADE data base and translated from money values into physical units (using the 1970 United States average unit price of $19.78 per ton). The new cement input coefficients were calculated as the ratio of apparent consumption to construction output. The input coefficients for cement in 1980 and 1990, reported both in dollars per dollar and in kilos per dollar of construction output, are shown in Tables 8.8 and 8.9, respectively.

Not surprisingly, North America has the lowest input coefficients for cement to construction. This fact reflects the maturity of the economy, the high share of construction of one-family dwellings, and the high share of maintenance construction. Between 1980 and 1988, there was a small decline in the cement input coefficient since the effect of a growing share of maintenance and one-family dwelling construction in the United States is partly offset by the rapid growth in cement-intensive road construction in the region.

All other developed economies have higher cement input coefficients than the United States, but these coefficients show a decided decline over time, probably reflecting higher shares of maintenance and one-family dwelling construction.

In the United States there has been an increase in the share of ready-mixed concrete, which in 1988 accounted for close to 75 percent of all cement consumed. This trend is not confined to the United States. In most cases, the use of ready-mixed concrete leads to savings of cement because of its uniform quality, and its use has contributed to the overall decline in the cement input coefficients in developed countries. While ready-mixed concrete may save cement, more transportation services are generally required. In most developing countries, with their poorly developed infrastructure and high transportation costs, the use of ready-mixed concrete is not significant. Most developing regions have substantially higher cement input coefficients than developed regions due to expansion of infrastructure and urbanization, a low share of maintenance and repair construction, and a low share of ready-mixed concrete.

For the two most developed regions in this category, the newly industrializing countries of Latin America and Asia, the cement coefficients seem to have peaked; for most others that are in earlier stages of development, they are still growing. For centrally planned Asia, major oil-producing countries, and North Africa and other Middle East, the coefficients increased rapidly between 1970 and 1988. These three regions, especially the latter two, have shortages of wood, which are also reflected in very low wood input coefficients. In centrally planned Asia (China), there has been very little emphasis on residential construction.

Table 8.8. Principal material input coefficients, except energy and metals, to construction for World Model regions in 1980 (dollars of input per dollar of output, 1970 prices)

	XX2 Residual resources	XX7 Wood products	XX14 Finished chemicals	XX15[a] Cement	XX16 Glass, stone, clay and concrete products	XX15[a] Cement (kilograms per dollar of output)
High-income North America	0.014	0.059	0.015	0.010	0.054	0.529
Newly industrializing Latin America	0.009	0.044	0.015	0.036	0.068	1.796
Low-income Latin America	0.009	0.044	0.014	0.040	0.067	2.027
High-income Western Europe	0.012	0.057	0.015	0.019	0.075	0.936
Medium-income Western Europe	0.009	0.048	0.015	0.035	0.070	1.778
Eastern Europe	0.011	0.025	0.015	0.030	0.048	1.521
Former Soviet Union	0.012	0.025	0.015	0.035	0.048	1.744
Centrally planned Asia	0.009	0.030	0.014	0.062	0.064	3.141
Japan	0.009	0.056	0.015	0.021	0.064	1.062
Newly industrializing Asia	0.009	0.069	0.015	0.023	0.070	1.178
Low-income Asia	0.009	0.078	0.014	0.045	0.064	2.270
Major oil producers	0.009	0.027	0.014	0.115	0.068	5.799
North Africa and other Middle East	0.009	0.017	0.014	0.096	0.064	4.866
Sub-Saharan Africa	0.009	0.057	0.014	0.045	0.064	2.286
Southern Africa	0.009	0.062	0.015	0.027	0.073	1.388
Oceania	0.012	0.062	0.015	0.012	0.088	0.628

a. Cement is shown in value terms, for comparison with XX2, residual resources. This includes minimally processed forms of materials not included in other sectors (like gravel).

Note: The first column corresponds to XX2, residual resources, as well as in physical units.

Source: Institute for Economic Analysis based on UNIDO, 1985c, 1985d; UN Industrial Statistics Yearbook, 1988; U.S. Department of the Interior, Bureau of Mines, Minerals Yearbook, 1978? UN COMTRADE data base.

Table 8.9. Principal material input coefficients, except energy and metals, to construction for World Model regions in 1990 (dollars of input per dollar of output, 1970 prices)

	XX2 Residual resources	XX7 Wood products	XX14 Finished chemicals	XX15[a] Cement	XX16 Glass, stone, clay and concrete products	XX15[a] Cement (kilograms per dollar of output)
High-income North America	0.014	0.059	0.017	0.010	0.054	0.489
Newly industrializing Latin America	0.009	0.044	0.017	0.033	0.068	1.666
Low-income Latin America	0.009	0.044	0.015	0.045	0.067	2.260
High-income Western Europe	0.014	0.057	0.017	0.016	0.075	0.797
Medium-income Western Europe	0.011	0.048	0.017	0.044	0.070	2.248
Eastern Europe	0.013	0.025	0.017	0.023	0.048	1.184
Former Soviet Union	0.014	0.025	0.017	0.021	0.048	1.063
Centrally planned Asia	0.009	0.030	0.015	0.101	0.064	5.130
Japan	0.014	0.056	0.017	0.018	0.064	0.902
Newly industrializing Asia	0.011	0.069	0.017	0.022	0.070	1.116
Low-income Asia	0.009	0.078	0.015	0.053	0.064	2.687
Major oil producers	0.010	0.027	0.015	0.148	0.068	7.467
North Africa and other Middle East	0.009	0.017	0.015	0.128	0.064	6.448
Sub-Saharan Africa	0.009	0.057	0.015	0.033	0.064	1.689
Southern Africa	0.010	0.062	0.017	0.030	0.073	1.525
Oceania	0.014	0.062	0.017	0.013	0.088	0.634

a. Cement is shown in value terms, for comparison with other materials, as well as in physical units.

Note: The first column corresponds to Sector XX2, residual resources. This includes minimally processed forms of materials not included in other sectors (like gravel).

Source: Institute for Economic Analysis estimates based on UNIDO, 1985c, 1985d; UN Industrial Statistics Yearbook, 1988; U.S. Department of the Interior, Bureau of Mines, Minerals Yearbook, 1981 UN COMTRADE data base.

Cement inputs in Sub-Saharan Africa have been declining. This is probably due to problems in the cement industry, which has experienced low rates of capacity utilization in many countries in the region, to balance of payments constraints that restrict imports of cement as well as inputs to the cement industry, and to high transportation costs.

Stone, Clay, Glass, and Concrete Products

Estimates of nonmetallic mineral inputs (including cement) to construction are provided by UNIDO for 1980. These data, together with the cement input coefficients, were used to develop the input coefficients of stone, glass, and clay into construction that are reported in Tables 8.8 and 8.9.

Discrepancies between the UNIDO regional classification and that of the World Model needed to be reconciled, and the price basis (1975 U.S. prices) was adjusted to that of the World Model (1970 U.S. prices).

New input coefficients for stone, glass, and clay products (excluding cement) were calculated for those developed regions with relatively low cement coefficients (high-income North America, high-income Western Europe, Eastern Europe, Japan, southern Africa, and Oceania) by subtracting the cement coefficients from Tables 8.8 and 8.9 from the UNIDO estimates for total nonmetallic mineral inputs. Eastern Europe was assumed to have the same coefficients as the former Soviet Union. For all other regions with high cement coefficients, and where the stone, glass, clay, and concrete products sector contains little ready-mixed concrete, the original World Model coefficients were used.

The resulting input coefficients for stone, glass, clay, and concrete products vary far less across regions than do the coefficients for cement, as the former are less dependent on the level of development and the composition of aggregate construction. Some confirmation that this is realistic is provided by Table 8.4, which shows that most types of construction in the United States had similar input coefficients for nonmetallic minerals other than cement/concrete even though the composition of the mix varied greatly. The input coefficients for glass, stone, clay, and concrete products are assumed to be the same in 1980 and in 1990.

Metals

According to UNIDO estimates, total metal inputs to the construction sector in 1980 varied within a very narrow margin in the developed market economies, between 0.12 and 0.14 dollars of input per dollar of output (in 1975 prices), while the formerly centrally planned economies had a coefficient of 0.11. With the exception of Sub-Saharan Africa (0.07), the coefficients for developing regions ranged between 0.10 and 0.14. The main difference between the developed and developing regions was the share of primary metals (processed and semifabricated) versus finished (fabricated) metals. While the share of finished metals was between 62 percent and 75 percent in the developed regions, it varied between 24 percent and 49 percent in the developing regions. This difference reflects the use of simpler metal structures, less elaborate facilities in the finished construction projects, and a smaller variety in the supply of metals, demanding more adjustment at the construction site.

The World Model includes both a metal processing sector (XX5) and several metal-fabricating sectors (XX17–XX24), each absorbing different metals and delivering its output to a variety of sectors, including the construction sector. Metal inputs from metal processing to construction are charged through the metal products sector, which is the main supplier of fabricated metals for construction. For input coefficients to the construction sector, we have maintained the original World Model estimates, which assume only minor changes in the coefficients between 1970 and 1990. This assumption seems reasonable in view of the small variation among regions at very different stages of development as reported by UNIDO.

We have, however, reestimated the metal input coefficients to the metal-fabricating sectors in order to capture increased levels of fabrication and quality of output reflected in declining metal inputs per unit of output over time in these sectors. This is discussed at length in Chapter 7.

Wood Products

Coefficients measuring inputs of wood products to construction, shown in Tables 8.8 and 8.9, were revised on the basis of the UNIDO data (UNIDO, 1983a, 1983b). The wood input coefficients are lowest in the regions that have the highest cement input coefficients.

Chemicals

While the input of industrial chemicals (XX12) to construction is neglible, the input of finished chemical products (XX14) such as plastics, paints, and glues is important. These products are used in very different parts of the construction sector. According to Table 8.4, plastics has its main use in new buildings, and the input of paints and allied products is highest in maintenance and repair construction.

The input coefficients for finished chemicals (mainly plastics, paints, and allied products) are somewhat higher in developed than in developing countries, presumably because of their higher share of maintenance and repair. The original World Model Model estimate for high-income North America for finished chemicals seems to be consistent with what is known from other sources for the United States, and it is reasonable to assume that other developed countries have similar coefficients. We have chosen to keep the original model estimates for industrial chemicals, finished chemicals, and petroleum products.

Other Minerals

The production of minimally processed products such as sand, stone, and gravel is included among the activities of the residual resources sector (XX2). The highest intensity of use of these materials for construction is in highway construction. Repair and maintenance activities also use these materials intensively.

At early stages of development, new road construction constitutes an important part of overall construction, but it subsequently declines. In the United States the level of new road construction is the same as it was thirty years ago, but the share of total construction has fallen from more than 8 percent to less than 5 percent. As the share of new road construction decreases, however, the share of sand- and gravel-intensive road maintenance increases. The net impact on coefficients is small, and we have decided to keep the original World Model input coefficients for residual resources.

Projections Under the ocf Scenario

The overall use of materials per unit of construction can be expected to decline due to the increasing importance of maintenance relative to new construction. For most processed materials the decline, as measured in raw material content, will be larger than the decline,in value because of increased fabrication, improvements in quality through better design, and higher strength for constant volume.

Increasing use of ready-mixed concrete is expected in developed regions, as well as in developing regions, as their infrastructure improves. These assumptions will reduce requirements for cement. With moderate rises in energy prices, however, the competiveness of cement is likely to increase, both as a bearing material compared to steel and cement and as a means of insulation in cold regions. Unlike metals, cement serves as a high-volume, low-price, bulk material, and there are unlikely to be dramatic changes in the way cement is used in the different fields of construction. The annual projected rates of change in cement and other input coefficients are reported in Table 8.10.

We expect the input coefficients for stone, glass, clay, and concrete products to be stable in the future in developed and developing regions. Building and maintenance construction is more glass intensive than other construction, so the share of glass is likely to increase, while the aggregate of the other products is declining. In developing countries, we assume that cement and concrete will substitute for structural clay products (e.g., bricks) in building construction as buildings increase in height. While the use of cement and concrete per unit of output is projected to decline, we assume that a larger share of concrete will be manufactured by the stone, clay, glass, and concrete products sector as prefabricated or ready-mixed concrete.

A sharp decline in metal inputs (measured in physical units) per unit of output is expected in developing countries and in the formerly centrally planned economies. This assumption corresponds to higher future levels of fabrication,

Table 8.10. Construction input coefficients under the OCF scenario in 2020 (average annual rate of change after 1990) (percentages)

	SE5 Copper	SE6 Aluminum	SE10 Iron	XX14 Finished chemicals	XX15 Cement
High-income North America	−1.50	0.50	−1.00	1.00	−0.50
Newly industrializing Latin America	−1.50	0.50	−2.00	1.00	−1.00
Low-income Latin America	−1.00	1.50	−2.00	1.00	0.00
High-income Western Europe	−1.50	1.00	−1.00	1.00	−1.00
Medium-income Western Europe	−1.50	0.50	−2.00	1.00	−2.00
Eastern Europe	−1.50	1.50	−2.00	1.00	−1.50
Former Soviet Union	−1.50	1.00	−2.50	1.00	−1.50
Centrally planned Asia	−1.50	1.00	−2.75	1.00	−0.50
Japan	−1.50	0.50	−1.00	1.00	−1.00
Newly industrializing Asia	−1.50	1.00	−2.00	1.00	−0.50
Low-income Asia	−0.50	1.50	−1.50	1.00	0.00
Major oil producers	−1.50	0.00	−2.75	1.00	−1.00
North Africa and other Middle East	−0.50	1.00	−1.00	1.00	−1.00
Sub-Saharan Africa	−1.50	0.00	−2.00	1.00	2.00
Southern Africa	−1.50	0.50	−1.00	1.00	−1.00
Oceania	−1.50	0.50	−1.00	1.00	−1.00

Note: Other material input coefficients—residual resources (XX2), wood products (XX7), and glass, stone, clay, and concrete products (XX16)—are assumed to remain unchanged.

Source: Institute for Economic Analysis.

better design, a larger use of higher-strength alloys and composite materials including nonmetals, and an increased share of customized products. In addition, other materials will be substituted for metals in the metal-fabricating sectors, notably ceramics, fiber optics, and plastics for coating, to mention just a few areas. The trend toward a higher share of maintenance in total construction also exerts a downward pressure on metal inputs.

We assume a substantial decline notably in iron and steel inputs, but also in copper. Copper will face increased competition in plumbing and other uses from plastics and fiber optics. Copper is used most intensively in public utility construction, which as a share of total construction is expected to decline. On the other hand, aluminum inputs are expected to grow steadily in most regions, reflecting increased substitution of aluminum for iron and copper in, for example, non-weight-bearing sections and wiring.

The input coefficients for finished chemicals, mainly plastics and paints, are projected to increase by 1 percent a year in all regions. Plastics might substitute for a number of materials in a wide array of uses, such as plumbing, frames, and fixtures. The use of paints is expected to increase with the increased importance of maintenance and repair construction. For residual resources, petroleum products, and finished chemicals, we assume that the input coefficients will be constant over the next thirty years.

Input coefficients for wood are expected to be constant over the period. The tendency toward increased production of one- and two-family dwellings in developed countries (as has been observed in the United States and Western Europe) is expected to be offset by the increase in maintenance. For developing countries, it is assumed that the major growth in residential construction will come in cement/concrete and brick buildings that will replace simple wooden structures. At present, as much as 30–40 percent of wood for construction in developing countries takes the form of poles and similar items, but this use is expected to decline. The value of the wood input per unit of construction is assumed to be unchanged because of the corresponding increase in the degree of processing of the wood that will be used for construction.

9

Cement

The Role of the Cement Industry

The word *cement* can be used to describe any substance that makes objects adhere to each other, but in common usage it refers to hydraulic cement, which has the property of hardening under water.

In the United States 95 percent of hydraulic cement production is portland cement, and most of the rest is masonry cement. Clinker is the base for cement; it is a mixture of calcium carbonate, silica, alumina, and usually iron oxide. Clinker is heated in a kiln to achieve partial fusion. To make portland cement, the processed clinker is ground with a small amount of calcium sulfate. The main energy inputs for making cement are fossil fuels used for clinkering; 10–25 percent of total energy consumption is in the form of electricity, mainly for crushing and grinding of feed and the final grinding of cement. The principal material and energy inputs are shown in Table 9.1.

In the production of cement, clinker can to some extent be replaced by other constituents such as granulated blast furnace slag, fly ash, and natural pozzolanas to make composite cements, saving fuel. The relative importance of such cements varies considerably among countries.

Except for oil wells and other minor uses, cement is delivered to the construction sector. The main use is for concrete, which is a mixture of sand, gravel, or stone bound together by a paste of cement and water. The common proportions of cement, sand, and gravel or stone are 1–2–4 and 1–3–5.

The main driving force in the demand for all materials in developing countries is the construction sector. Developing countries account for a much larger share of world cement production and consumption than of metals and most other energy-intensive materials. In 1988 their share of cement production was

Table 9.1. Main material and energy inputs to cement

SE11	Petroleum
SE12	Natural gas
SE13	Coal
XX 2	Residual resources
XX12	Industrial chemicals
XX25	Electric power

136

46 percent, and they accounted for half of world consumption. On a per capita basis, however, production in the developed market economies was 426 kilos in 1988; in the newly industrializing countries it was 202 kilos, and in other developing countries, 112 kilos.

The production of cement is highly energy intensive. Energy inputs can account for as much as 40 percent of overall production costs. Even though energy consumption for making a ton of cement is only approximately 20 percent of what is required for making of a ton of crude steel, world cement production is 50 percent higher than world steel production and is growing rapidly in developing countries. The developing countries' share of world steel production is around 20 percent compared to around 50 percent for cement, and energy consumption in the cement industry in developing countries is approximately 67 percent of that in the steel industry. Consequently, the cement industry is one of the major industrial energy consumers in developing countries. For example, the cement industry in India accounted for 17 percent of total industrial coal demand in 1981 and 4 percent of electricity, while the U.S. cement industry accounted for only 3.5 percent of the total energy purchased by all manufacturing industries.

Regional Distribution of Production and Use of Cement

The principal source used for cement production statistics is the UN's *Industrial Statistics Yearbook*. The *Minerals Yearbook,* published by the U.S. Bureau of Mines, also has detailed country production levels. The unit of measure in these sources is weight, and the *Minerals Yearbook* also gives unit prices in U.S. dollars: in 1970 the average U.S. price per ton of hydraulic cement was $19.78 at the factory gate. The UN COMTRADE data base provides trade figures in dollars. The current World Model unit is constant United States prices; in future work, it will be measured in tons.

The production of cement by region, measured in tons, is shown in Table 9.2 for 1970, 1980, and 1988. Over this period, most of the increase in world cement production occurred in the developing regions. Their share rose from 31 percent to 46 percent between 1980 and 1988, reaching an annual rate of 500 million tons. As recently as 1970, the total share of developing countries was only 17 percent. The most spectacular increase was in centrally planned Asia, which more than doubled its production to a share in excess of 20 percent of the world total in 1988.

Production and trade in cement (measured in constant U.S. prices), as well as apparent consumption and self-sufficiency (production divided by consumption), are reported in Tables 9.3 and 9.4 for 1980 and 1988, respectively. The developing countries are net importers, but their rate of self-sufficiency as a group increased from 78 percent in 1980 to 91 percent in 1988. Omitting the oil-rich countries, the developing countries were net exporters by 1988. Regional export shares and import coefficients are summarized in Tables 9.5 and 9.6.

The main uses of cement in the United States in 1988 were for the production of ready-mixed concrete, which accounted for close to 75 percent of the

Table 9.2. Cement production in World Model regions in 1970, 1980, and 1988 (millions of tons)

Region	1970	1980	1988
High-income North America	77	80	85
Newly industrializing Latin America	25	57	63
Low-income Latin America	9	18	21
High-income Western Europe	150	152	140
Medium-income Western Europe	35	70	76
Eastern Europe	42	67	65
Former Soviet Union	95	125	135
Centrally planned Asia	14	88	220
Japan	57	88	72
Newly industrializing Asia	10	32	62
Low-income Asia	18	28	52
Major oil producers	7	27	48
North Africa and other Middle East	10	16	27
Sub-Saharan Africa	5	7	7
Southern Africa	6	7	7
Oceania	6	6	7
World	566	868	1,087
Developing regions	98	273	500
Share (percentage)	17	31	46

Source: UN, *Industrial Statistics Yearbook,* 1979, 1988.

Table 9.3. Production, consumption and trade of cement in 1980 (billions of dollars, 1970 U.S. prices)

Region	Production	Exports	Imports	Apparent consumption	Production/ consumption
High-income North America	1.58	0.15	0.21	1.63	0.97
Newly industrializing Latin America	1.13	0.03	0.06	1.17	0.97
Low-income Latin America	0.35	0.15	0.11	0.31	1.12
High-income Western Europe	3.00	0.70	0.29	2.60	1.16
Medium-income Western Europe	1.39	0.73	0.05	0.71	1.96
Eastern Europe	1.32	0.00	0.00	1.32	1.00
Former Soviet Union	2.47	0.09	0.00	2.38	1.04
Centrally planned Asia	1.74	0.13	0.00	1.62	1.08
Japan	1.74	0.40	0.00	1.34	1.30
Newly industrializing Asia	0.63	0.42	0.36	0.57	1.10
Low-income Asia	0.55	0.05	0.19	0.70	0.79
Major oil producers	0.54	0.05	1.31	1.80	0.30
North Africa and other Middle East	0.31	0.00	0.28	0.60	0.53
Sub-Saharan Africa	0.14	0.11	0.15	0.18	0.77
Southern Africa	0.14	0.01	0.01	0.14	1.02
Oceania	0.12	0.02	0.01	0.11	1.09
World	17.17	3.04	3.04	17.17	1.00
Developing regions	5.40	0.93	2.47	6.94	0.78
Share (percentage)	31%	31%	81%	40%	78%

Source: Institute for Economic Analysis based on UN, *Industrial Statistics Yearbook,* 1988; U.S. Department of the Interior, Bureau of Mines, *Minerals Yearbook,* 1981; UN COMTRADE data base.

Table 9.4. Production, consumption and trade of cement in 1988 (billions of dollars, 1970 U.S. prices)

Region	Production	Exports	Imports	Apparent consumption	Production/ consumption
High-income North America	1.67	0.29	0.58	1.97	0.85
Newly industrializing Latin America	1.25	0.26	0.01	0.99	1.25
Low-income Latin America	0.42	0.17	0.11	0.36	1.16
High-income Western Europe	2.78	1.00	0.54	2.32	1.20
Medium-income Western Europe	1.51	0.56	0.08	1.03	1.47
Eastern Europe	1.28	0.00	0.00	1.28	1.00
Former Soviet Union	2.67	0.25	0.01	2.43	1.10
Centrally planned Asia	4.36	0.01	0.03	4.37	1.00
Japan	1.43	0.18	0.11	1.36	1.05
Newly industrializing Asia	1.22	0.65	0.22	0.79	1.54
Low-income Asia	1.03	0.09	0.25	1.19	0.86
Major oil producers	0.96	0.07	1.26	2.14	0.45
North Africa and other Middle East	0.53	0.10	0.43	0.86	0.62
Sub-Saharan Africa	0.14	0.14	0.14	0.15	0.94
Southern Africa	0.13	0.00	0.01	0.14	0.98
Oceania	0.14	0.01	0.01	0.14	1.03
World	21.51	3.78	3.78	21.51	1.00
Developing regions	9.89	1.49	2.45	10.85	0.91
Share (percentage)	46%	40%	65%	50%	91%

Source: Institute for Economic Analysis based on UN, *Industrial Statistics Yearbook,* 1988; Bureau of Mines, *Minerals Yearbook,* 1989; UN COMTRADE data base.

Table 9.5. Export shares for cement for World Model regions in 1980 and 1990

Region	1980	1990
High-income North America	0.05	0.08
Newly industrializing Latin America	0.01	0.07
Low-income Latin America	0.05	0.04
High-income Western Europe	0.23	0.26
Medium-income Western Europe	0.24	0.15
Eastern Europe	0	0
Former Soviet Union	0.03	0.07
Centrally planned Asia	0.04	0
Japan	0.13	0.05
Newly industrializing Asia	0.14	0.17
Low-income Asia	0.02	0.02
Major oil producers	0.02	0.02
North Africa and other Middle East	0	0.03
Sub-Saharan Africa	0.04	0.04
Southern Africa	0	0
Oceania	0.01	0
World	1.00	1.00
Developing regions	0.31	0.40

Note: The export share is the regions's share of total world exports of cement.

Source: Tables 9.3 and 9.4.

Table 9.6. Import coefficients for cement for World Model regions in 1980 and 1990 (imports per unit of domestic production)

Region	1980	1990
High-income North America	0.13	0.35
Newly industrializing Latin America	0.06	0.01
Low-income Latin America	0.32	0.26
High-income Western Europe	0.10	0.20
Medium-income Western Europe	0.04	0.05
Eastern Europe	0	0
Former Soviet Union	0	0
Centrally planned Asia	0	0.01
Japan	0	0.07
Newly industrializing Asia	0.56	0.18
Low-income Asia	0.35	0.25
Major oil producers	2.41	1.32
North Africa and other Middle East	0.90	0.81
Sub-Saharan Africa	1.12	1.05
Southern Africa	0.04	0.04
Oceania	0.06	0.04
World	0.18	0.18
Developing regions	0.46	0.25

Note: A region's import coefficient is defined as cement imports divided by domestic production.

Source: Tables 9.3 and 9.4.

total U.S. demand of 84.6 million tons, and of concrete products, accounting for 11 percent of the demand. These are two components of the World Model Sector XX16, stone, clay, glass, and concrete products. The balance of use is accounted for by purchasers who mix their own concrete, such as highway and other contractors or government agencies, and by building-material dealers selling to the construction industry.

Production Technology

The main inputs for making cement are limestone (1.3 tons per ton of cement) and clay (0.3 ton per ton of cement). Most countries have large reserves of the raw materials, which are generally mined using low-cost, open-pit mining. From the mine, rock is transported to crushers that reduce the stone to feed size. The main processes for making portland cement include crushing, grinding, and mixing of raw materials; burning raw materials in a kiln to produce clinker; cooling and grinding the clinker; and adding gypsum or anhydrite. The most energy-intensive step is the combustion of clinker.

There are two different types of grinding processes, wet and dry. In the dry process, the raw materials are dried and pulverized; in the wet process, water is added to produce a slurry consisting of 67 percent solids. The wet process involves a simpler technological scheme for raw mix preparation, is less labor intensive, and leads to less dust pollution than the dry process. However, due to the price increases of fossil fuels in the 1970s, the dry process is becoming increasingly dominant due to its substantially higher energy efficiency.

Two types of kilns are used for burning clinker, vertical kilns with average capacities of 60,000 tons/year and rotary kilns with an optimal capacity that well exceeds 1 million tons/year. At present, a large majority of world cement production is based on rotary kilns. A notable exception among major cement producers is China, which produces 75 percent of its cement from vertical kilns with an average capacity of 30,000 tons/year. Vertical kilns are simple to construct, can be built using local technology and resources, and are quite energy efficient. However, this is a very labor-intensive way of producing cement. The future role of vertical kilns in developing countries is controversial.

The rotary kiln is a cylindrical steel shell rotating slowly around an axis with a small slope. Rotary kilns can be used for both wet and dry processes, but vertical ones are used for dry processes only. In the wet process, the slurry is fed into the upper end of the kiln and moves slowly at progressively increasing temperatures as the material approaches the firing, or discharging, end of the kiln. In the first part, water is vaporized, followed by the combustion of organic material and calcination. Clinkering takes place in the burning zone. While the exit gases have a temperature of 250–350° C, the temperature in the burning zone may be 1500° C.

Drying in the traditional dry-process kiln is shorter, and therefore less energy intensive, than in the wet-process one, as the former omits the water evaporation stage. Modern dry-process kilns with preheating systems shorten the process and reduce energy requirements even more. The exit gas from the kiln, which is 1,000° C, is returned for use in the preheater (the suspension type being the most efficient) to start combustion and calcination, and the feed enters the kiln at 800° C. The latest important development is the introduction of preheaters with precalciners. Now the firing is accomplished in two phases. The primary firing, at the discharge end of the kiln, supplies only the heat for final sintering of the material. The secondary firing, at substantially lower temperatures, takes place in the precalciner and leads to decarbonation of the input of up to 90 percent. Even though the reduction in fossil fuel requirements is small and electricity requirements may rise, the use of precalciners is growing rapidly in both developed and developing countries. The advantage is that the kiln volume can be reduced by 60 percent for the same output because decarbonation takes place in the precalciner. Furthermore, since the temperature requirement in the secondary firing is lower, lower-grade fossil fuels can be used and the potential impurities from the fuel can be contained in the clinker. With the use of precalciners, nitrogen oxide emissions are also decreased.

Energy Consumption

Fossil fuel consumption per ton of clinker and cement in 1980 and 1990 and the use of secondary constituents in final cement are reported in Table 9.7 for all regions. The average use of fossil fuels in the OECD area in 1973 for making a

Table 9.7. Fossil fuel consumption and share of secondary constituents in cement in World Model regions in 1980 and 1990

	1980			1990		
	tce/ton of clinker	Share of secondary constituents	tce/ton of cement	tce/ton of clinker	Share of secondary constituents	tce/ton of cement
High-income North America	0.22	0.01	0.22	0.15	0.01	0.15
Newly industrializing Latin America	0.17	0.10	0.15	0.14	0.10	0.13
Low-income Latin America	0.20	0.10	0.18	0.18	0.10	0.16
High-income Western Europe	0.14	0.15	0.12	0.13	0.15	0.11
Medium-income Western Europe	0.14	0.15	0.12	0.13	0.15	0.11
Eastern Europe	0.17	0.20	0.14	0.15	0.20	0.12
Former Soviet Union	0.22	0.22	0.17	0.20	0.22	0.16
Centrally planned Asia	0.14	0.10	0.13	0.13	0.10	0.12
Japan	0.12	0.03	0.12	0.11	0.03	0.11
Newly industrializing Asia	0.16	0.10	0.14	0.13	0.10	0.12
Low-income Asia	0.18	0.10	0.16	0.14	0.10	0.13
Major oil producers	0.17	0.10	0.15	0.14	0.10	0.13
North Africa and other Middle East	0.21	0.10	0.19	0.18	0.10	0.16
Sub-Saharan Africa	0.22	0.10	0.20	0.20	0.10	0.18
Southern Africa	0.14	0.10	0.13	0.13	0.10	0.12
Oceania	0.14	0.01	0.14	0.13	0.01	0.13

Note: Fossil fuel consumption per ton of cement is equal to fossil fuel consumption per ton of clinker multiplied by the share of clinker (1 minus the share of secondary constituents).

Source: Institute for Economic Analysis based on UN, *Minerals Yearbook*, various years; OECD, 1982; Sterner, 1990; Stewart and Muhegf, 1989; UNIDO, 1985c; Wilson, 1983.

ton of clinker was 0.18 tce/ton. However, there were considerable differences in the use of energy in different regions, ranging from 0.15 tce/ton in Japan to 0.23 tce/ton in North America. By 1980 the average OECD usage was down to that of Japan in 1973. Japan used 0.12 tce/ton of clinker in 1980, while North America still required 0.21 tce/ton according to OECD. The differences in energy consumption for clinker production are due to differences in kiln feed, prices of fossil fuels, the age of the capacity, levels of preheating and precalcination, and the share of wet processes.

According to the *Minerals Yearbook,* average kiln consumption per ton of clinker was 0.22 tce in the United States in 1980. In kiln firing in wet-process plants it was 0.23 tce compared to 0.19 tce in dry-process plants, and 45 percent of clinker was produced by the dry process. Fuel consumption in plants with suspension preheaters was 0.18 tce/ton.

Average fuel consumption per ton of clinker in the United States in 1988 fell to 0.15 tce/ton: 0.19 tce/ton in wet-process plants and 0.13 tce/ton in dry-process plants, which now account for 64 percent of production.

The increase in fuel oil prices has led to a major substitution of coal for oil and gas for kiln firing. In 1973 only 15 percent of the energy in Western Europe came from coal, while the share in North America was 38 percent. By 1980 coal provided 44 percent of the energy in Western Europe, 69 percent in North America, and 58 percent in Japan. By 1988, 93 percent of the fuel for kiln firing in the United States was coal, 4 percent was natural gas, and the rest was oil and waste fuel.

While there have been great savings in fossil fuel use in the kiln, there has been no decline in the use of electricity in the United States. In 1972 electricity consumption per ton of cement was 127 kwh or 0.044 tce/ton (assuming a conversion factor of 0.4). In 1980 the use was 0.055 tce/ton, declining by 1988 to 0.051 tce/ton or one quarter of total energy consumption in cement production. The main reason for these developments is that fuel-saving technologies tend to be electricity-intensive.

Even though the share of clinker produced in Japan by wet processes fell from 14 percent in 1973 to zero in 1984 and the share produced in kilns with precalciners increased from 10 percent to 82 percent (vs. only 6 percent in the United States in 1984), electricity requirements have fallen from 117 kwh/ton to 108 kwh/ton of cement—and as low as 90 kwh ton in the most efficient plant (Kahane, 1986). There are two dominant reasons for the different electricity requirements in the United States and Japan: differences in feed and specification of cement and the greater use of advanced energy-saving technology in Japan in the stages of grinding, pyro-processing, and final grinding. Japan has finer feed and greater usage of roller mills in grinding. In the pyro-processing stage, United States producers need gas-bypass systems to reduce the high alkali content of their raw material. In final grinding, energy requirements are lower in Japan because of the installation of improved classifiers and because of lower final product surface area specifications.

Most Western European countries use dry processes and have an energy efficiency in cement production close to that of the Japanese. A notable exception is the United Kingdom, which relies heavily on wet processes due to the quality of the feed.

In developing countries, the main reason for differences in fossil fuel consumption per ton of clinker seems to be the share of dry processes. Around 1980 dry-process plants used 0.13 tce/ton of clinker in India, while wet-process plants, which made up 65 percent of total plants, used 0.21 tce/ton. Similar differences, amounting to 50–75 percent higher fuel consumption in wet compared to dry processes, are common in other developing countries. These countries have not implemented many of the measures taken in the industrial countries to improve the energy efficiency of wet-process plants.

As late as 1978, about 33 percent of the rotary kilns in the newly industrializing countries of Latin America, as well as in Asia, Sub-Saharan Africa, and oil-rich countries used wet processes. For North Africa and low-income Asia the share was 67 percent, while low-income Latin America had a share of 55 percent. Since then, all shares have declined sharply. There has been a rapid increase in cement production in most developing regions, and the new capacity that has been put in place uses the dry process. Also, a substantial share of the wet-process capacity has been scrapped because of age or for economic reasons, and some conversion of existing wet capacity to dry capacity has taken place. Conversion is very expensive, however, sometimes amounting to 60 percent of the cost of building a new kiln.

In the countries of newly industrializing Latin America, the share of wet processes in the mid 1980s ranged from 7 percent to 29 percent, and typical fossil consumption per ton of clinker was 0.15–0.16 tce/ton. In low-income Latin America, where the share still was very high, typical consumption was 0.19–0.23 tce/ton.

In Africa, energy efficiency may be even lower. It is suggested that even for a new dry-process cement plant in Tanzania, the coal requirement is 0.172–0.196 tce/ton of cement, with electricity requirements of about 120–125 kwh/ton.

In the Soviet Union in 1980, only 15 percent of cement was produced by dry processes due to problems in reducing the moisture in the feed to suitable levels. Consequently, average energy consumption per ton of clinker was in excess of 0.22 tce. The target was to produce 22 percent by dry processes for 1990 and 40 percent by 2000, with fuel consumption per ton of clinker falling to 0.19 tce/ton. The Soviet Union had large supplies of natural gas, and the share of natural gas reached 60 percent of fuel use for making clinker in 1975.

Unlike the former Soviet Union, Eastern Europe uses mainly dry and semi-dry processes. In 1980 the cement produced by such methods had shares of production in the German Democratic Republic, Hungary, and the Czech Soviet Socialist Republic of 87, 82, and 69 percent, respectively. Fuel consumption in the average kiln in Hungary and the Czech Soviet Socialist Republic per ton of clinker was about 0.17 tce. The most efficient new kilns in these countries had a fuel consumption of only 0.11 tce/ton.

Centrally planned Asia (China) produces 75 percent of its cement in small-scale, vertical kilns. These kilns are also in operation in India and some other developing countries. This simple, labor-intensive technology, based on coal, was phased out in developed countries with the introduction of large-scale rotary kilns. Due to the basic efficiency of direct heat transfer in the vertical kiln, it is estimated that these kilns consume only 0.13–0.14 tce/ton of clinker.

The most efficient new kilns in the developing regions are probably found in newly industrializing Asia. In 1980 the most efficient kiln in Thailand, a suspension preheater dry kiln, had fuel consumption per ton of clinker of only 0.111 tce. This was less than 10 percent more than the world's most efficient kilns and below the average energy consumption in Japanese kilns (0.118 tce/ton) at that time.

In 1978 the main fuel for clinker production in developing countries was oil. Most countries used only this fuel for rotary kilns. Countries with abundant coal, like China, used coal to varying degrees, while gas-rich countries relied on natural gas, although only a few countries with small cement capacity relied exclusively on gas. As in the developed economies, there has been a switch from oil to coal during the last decade.

Cost Structure

Rotary kilns exhibit substantial economies of scale up to a capacity in excess of 1 million tons/year. Compared to smaller rotary kilns (a few hundred thousand tons per year of capacity), the even smaller vertical kilns have a lower overall cost per ton and lower fossil-fuel requirements.

Compared to the value of cement at the factory gate, the transportation cost per ton is very high. The cheapest transport is by sea or river. The cost of rail-road transportation might be 4–5 times, and that of road transportation might be 10–20 times, the value of the product itself in developed countries, where 1,000 kilometers of road transport can double the price of cement. In developing countries with poor roads and reliance on smaller vehicles running at lower speeds, a road transportation distance of 150 kilometers might double the cost compared to the price at the factory gate.

The high transportation cost and lower demand in many developing countries in most cases make the optimal plant size substantially smaller than in developed countries, except in the vicinity of large urban centers. Urbanization and the expansion of infrastructure have a double effect on cement production. Both phenomena increase demand directly. They also reduce production and transportation costs, further increasing the use of cement.

Projections Under the OCF Scenario

We assume that in 2020 most regions will rely entirely on dry processes and that, in the remaining regions, only a neglible share of clinker will be produced using wet processes. To achieve this, countries like the United States, the United Kingdom, and the countries of the former Soviet Union will need to solve their problems with feed quality. The rapid increase in energy prices in the former Soviet Union will substantially speed up the transition from wet to dry processes, and both in this region and in Eastern Europe, new energy-efficient dry-process kilns with preheaters will be installed in the coming decades.

Projections of fossil fuel consumption per ton of clinker and cement in 2020, and the shares of secondary constituents in final cement, are reported in Table 9.8. We assume that by 2020 the average energy consumption per ton of clinker in developed regions and in newly industrializing Asia and Latin America will be 0.10 tce/ton, equal to the efficiency of new kilns presently being built in several of these regions. This estimate is conservative since it does not take into account possible improvements in insulation of kilns, increases in heat recovery, and changes in feed that reduce heat requirements compared to today's best practice.

We also assume that new capacity in developing regions other than the newly industrializing ones will be dry process, with basically the same technology as in the developed regions. Only centrally planned Asia will probably have a substantial share of vertical kilns. Typically, developing regions have a lower operating energy efficiency for the same equipment and are less able to introduce new energy-saving measures in existing capacities and processes. We assume that the developing regions except sub-Saharan Africa will use 0.115 tce/ton in 2020. For sub-Saharan Africa we assume that energy consumption will be 0.13 tce/ton.

With the exception of the oil-rich Middle East, the conversion to coal for kiln firing will be complete by the year 2000. This is also assumed for the for-

Table 9.8. Projected fossil fuel consumption and share of secondary constituents in cement under the OCF scenario in 2020

	tce/ton of clinker	Share secondary constituents	tce/ton of cement	As a percentage of 1990 tce/ton of cement
High-income North America	0.100	0.20	0.080	54
Newly industrializing Latin America	0.100	0.20	0.080	64
Low-income Latin America	0.115	0.20	0.092	57
High-income Western Europe	0.100	0.30	0.070	63
Medium-income Western Europe	0.100	0.30	0.070	63
Eastern Europe	0.100	0.30	0.070	58
Former Soviet Union	0.100	0.30	0.070	45
Centrally planned Asia	0.115	0.20	0.092	79
Japan	0.100	0.20	0.080	75
Newly industrializing Asia	0.100	0.20	0.080	68
Low-income Asia	0.115	0.20	0.092	73
Major oil producers	0.115	0.20	0.092	73
North Africa and other Middle East	0.115	0.20	0.092	57
Sub-Saharan Africa	0.130	0.20	0.104	58
Southern Africa	0.100	0.20	0.080	68
Oceania	0.100	0.20	0.080	62

Note: Fossil fuel consumption per ton of cement is equal to the fossil fuel consumption per ton of clinker multiplied by the share of clinker (1 minus the share of secondary constituents).

Source: Institute for Economic Analysis.

mer Soviet Union, which will place substantially higher value on the use of gas in areas other than cement. We assume that the oil-rich Middle East will use half coal and half natural gas after 2000.

Clinker can to some extent be substituted for by other components such as granulated blast furnace slag, fly ash, and natural pozzolanas; this substitution leads to proportionately lower use of fossil fuel per ton of cement, although it also results in lower strength. Blends containing 20 percent pozzolana are suitable for ordinary concrete works, and blends containing 40 percent are suitable for low-grade cements. In the early 1980s, the proportions of such materials were less than 1 percent in North America, 3 percent in Japan, 15 percent on average in Western Europe with as much as 50 percent in the Netherlands, and 20 percent in the Soviet Union and Eastern Europe. The OECD study *The Use of Coal in Industry* (1982) projected that Western Europe would reach a share of additives of 30 percent by 2000, while North America and the Pacific OECD countries would reach 20 percent. The high expectations for a sharp increase in the use of additives in the early 1980s have not been fulfilled, probably because of declining fossil-fuel prices; the levels in 1990 are approximately the same as those a decade ago.

With the increase in energy prices that is assumed under the OCF scenario, the use of additives will be increasingly attractive. We assume that by 2020 the use of additives will have reached an average content of 20 percent in manufactured cement in all regions except those of Europe, where it is expected to reach 30 percent (see Table 9.8).

We assume that electricity consumption per ton of cement will decline in all regions through improvements in grinding of raw material and final output. The decline will be partly offset by increased use of electricity for pollution control.

We assume no changes in the value of feed from sector XX2, residual resources (nonmetal mining), or from sector XX12, industrial chemicals, per unit of cement output.

10

Pulp and Paper

Paper is one of the most energy-intensive commodities since it has large direct energy requirements, as well as substantial indirect energy use through its reliance on chemical inputs. While the paper industry has been dominated by developed countries, the developing countries with large forest resources are rapidly increasing their capability for domestic processing of the wood products they traditionally exported. Domestic consumption of paper for uses such as newspapers is expected to increase rapidly in developing regions in the future; such uses of paper are near saturation levels in developed regions.

Production and consumption of paper are discussed in this chapter. The production of paper is likely to undergo significant technological changes in the future, largely related to increased recycling of paper in response to environmental concerns. Projections of future input coefficients are developed based on assumptions about rates of recycling in different regions and the impact of increased recycling on the average technology of the paper industry.

Description of the Sector

Paper is represented by a single sector, paper and pulp (XX9), in the World Model. Table 10.1 indicates the principal subsectors and inputs of the paper and pulp sector and the main purchasing sectors. In food processing and trade, paper is used primarily for wrapping and packaging. Households use mainly sanitary paper products, included the paper and paperboard subsector. Services and the government sector use mainly printing and writing paper.

In the period 1981–90, world consumption of paper and paperboard increased at an average annual rate of 3.7 percent, up from 3.2 percent in the 1970s (see Table 10.2). The fastest-growing part of the industry has been printing and writing paper, in response to the demand for paper and printed matter by the service sector. The latter demand grew at an average annual rate of 5 percent in the 1980s.

Most paper is produced and consumed in the developed countries, which accounted for 83 percent of production and 80 percent of consumption in 1990. Low production and consumption in developing countries result from relatively large economies of scale in production, which favor developed countries, lower

Table 10.1. Principal subsectors, material inputs, and purchasing sectors for paper (XX9)

Subsectors	Material inputs		Purchasing sectors	
Newsprint	SE11	Petroleum	XX3	Food processing
Other printing and writing paper	SE12	Natural gas	XX10	Printing and publishing
Other machine-made paper	SE13	Coal	XX27	Trade
and paperboard	XX6	Textiles	MA2	Consumption
Production of pulp	XX7	Wood products	MA5	Government
	XX11	Rubber products		
	XX12	Industrial chemicals		
	XX25	Electricity		

availability of suitable fiber inputs for quality paper, and low demand for newspapers. However, paper production and consumption are growing most rapidly in developing regions (7 percent), nearly double the world average rate in the 1980s, and developing regions increased their share of world production from 11 percent to 15 percent over this period. The growth of paper production was especially high in centrally planned Asia and newly industrializing Asia.

Recycling Technology

One of the most important developments in the paper and pulp industry concerns the recycling of waste paper. While the demand for virgin pulp increased at an average annual rate of 2.5 percent between 1970 and 1988, the demand for recycled fibers grew twice as fast. Recycling has two components, the recovery of waste paper and the utilization of this material in the production of paper. These components are quantified in Table 10.3, which indicates that the use of recycled fibers in place of virgin fibers is significant in all geographic regions. In 1988, recycled fibers accounted for 33 percent of fiber input in paper production worldwide. In North America, recovery is higher than utilization because some of the recovered waste paper is exported to other countries, which currently utilize more waste paper in production than they are able to recover domestically.

Because recycling requires fewer of most of the major inputs than the manufacture of paper from virgin fiber, some recycling has always been cost effective, particularly for papers such as newsprint, which need not be of high quality, and cardboard, which does not require much de-inking. Recycling has also been significant in wood-deficit areas such as Japan, where virgin fibers must be imported. However, the rate of recycling can be increased substantially in most regions. The maximum rate of collection of wastepaper is estimated at 80–85 percent, though the practical limit may be lower. The remaining wastepaper consists of sanitary and household tissues and books. Cardboard has the highest current rate of recycling; mixed paper, which requires labor-intensive sorting, the lowest.

Recycling technology itself faces serious obstacles, especially in the de-inking stage. It is difficult to handle certain types of paper (e.g., magazines, which have different qualities of inks and paper in the same issue). Further-

Table 10.2. Production of paper in World Model regions in 1980 and 1989 (thousands of metric tons)

Region	1980				1989			
	Newsprint	Other printing and writing paper	Other machine-made paper and paperboard	Total	Newsprint	Other printing and writing paper	Other machine-made paper and paperboard	Total
High-income North America	12852	15340	42026	70218	15144	22509	48359	86012
Newly industrializing Latin America	405	1680	4781	6866	840	2273	6748	9861
Low-income Latin America	1	193	596	790	0	297	836	1133
High-income Western Europe	5723	12597	21086	39406	7621	19850	26578	54049
Medium-income Western Europe	248	1245	3418	4911	343	1443	4401	6187
Eastern Europe	381	841	4157	5379	278	1077	4461	5816
Former Soviet Union	1535	1141	6238	8914	1719	1571	7364	10654
Centrally planned Asia	376	1856	4676	6908	387	3558	11140	15085
Japan	2674	4137	11277	18088	3217	8828	14764	26809
Newly industrializing Asia	215	488	1643	2346	590	1216	3825	5631
Low-income Asia	171	670	662	1503	415	1060	1065	2540
Major oil producers	0	58	71	129	0	59	74	133
North Africa and other Middle East	5	180	322	507	1	218	518	737
Sub-Saharan Africa	21	22	105	148	19	51	167	237
Southern Africa	226	177	796	1199	350	315	971	1636
Oceania	540	243	1321	2104	697	383	1564	2644
World	25373	40868	103175	169416	31621	64708	132835	229164
Share of developing countries	0.047	0.126	0.125	0.113	0.071	0.135	0.183	0.154

Source: Institute for Economic Analysis based on UN *Industrial Statistics Yearbook*, 1989.

Table 10.3. Wastepaper recovery and utilization rates in paper production in 1988 (percentages)

Region	Recovery of waste paper	Utilization of waste paper in production
North America	29.4	22.8
Western Europe	35.8	34.4
Eastern Europe and former Soviet Union	29.0	27.1
Oceania	24.8	28.2
Latin America	33.6	45.3
Japan	48.0	50.9
China	20.4	24.4
Other Asia	34.2	68.5
Africa	16.5	26.9
World	32.7	32.8

Source: Veverka, 1991.

more, de-inking can be more polluting than pulping, depending on the composition of the inks (Hoekstra, 1991).

Projections Under the OCF Scenario

Under the OCF scenario, we assume that the rates of fiber recycling will continue to grow in response to environmental regulation, improvements in technology that will improve the quality of recycled fibers, and increasing scarcity of virgin fibers. Recycling is projected to further reduce virgin fiber input (producted by the wood products sector, XX7) by 40 percent in all regions by the year 2020. Production of paper products from recycled materials will also reduce energy inputs but can be expected to increase requirements for chemicals. The projected changes in input coefficients are given in Table 10.4.

Table 10.4. Changes in input coefficients to pulp and paper (XX9) due to recycling under the OCF scenario in 2020 (percentage change from 1990 coefficient)

Input	
SE11 Petroleum	−15
SE12 Natural gas	−15
SE13 Coal	−15
XX7 Wood products	−40
XX12 Industrial chemicals	+15
XX25 Electricity	−15

Note: The same percentage changes were assumed for all regions.

Source: Institute for Economic Analysis estimates based on personal communication with paper industry expert.

11

Chemicals

Description of the Sectors

While all case studies face data problems, the lack of systematic information is particularly severe in the case of the chemical sectors because of the great diversity of products, the overlapping classification schemes used in different sources, and the lack of a common physical unit that can be useful at this degree of aggregation. For these reasons, this case study is more preliminary than the others.

The chemical sectors are among the most energy-intensive sectors in an economy and play an important role in development because of their strong linkages to other sectors, their importance in trade, and the regulatory issues raised by safety, environmental, and property-right (i.e., patenting) considerations.

Chemicals are represented in the World Model in terms of three sectors: industrial chemicals (XX12), fertilizers and agricultural chemicals (XX13), and finished chemical products (XX14). These sectors produce an extremely diverse array of outputs covered by the three-digit ISIC codes 351 and 352. The World Model sectors are identified with the corresponding subsectors in Table 11.1. The total value of world production of chemicals amounted to about $900 billion a year in the late 1980s, of which more than one-fifth (in value) entered into international trade. Order of magnitude estimates of the relative sizes of the different parts of the industry circa 1987, pieced together from various sources, are shown in Table 11.1.

The industrial chemicals (XX12) include the basic building blocks that serve as inputs to the rest of the chemical industry. Prominent among them are the bulk petrochemicals, which are high-volume, low-price (a few hundred dollars a ton) intermediate products. The other main category is the bulk inorganics, not containing carbon, such as chlorine, ammonia (used mainly for fertilizer production), sulfuric acid, and phosphoric acid. More specialized, or fine, chemicals of lower volume and higher price are also included.

Fertilizers are also bulk products. They are made from ammonia and minerals like phosphate rock and potashs. They and the agricultural chemicals are often classified together (XX13). While the latter are more expensive on a per pound basis, their total tonnage is small compared to that of fertilizers.

Prominent among the finished chemical products (XX14) are the plastics, which are rapidly being substituted for other materials especially in developing

Table 11.1. Chemical sectors and subsectors and approximate sales around 1987 (billions of dollars)

		Sales
XX12 Industrial chemicals		$390
3511	Bulk organics: ethylene, styrene, aromatics, propylene, etc.	130
	Bulk inorganics: chlorine, sodium hydroxide, sodium carbonate, titanium dioxide, hydrogen peroxide, ammonia, etc.	130
	Fine industrial chemicals	130
XX13 Fertilizers and agricultural chemicals		70
3512 except 351216	Nitrogen, phosphatic, and potassic fertilizers	50
351216	Herbicides, insecticides, fungicides, disinfectants, plant growth regulators	20
XX14 Finished chemicals		440
3513	Plastics: polyethylene, polypropylene, polystyrene, polyvinyl chloride, and others	130
	Synthetic fibers	30
	Synthetic rubber	20
352	Other chemical products	
3521	Paints	30
3522	Pharmaceuticals	130
3523	Cleaning products (soaps, etc.)	35
3529	Photographic chemicals	10
3560 and parts of others	Products not elsewhere classified	55
Total		900

Note: Estimates in the last column are extremely rough because figures reported in different sources, and often in different places within the same source, vary considerably.

Source: Institute for Economic Analysis estimates based on UNIDO, *Industry and Development Global Report*, 1987, 1988, 1989, 1990.

economies and even in the developed economies, where it had been thought that the process was nearly completed. The pharmaceuticals are another major category; they involve significant research and development expenditures that are generally recovered through patenting. These products can cost up to several hundred thousand dollars a ton. A wide assortment of other products of less economic importance, from cleaning agents to dyes and explosives, are also included in this sector. Direct consumer purchases of finished chemicals increase with income: this is true in particular for pharmaceuticals, personal-care products, and synthetic cleaning products.

A more refined analysis would require further disaggregation of sectors XX12 and XX14, into the bulk organics, bulk inorganics, plastics, and pharmaceuticals. Then outputs could be measured in tons.

Regional Distribution of Production and Use of Chemicals

Chemicals are still largely produced and used in the rich, developed countries, which accounted for about 70 percent of world production, over 80 percent of world exports, and 70 percent of use in the late 1980s. A rough breakdown of sales in 1987 is shown in Table 11.2.

Starting from a small base, however, both production and demand have been growing rapidly in the developing countries and will continue to do so as these countries strive to reduce their dependence on imports, both autonomously and through joint ventures. The developing countries, especially those countries that are rich in raw materials or have large domestic markets, have moved first into production of bulk chemicals. Countries with large domestic markets are able to exploit economies of scale in these capital-intensive industries where the capacity of the average new production unit is large and growing. Furthermore, because the bulk chemicals have a low price per ton, there is an advantage to locating close to market to minimize transport costs. The newly industrializing Asian countries are an exception. They have neither the raw materials nor the domestic markets, but they have achieved rapid growth in chemical production for export.

Bulk fertilizer production is already relatively decentralized geographically. It will be more difficult, however, for developing countries to manufacture insecticides and other agricultural chemicals, as these products require a developed organic chemicals industry for their active ingredients. It may prove possible, however, to manufacture such products from locally available raw materials.

The developed countries will probably add little new capacity for the production of chemicals in the next decade, but they will intensify research and development and concentrate on specialty niches. Principal objectives will be to increase flexibility in the choice of feedstock, improve energy efficiency, and install computer control systems.

Production Technology

The major inputs for the production of chemicals are the feedstock (hydrocarbons for the petrochemicals, chlorine, phosphate rock, etc.), a source of energy, and capital goods. While the chemical sectors are rightly known to be very energy-intensive, this is mainly true for the production of the bulk or commodity chemicals such as ethylene and benzene (included in sector XX12) and polyethylene

Table 11.2. Geographic distribution of the sales of chemicals in 1987 (billions of dollars)

Region	Sales	Percentage of total
Western Europe	$300	33
North America	240	26
Japan	120	13
Soviet Union, Eastern Europe, and China	100	11
Africa and India	60	7
Latin America	50	5
Newly industrializing Asia and Oceania	50	5
World	920	100

Source: Institute for Economic Analysis based on UNIDO, 1990, p. 173.

(in sector XX14). Furthermore, production has historically relied on the premium fuels, oil and gas. The six most energy-intensive processes, which are common to many chemical products, are electrolysis, fuel-heated reaction, distillation, refrigeration, evaporation, and machine drive (OTA, 1983, p. 119, based on work by R. U. Ayres).

Reducing energy intensity has been an industry objective since the early 1970s in the developed economies and has been achieved largely in the absence of major process changes. In the United States, for example, energy use in the chemical industry per unit of product fell by about 24 percent between 1972 and 1981, and it was estimated (in 1983) that it would fall another 10–20 percent between 1980 and 1990 (OTA, 1983). The principal avenues have been computer control, with feedback optimization, of steam generation and distribution; recovery of energy, such as heat from exothermic reactions (using heat recuperators and exchangers); and improved physical separation in distillation columns (which economizes feedstock as well as fuel). Improvements are also attributable to more timely maintenance and repair, and to the more precise matching of the capabilities of different pieces of equipment.

Generally, energy savings have been achieved by incurring additional capital costs, but the payback periods to date have been extremely short in many instances, as the easiest, most cost-effective measures were adopted earliest. Considerable further energy savings can be anticipated but at greater capital costs.

Another aspect of changes in production is the shift in the mixes of fuels and feedstocks. In the United States, an important producer, there has been a shift from oil and gas as fuels to electricity and coal. With regard to feedstock, there is likely to be increasing use of those of biological origin, and of various categories of recovered wastes, in response to both economic and environmental pressures.

General cost reductions, particularly energy savings, will also be achieved by further integration of the production processes. The cogeneration of heat and electricity, for example, will be increasingly important. Many intermediate products, now produced by the chemical sectors, will instead be produced in petroleum refineries, especially in the oil-rich, developing countries. This is part of a more general shift in product mix: the developed countries will continue to move away from the energy-intensive bulk items and will increasingly specialize in research-intensive specialty products.

There will be heightened concern with avoiding environmental problems and more recycling of chemical products, including plastics. New products and processes will be developed using biological technologies in the industrial countries and also in some of the larger developing countries.

Use of Chemicals

The industrial chemicals (XX12) are used throughout the economy but mainly by the two other chemical sectors—(fertilizers and agricultural chemicals,

XX13, and finished chemical products, XX14)—and by food processing, paper, and electronic and communications equipment.

Fertilizers and agricultural chemicals are used by the four agricultural sectors (SE2–4 and XX1), and natural fertilizers are produced by the livestock sector (SE1). Modernization has invariably been accompanied by increased use not only of these products, improving yields, but also of plastic sheeting and piping, which are included in finished chemicals. These changes are accompanied by increased use of water and capital goods and by less intensive use of labor and/or land per unit of output. Over the next several decades, adoption of these practices is anticipated in all developing regions.

Finished chemical products include materials that substitute for cloth, paper, glass, metal, wood, and rubber in the production of apparel and items like carpets; containers and packaging for food and a wide variety of other products; production of appliances and furnishings; bodies, components, and accessories for automobiles and other transportation equipment; and inputs for the construction industry. Plastics and synthetic fibers will continue to substitute for other materials in packaging, clothing, housewares, construction, and autos.

Major chemical-using sectors are food processing (XX3), furniture and pixtures (XX8), paper (XX9), motor vehicles (XX17), and construction (IN2). In all of these, finished chemicals (plastics, synthetic fibers, etc.) will increasingly substitute for metals (SE5–10), textiles (XX6), wood and cork (XX7), paper (XX9), rubber (XX11), cement (XX15), and glass (XX16).

Prospects for the Future

Production and international trade of chemicals grew rapidly in the 1970s and 1980s, and there is some concern about overcapacity in the 1990s. Nonetheless, it is expected that future growth in demand will average over 3 percent a year in the developed countries and 6 percent in the developing countries, mainly East Asia and Latin America, and in Eastern Europe at least over the next decade. The developing countries will progress from the production of individual products to more integrated chemical industries.

Specific subsectors can be expected to grow rapidly. Developing country demand for bulk petrochemicals will be significant and will increasingly be satisfied by production in the developing countries.

Demand for fertilizers and agricultural chemicals may grow extremely quickly in Latin America and especially in sub-Saharan Africa, which is starting from a very low level of use.

Among finished chemical products, demand for plastics and synthetic fibers is likely to grow at an annual rate of 9 percent in developing countries in the next decade. Production of bulk plastics will shift decisively to oil-rich, developing countries, which until now have relied mainly on cheap gas for feedstock compared to the use of expensive oil in the developed countries. While over half of the world output of fibers is now synthetic, natural fibers still predominate in the developing countries. Repercussions will be felt in agriculture as synthetic fibers displace cotton and wool in the production of textiles and apparel even in developing countries.

Developing countries may be able to begin production of paints and synthetic cleaning products; the latter will displace the use of natural soaps. The use of synthetic powders is expected to grow at about 10 percent a year in China and India, where changing demographics and urbanization are accompanied by the use of washing machines. For the longer term, renewable fats and oils of tropical origin may be more suitable than petrochemical feedstocks for fatty alcohols used in detergents and cosmetics. In the developed countries, environmentally safer additives will come into use: for example, citrate rather than phosphate builders and hydrogen peroxide rather than chlorine.

The pharmaceutical industry will also continue to grow quickly, especially in developing countries. The high-technology end will remain in the developed countries, while a basic industry, producing a limited range of low-cost drugs, is established in the developing countries. India and several of the newly industrializing Latin American countries already produce active ingredients. In the future, the use of natural feedstock of plant origin can be expected to increase, especially in these countries. As their research capability is established, the emphasis will be on tropical diseases like hepatitis and malaria. The use of health and personal-care products will increase in developing countries as income rises.

Assorted intermediate plastic products, like molds and dies, are already being produced in many developing countries in Asia and Africa. High-performance engineering plastics, however, which are modified by alloying and blending with different polymers, are produced and used essentially in North America, Western Europe, and Japan. Their production and use in developing countries will proceed very slowly.

Updating Parameters

When it comes to evaluating existing World Model parameters for possible revision (or to projecting parameters for the future), the most accessible of the three chemical sectors is fertilizers and agricultural chemicals (XX13) since its output is relatively homogeneous (compared to the other two chemical sectors) and is measured in physical units (metric tons) both in the World Model and in most data sources. For 1980 and 1990, new import coefficients and export shares were calculated on the basis of data obtained from the UN COMTRADE data base and the Food and Agriculture Organization. Fertilizer and agricultural chemical inputs to the agricultural sectors were also revised for these years by scaling the original coefficients, so that total use of fertilizer and agricultural chemicals in each region matched the corresponding control totals. These parameters were simply repeated for the future, although it would clearly be desirable to make detailed alternative assumptions about future changes in diet, crop mix, and agricultural technologies that would affect fertilizer use directly and indirectly.

The major change in the production of fertilizers and agricultural chemicals is likely to be conservation of energy inputs. This subject is covered in the case study on industrial energy conservation reported in Chapter 6. Based on that work, we have assumed that direct energy inputs to this sector will fall by 30 percent per ton of output between 1990 and 2020.

As for the two other chemical sectors, the numbers reported in Tables 11.1 and 11.2 were compared with World Model computations for 1990 and earlier years. While total world production of chemicals matched relatively well, the clearest discrepancy with the admittedly crude control totals was that the World Model had underestimated the growth of finished chemicals (XX14) while over-estimating that of the bulk commodities included in industrial chemicals (XX12). Based on an examination of input-output tables for several countries, we made rough estimates of the rates of change in the use of finished chemicals by the major using sectors in the rich, developed economies and assumed that these practices were adopted with a ten-year lag in other regions. The figures are shown in Table 11.3.

Table 11.3. Changes in inputs of finished chemicals to other sectors in 1980 and 1990 (average annual rate of change since preceding decade[a]) (percentages)

XX 8	Furniture and fixtures	2
XX12	Industrial chemicals	−2
XX17	Motor vehicles	1
XX19	Aircraft	1
XX26	Construction	1

a. These rates are applied to input coefficients for 1980 and subsequent years for the rich, developed regions. Resulting coefficients are used with a ten-year lag for other regions.

Source: Institute for Economic Analysis.

12

Household Energy Conservation

Future energy use by households will depend on the level and specific mix of energy services that are utilized and on the energy required to deliver those services in the future. For most developed regions, where the population is growing very slowly and a relatively high standard of living has already been achieved, we assume relatively little change in per capita energy services; the change in energy requirements will reflect primarily the changing energy needed to deliver these services. In developing regions, by contrast, average per capita energy services will increase substantially, although these increases will be to some extent offset by expected gains in energy efficiency. New technologies in developed regions, and factors affecting energy use in developing regions, are discussed below and are the basis for new projections of fossil fuel and electricity input coefficients to consumption. Because the household consumption vector includes petroleum used for private transportation, this chapter draws on work reported in Chapter 13 to project future oil input coefficients.

Energy Use in Developed Regions

A number of analysts have identified residential and commercial energy use as the most attractive target for energy conservation in the developed countries: the volume is large (accounting for 25–33 percent of total energy use), the conservation methods depend on proven technologies, little or no sacrifice of convenience is allegedly involved, and the changes are said to be cost effective for the user. Most of these studies have examined direct energy savings at the point of use only and have estimated the potential for conservation to be at least 20–50 percent (EPA, 1990, pp. VII–91; Hirst and Hannon, 1979).

Some observers question whether it is possible to improve energy efficiency costlessly, as a number of energy specialists have claimed. The counterargument is that if these energy saving technologies were cost effective, they would already be implemented. OTA (1991) has shown that both the real cost and the energy efficiency of major appliances have been falling over the last thirty years. The following reasons have been given for the slow rate of implementation of some of these improvements (Geller, 1989, p. 742):

159

160 *Case Studies*

- Lack of information or awareness among consumers
- Uncertainty about savings and payback
- Lack of capital and resistance to buying equipment with a greater first cost
- Rapid payback and high rate-of-return requirements of building owners, occupants, and businesses
- Separation of responsibilities for making capital investments and paying operating costs.

It is safe to assume that electric utilities will play an increasingly important role in the future in promoting the use of energy-saving technologies described below as an alternative to expanding capacity. Initial experiments in utility-initiated conservation incentive programs in the United States have been quite successful. In addition, regulatory agencies are expected to update energy efficiency standards for construction and appliances and expand their scope to include lighting.

The production of energy use associated with specific household activities is similar in all rich, developed economies (EPA, 1990; Schipper, Ketoff, and Kahane, 1985). The distribution is shown for the United States in Table 12.1.

Energy requirements for space conditioning (heating, cooling, and ventilation), the single largest residential use of energy, depend on climate, habits of the occupants, building characteristics, and attributes of the heating and cooling equipment. Characteristics of new buildings are directly reflected in the input structures of the residential and commercial construction sectors. The most significant changes affect the following inputs:

- Materials for shell construction, more extensive use of thermal insulation, and structural components such as windows
- Automated systems to monitor and control space conditioning
- Greater reliance on customized designs to exploit the potential for passive solar energy or for cooling provided by landscaping.

Substantial improvements are possible in the energy efficiency of commonly used gas and oil furnaces (Geller, 1988). Gas and oil furnaces that are 95 percent efficient, rather than the average of 75 percent, are already being marketed in the United States and Europe. Their use would lead to a reduction of roughly 25 percent in energy for space heating (Geller, 1988). It can also be

Table 12.1. Uses of residential and commercial energy in the United States in 1985

	Exajoules	Percentage of total
Space heating	10.0	35.1
Air conditioning and ventilation	5.3	18.6
Lighting	4.2	14.7
Hot water heating	3.2	11.2
Refrigeration	2.1	7.4
Other appliances	3.7	13.0
Total	28.5	100.0

Source: EPA, 1990.

cost effective to invest in alternative energy systems like heat pumps, air-to-air heat exchangers, and passive solar systems with thermal storage.

The average new house in the United States requires about 40 percent less energy to maintain a given internal temperature than the average existing house because of more weathertight design and materials (Goldemberg, Johansson, Reddy, and Williams, 1987). Unfortunately, however, the housing stock turns over slowly in developed regions, where population growth is slow. The existing housing stock will dominate the residential stock for the time frame of this study. Conservation will depend on retrofitting improvements into the existing stock. Storm windows and doors, added insulation, clock thermostats, and heating system improvements can reduce energy requirements for space conditioning of older structures by 20–30 percent according to Goldman (1984). These savings are achieved at a cost of about $1,000 to $1,300 (in 1980 prices). It has been estimated that this entire package of energy conservation measures can reduce the space conditioning energy requirements of a new building by 70 percent to 90 percent (Bevington and Rosenfeld, 1990; Claridge and Mowris, 1985; Hirst, Clinton, Geller, and Kroner, 1986; Rosenfeld, 1985; Rosenfeld and Hafemeister, 1985; Schipper, Meyers, and Kelly, 1985).

Lighting is said to offer some of the most cost-effective opportunities for conservation (Berman, 1985; McGowan, 1990; Rosenfeld and Hafemeister, 1985). Many technological alternatives take the form of replacement lamps or parts that can be used with little or no modification to existing installations. Some of the most promising products and practices are identified in Table 12.2. Energy-saving incandescent and fluorescent lights still represent half of the lamps sold in the United States, and most of those are purchased by the commercial sector. While many of the lighting alternatives are currently more suitable for commercial than for household application, the compact fluorescent lamps and bulbs are appropriate for household use.

Every type of major household appliance is already more energy efficient than earlier models in all developed economies (Geller, 1985, 1988; Jannsen and Milkop, 1987; Kanoh, 1987), and in the 1990s the most energy-intensive appliances are expected to use considerably less energy than those produced in the 1980s (see Table 12.3). These energy savings are largely attributable to increased use of insulation and electronic controls in their manufacture. The two most important items are refrigerators and water heaters.

The assumptions about future energy conservation through the introduction of specific technologies in developed regions are listed in column 1 of Table 12.4. All of these assumptions are conservative in that they are based on technologies that are currently available; no attempt is made to anticipate new sources of energy savings that will probably be developed in the coming decades. All furnaces in the existing stock of dwellings are expected to be replaced by more efficient ones by 2020, reducing energy requirements for heating by 25 percent from 1990 levels. The existing housing stock is also assumed to be weatherized sufficiently to reduce energy requirements for space heating by an additional 25 percent. New dwellings are assumed to be constructed with an energy efficiency improvement equal to the lower bound of what is currently

Table 12.2. Energy-saving lighting technologies

Incandescent lighting

Halogen, with a filament tube containing high-pressure halogen gas inside the bulb (lamp within a lamp), improves efficiency of general service lamps by 10 percent.

Coating the filament tube with infrared-reflecting film (irf) to keep heat concentrated near the filament; requires less energy to keep the filament hot. For technical reasons, irf is not suitable for low-wattage applications but is good for flood and area lighting, as well as stage and studio lighting.

Compact fluorescent lamps

Designed to screw into existing incandescent fixtures, they are 60–70 percent more energy efficient than incandescent lamps.

High-intensity discharge lamps

These are primarily for commercial use in warehouses, factories, and street lighting, not household use; they achieve 45–60 percent savings over currently used mercury vapor or fluorescent lighting.

Electronic ballasts

These serve as a replacement for the electromechanical ballast currently used in fluorescent lights, reducing power consumption by 20–35 percent.

Daylighting

This is a design approach for new structures that takes advantage of natural light.

Others

Electronic lighting controls, occupancy sensors, time clocks; task lighting for specific areas, use of reflectors to direct light to area where it is most needed.

Source: Institute for Economic Analysis based on EPA, 1990; McGowan, 1990.

possible, 50 percent. Together, the energy requirements for space heating will be reduced by 50 percent from 1990 levels. While the assumptions about retrofitting the existing stock may overestimate energy conservation, the assumption about new stock is an underestimate (the range given in the literature is a 50–90 percent reduction in energy requirements).

Major appliances have roughly a twenty-year life span, so that most of the stock underlying the appliance energy requirements reported in Table 12.3 will

Table 12.3. Energy requirements for advanced-technology appliances in the United States (kWh/year)

Appliance	Stock in 1986[a]	Best in 1986[b]	Advanced technology for mid-1990s[c]
Refrigerator	1,450	750	300–500
Freezer	1,050	430	200–300
Central air conditioning	3,500	1,800	1,200–1,500
Room air conditioning	900	500	300–400
Electric water heating	4,000	1,600	100–1500
Gas water heating	270	200	100–150
Other appliances			
Electric stove	800	700	400–500
Gas stove	70	40	25–30
Electric dryer	1,000	800	250–500

a. Average energy consumption per unit for the stock of appliances in 1986.

b. Energy consumption for the best model mass produced in 1986.

c. Energy consumption possible for new models in 1990s.

Source: Geller, 1988.

Table 12.4. Reduction in residential energy requirements in developed regions under the OCF scenario between 1990 and 2020 (percentages)

Activity	Reduction of energy requirements relative to 1990[a]	Distribution of residential use of energy			
		Electricity (XX25)	Oil (SE11)	Gas (SE12)	Coal (SE13)
Space heating	50	n.a.	50.0	100.0	100.0
Air conditioning	37	28.7	n.a.	n.a.	n.a.
Refrigeration	73	11.4	n.a.	n.a.	n.a.
Hot water heating	53	17.3	n.a.	n.a.	n.a.
Other appliances	55	20.0	n.a.	n.a.	n.a.
Lighting	40	22.7	n.a.	n.a.	n.a.
Total	48.2	51.0	50.0	50.0	

a. Including a 52 percent reduction in energy requirements for transportation, which accounts for the remaining 50 percent of household oil use. (See Chapter 13 for a discussion of transportation.)

Notes: 1. Reduction of energy requirement relative to 1990 assumes that by 2020 100 percent of households are using the best technology available for the mid-1990s, but that only 50 percent of the lighting fixtures will use such technology (compact fluorescent with electronic ballasts, or the equivalent in terms of energy efficiency).

2. Retrofit of existing dwellings with new furnaces and weatherizing reduce heating energy requirements by 50 percent, and new construction reduces energy requirements for heating by 50 percent.

3. The distribution of residential energy use was based on Table 12.1, assuming that space heating is provided by fossil fuels and the remaining energy services are provided by electricity. All gas and coal are used for sspace heating, while half of oil is used for transportation.

Sources: Institute for Economic Analysis estimates based on Tables 12.1, 12.2, and 12.3.

be replaced by 2010 and all of the stock can be assumed to be replaced by 2020. While households cannot be expected to purchase the most energy-efficient model available in a given year (in 1986, the energy efficiency of the typical model bought was 50–80 percent of the best model available), if current trends continue, the *average* model purchased in 2020 can be expected to be at least as efficient as the *most efficient* model available twenty-five years earlier, in the mid-1990s.

The increased use of fluorescent lights by households is difficult to project. They are cheaper than incandescent bulbs because they have a longer lifetime as well as saving energy, but the higher initial cost (and perhaps limited information and availability) seems to have deterred consumers. Compact fluorescents, which can be used with many, but not yet all, incandescent fixtures, have only recently become widely available. It is likely that, in the future, governments will mandate efficiency standards for lighting similar to those enacted for appliances and new construction, and that these standards will result in increased use. As an energy conservation measure, electric utilities have been offering residential consumers compact fluorescent lighting on concessional terms in order to acquaint them with a new technology they might not otherwise be inclined to try (Williams, 1989). A conservative estimate of a 50 percent share of lighting fixtures using these fluorescent technologies, or other similarly energy-efficient lighting technologies, is assumed for 2020.

The share of residential energy use associated with each of the activities or energy services in Table 12.4 is given in columns 2–5 of Table 12.4 for each source of energy: electricity, oil, gas, and coal. For quantifying the OCF scenario it was assumed that 100 percent of use of gas and coal and 50 percent of oil are for space heating, the primary residential use of these fuels except in Oceania, where only 10 percent of oil is for space heating. (The amounts of oil and gas used for hot-water heaters and other appliances are negligible.) Improvements in energy efficiency affecting these energy services are expected to be similar in magnitude to improvements for space heating. The other 50 percent of household oil use was assumed to be used for personal transportation.

The reduction in each energy input coefficient is calculated as the reduction in energy requirements for each activity weighted by the proportion of energy used for this activity. These reductions are given in the last row of Table 12.4. (The reduction in household use of oil also takes into account the assumptions about changes in the fuel efficiency of motor vehicles, which are discussed in Chapter 13.) Energy input coefficients for 2020 are calculated by multiplying the 1990 coefficients by 1 minus the percentage energy reductions in the last row of Table 12.4. These coefficients are then adjusted to reflect the levels of per capita energy services projected for the future.

In the OCF scenario, per capita energy services are projected to increase 10 percent in high-income North America, high-income Western Europe, Japan, and Oceania, reflecting some increased use of motor vehicles, increased average house size, appliance size, space heating, and air conditioning. In medium-income Western Europe and southern Africa, energy services per capita are expected to double, since these regions start out from a much lower level of energy use (including motor vehicle density) than other developed regions.

New construction and retrofit of the residential housing stock are expected to increase other inputs but not substantially. Household investment requirements increase 0.25 percent annually after 1990 under the OCF scenario.

Energy Use in Eastern Europe and the Former Soviet Union

Very little detailed information is available about these regions, and their future is highly uncertain. Household use of energy services is expected to increase in the former Soviet Union and Eastern Europe. While there are substantial opportunities for greater energy efficiency, the increased demand for lighting, electric appliance, heating, and hot water energy services are expected to result in a net increase in per capita energy use. Households in Eastern Europe will raise their per capita use of total fossil fuels by 50 percent between 1990 and 2020, increasingly substituting gas and oil for coal, and will triple use of electricity (Jaczewski, 1991). The same increases in per capita use of fossil fuels are projected for the former Soviet Union but electricity use per capita is expected to increase only 2.5 times over the period (Volfberg, 1991).

Energy Use in Developing Regions

Much less information is available about household energy use in developing regions, where per capita consumption of commercial energy services is still far below that of developed regions. Cooking is the single most important use, accounting for 50 percent of residential energy, followed by lighting, space conditioning, and energy use for other appliances. Most households switch from traditional to commercial fuels for cooking as soon as these fuels are available and affordable. As income increases, fuel use usually proceeds from wood or charcoal to kerosene to gas or electricity; the latter options offer many benefits, including reduced time and labor to obtain fuel, reduced indoor air pollution, cleaner pots, and reduced fuel required for cooking. The transition to modern fuels requires not only the availability of these fuels but also a substantial initial capital investment in items like gas bottles, new stoves, and better pots.

Energy use for lighting follows a similar progression as income increases, from candles and kerosene to electricity. In contrast to the developed regions, lighting currently accounts for a relatively small amount of total fuel and electricity used in residences in developing regions. The high initial capital costs prevent the rural and urban poor from obtaining more efficient lamps or electric lights.

After lighting installations, the typical progression of major appliance acquisition is fans, refrigerators, and televisions. Ownership of electric fans increases substantially in urban areas of developing regions as traditional building materials and designs are abandoned for modern ones and the supply of electricity becomes more reliable. Household use of air conditioners is still uncommon but will increase in the future.

Heating is a relatively insignificant use of energy in developing regions except for China. In China buildings are so poorly insulated that the interior temperature is near the freezing point in winter despite the use of substantial amounts of fuel for heating (ota, 1990). Better insulation and more efficient stoves will result in more comfortable interior temperatures in the future, but the use of fuel is unlikely to fall.

The major pressures for higher per capita energy use result from an increase in urban population, the substitution of commercial for biomass fuels in both rural and urban areas, and an improvement in the standard of living. Differences in per capita energy use are closely associated with the share of the population in urban areas. There are striking similarities in per capita energy use in villages throughout the developing world in terms of the nature of the energy services provided (mainly for cooking and subsistence agriculture) the sources of fuel, and the quantity used. Energy use by urban dwellers in developing regions, however, is closer to that of the developed regions in terms of quantity (within an order of magnitude), source (more commercial fuels, less biomass), and services provided (lighting and appliances, industrial goods, personal transport). These differences between rural and urban energy use can be attributed to the higher average incomes of urban dwellers, as well as to better energy distribution systems in urban areas (Leach, 1987). According to extensive household energy surveys in South Asia, the average urban inhabitant used four to six times more commercial energy than the average rural dweller (Leach, 1987).

Substitution of commercial fuels for biomass increases with income even in rural areas. Total energy use subsequently rises, despite the greater efficiency of modern fuels, because of increased demand for energy services for lighting, appliances, and autos. This substitution is projected to accelerate as incomes rise, as energy distribution networks expand, and, in some cases, as biomass becomes more scarce (Romain-Frisch, 1989). Improved material standards of living in the developing regions between 1990 and 2020 can be expected to result in expanded ownership of consumer appliances and motor vehicles that are generally not very efficient. Typically, the technology is a generation or more behind current technology in developed regions. While improvements are expected, they will be small and slow in the absence of a systematic program for large-scale technology transfer.

Detailed information on future use of energy by households in developing regions is difficult to obtain. The case study on transportation (Chapter 13) was only partially successful in projecting future parameters for developing regions. The projections about household energy use under the OCF scenario are based roughly on country studies carried out at the Lawrence Berkeley Laboratories under the direction of J. Sathaye and N. Goldman (1991) and are generally consistent with the work reported in Chapter 13. The case studies for India and China were used to generalize for the regions low-income Asia and centrally planned Asia and are discussed below.

Currently, urban households in China use about six times as much commercial fuel and four times as much electricty as rural households, even though China has a much higher proportion of electrified villages than most developing countries (Smil, 1988; World Bank, 1985). China plans to increase the energy services available to households, notably for space heating, hot water, and appliances such as refrigerators. The decline in the average number of persons per household will also tend to increase per capita energy use.

Residential electricity use in China is projected to increase nearly eightfold per capita between 1985 and 2025 for rural and urban households combined; the use of coal by urban households will decline and will be replaced by gas, but coal use in rural areas will increase dramatically (more than threefold) as it replaces nearly two-thirds of the biomass fuels. Oil use per household is projected to increase two and a half times. Residential use of natural gas will expand significantly by 2020 from near zero per capita use in 1990.

A similar study in the series by Sathaye and Goldman projected increases in per capita energy use for India and was used for low-income Asia: coal use per capita only doubles, but oil use increases nearly fivefold and household use of natural gas increases (from a very low initial base) thirtyfold. Use of electricity increases eightfold. The use of energy for personal transport is expected to increase fairly slowly in China, but the number of vehicles per capita and the use of oil for personal transport are projected to grow more rapidly in other developing regions.

Case studies were conducted by Sathaye and Goldman for Indonesia and Korea but were difficult to generalize from, since these countries account for only half of the energy use in the region (newly industrializing Asia) and the projections for household energy use in each of these two countries are strikingly different. It was not possible to generalize to a World Model region from the case studies of other countries. However, the trends in these case studies were used as guidelines to evaluate and revise, if necessary, the coefficients in the original World Data Base. If the original coefficients provided increases in per capita energy use considered within the range of expected increases (two to four times for fossil fuels, four to six times for electricity), they were kept; otherwise, they were adjusted upward. The exception to this trend is sub-Saharan Africa, where per capita energy use will increase relatively little (about 15 percent between 1990 and 2020) because per capita GDP is almost constant under the OCF scenario.

13

Motor Vehicles

A country needs freight transport to develop its industrial base, and passenger transportation provides the mobility necessary for social development. Without good transportation facilities, it is, for example, impossible to benefit from economies of scale in production or to provide medical services and education to rural communities. Generally, road transport is the most important mode of transportation for both freight and passengers, except in China and India, where railroads are more important. However, even in these countries, there is an increasing reliance on road transport (OTA, 1991, p. 79).

While there are significant variations among countries, road transport accounts on average for more than 30 percent of a country's use of petroleum and is an important source of nitrogen dioxide and carbon dioxide emissions. In OECD countries, 47 percent of nitrogen oxide emissions in 1980 were attributed to motor vehicles (Walsh, 1990, p. 218), and motor vehicles produced 14 percent of world carbon dioxide emissions originating from fossil fuels in 1990. In the United States, where automobile density is the highest in the world, this figure was 24 percent (Bleviss and Walzer, 1990, p.55).

Representation of Road Transportation in the World Model

The objective of this case study is to develop a framework to represent scenarios about the future use of road transport and their implications for energy and the environment in the World Model. The study involves several sectors: transportation equipment (XX17), which manufactures motor vehicles; transportation services (XX28), which purchases motor vehicles to provide commercial transportation; and households (MA2), which purchase motor vehicles for private transportation. We first project the future stock of motor vehicles and the annual production levels of the motor vehicles sector needed to achieve or maintain this stock. The latter is based on a relationship derived for historical years between the stock of motor vehicles and annual sales.

We then derive the parameters governing fuel use for transportation: the use of motor vehicles (determined by the size of a region's motor vehicle fleet and the average number of miles driven per vehicle) and the technical features of the average motor vehicle (the average fuel efficiency). We examine the like-

168

ly future technology of motor vehicles, notably shifts in the material inputs that increase fuel efficiency.

Quantifying these parameters about future fuel use in the system of classifications and units of measurement of the World Data Base requires additional information about fuel use, that is discussed at the end of the chapter. The final step, relating emissions to energy use, is achieved automatically because of the way in which the emission coefficients are applied (see Chapter 4).

Most of the other case studies in this volume deal with the changing energy requirements associated with the production of a commodity or service, like tons of steel or kilowatt-hours of electricity, and with the changing energy requirements associated with its use per unit of output of the principal sectors using that commodity or service. These changes in energy use are generally associated with the requirements of specific technologies. So, for example, the change in the amount of energy (as well as iron, scrap steel, and other inputs) required to produce a ton of steel will be determined within a relatively narrow range if we assume a switch to electric arc technology from the basic oxygen furnace.

The case of transportation is much more difficult both for conceptual reasons and because of the usual practical problems associated with balancing a level of detail adequate for the analysis with limited data. The input structure for producing transportation equipment is largely determined by technological choices, like other sectors. But representing the use of this equipment, and especially the energy associated with its use, is unusually problematic. An added complication is that transportation equipment is used both by households and by industry, and their patterns of use, and therefore of energy use, are very different.

Despite these difficulties, the conceptual framework presented here proved useful for developing the necessary parameters for transportation and can provide the basis for future work by ourselves and other researchers. Most of the parameters were quantified in at least a preliminary way and have been incorporated in the data base.

Regional Distribution of Production, Fleets, and Sales of Motor Vehicles

The use of road transport in each region depends on the number of motor vehicles and the number of miles they are driven. Annual deliveries of motor vehicles are the sum of deliveries to business establishments as investment goods (parts are purchased on current account) and to households and government. This total is defined as sales in most data sources.

However, for capital items like motor vehicles, use depends on the stock, not just on the flow on current account. In the World Model, stock is defined to include only the commercial motor vehicle fleet, not household and government stock, because, as in other economic models and in the National Accounts, deliveries to households and government are treated as flows on current account. Consequently, we need to construct a region-specific parameter to relate the stock of motor vehicles to annual motor vehicle sales: the fleet-to-sales ratio. Future stocks of motor vehicles are projected, based on anticipated motor vehicle densities and population growth, and then the stock-flow parameter is used to project future annual sales.

Production of Motor Vehicles

The principal subsectors of the motor vehicle sector are identified in Table 13.1, which also shows the major material inputs and the main sectors purchasing motor vehicles. In most World Model regions, households and investment account for more than 60 percent of all motor vehicle purchases. The use of motor vehicles by other sectors is represented by their purchases of transportation services.

The motor vehicle sector in the World Model is defined to include passenger cars, trucks and buses, motorcycles, and engines for motor vehicles. Although in several developing countries the motorcycle is an important mode of transport, only passenger cars, trucks, and buses are addressed in this case study.

There are several sources of statistics on motor vehicle production. Production in the developed world is well documented, although figures for the rest of the world are fragmentary. Most published sources calculate the world total without estimating production for the missing countries. Stark (1981) estimates production in 1979 in the unlisted countries at less than 0.2 percent (fewer than 75,000 units) of production in the listed countries (42,362,219 units). This estimate suggests that nonreporting countries have little if any production, and our estimates for motor vehicle production in 1980 and 1988 rely on the production of reporting countries. These figures are shown in Table 13.2 for World Model regional groupings. The figures in the source documents represent number of vehicles; this unit is converted to 1970 U.S. dollars using a unit price of $3,359. This price was calculated as the ratio of the World Model world motor vehicle output in 1970 (in 1970 U.S. dollars) to the source document world production

Table 13.1. Principal subsectors, material inputs, and purchasing sectors for motor vehicles (XX17)

Subsectors		Material inputs		Purchasing sectors	
Engines for motor vehicles	SE5	Copper	IN1	Equipment investment	
Passenger car production and assembly	SE6	Bauxite	MA2	Household expenditure	
Motor coaches, buses, and trucks	SE7	Nickel	MA5	Government expenditure	
Motorcycles	SE8	Zinc	XX28	Transportation services	
	SE10	Iron			
	XX5	Primary metal processing			
	XX11	Rubber			
	XX14	Plastic			
	XX20	Metal products			
	XX21	Machinery			
	XX22	Electric machinery			

Table 13.2. Motor vehicle production for World Model regional groupings in 1980 and 1988 (in millions of units and in billions of dollars, 1970 U.S. prices)

	1980		1988	
	Units	$	Units	$
Rich, developed economies	33.3	111.9	41.7	140.1
Newly industrializing economies	2.4	7.9	3.1	10.3
Eastern Europe and former Soviet Union	3.0	10.4	3.0	10.1
Other developing economies	0.4	1.4	0.9	3.1
World	39.2	131.6	48.7	163.6

Note: A 1970 unit price of $3,359 is assumed.

Source: Institute for Economic Analysis based on MVMA, 1981 and 1990, and Yannis, 1990.

in 1970 (in units), assuming that both figures are correct. The implicit price, which includes both cars and more expensive commercial vehicles, compares favorably to the average price paid for a new passenger car in 1970, $3,025 (MVMA, 1975, p. 33).

The distribution and growth rates for motor vehicle production are shown in Table 13.3. Although the rate of growth for other developing economies is the largest, these economies still count for only 2 percent of world production. The share of rich, developed economies in world production continued to increase between 1980 and 1988.

Fleets and Sales of Motor Vehicles

The objective in this section is to develop projections of future fleet size, fleet-to-sales ratios, and sales of motor vehicles under the OCF scenario. Published data about motor vehicle sales by region or country are complete for high-income North America, high-income Western Europe, and Japan; those for medium-income Western Europe, southern Africa, Oceania, and newly industrializing Latin America are almost complete. Information for other regions is fragmentary (see Table 13.4). Because total world sales are approximately equal to total production, unreported sales can be quantified and distributed among the World Model regions; this is shown in Table 13.5.

The future motor vehicle fleet depends on motor vehicle density and on population. Density is often used as an indicator of the extent to which a country's transportation needs are satisfied, and political goals concerning road

Table 13.3. Distribution and growth rates of motor vehicle production regional groupings in 1980 and 1988 (percentages)

	1980	1988
Rich, developed economies	85	85
Newly industrializing economies	6	6
Eastern Europe and former Soviet Union	8	6
Other developing economies	1	2
World	100	100

Source: Table 13.2.

Table 13.4. Sales of motor vehicles for regions and countries in 1980 and 1988 (thousands of units)

	1980	1988
High-income North America	12,523	17,231
Oceania	691	608
High-income Western Europe	10,418	13,008
Japan	5,016	6,721
Medium-income Western Europe (Greece, Portugal, Spain)[a]	880	1,662
Eastern Europe (GDR, Poland 1980)	650	187
Southern Africa	4058	358
Newly industrializing Latin America (Mexico, Argentina, Brazil)	1,720	1,252
Soviet Union	–	–
Major oil producers (Kuwait)	43	–
Newly industrializing Asia (Korea, Taiwan 1988, Malaysia 1980, Hong Kong 1980)	346	1,369
Low-income Latin America	–	–
North Africa and other Middle East (Morocco)	22	12
Low-income Asia (India, Philippines 1980)	169	382
Sub-Saharan Africa	–	–
Centrally planned Asia	–	737
Sum of above	32,908	43,526
World total production	39,179	48,702

a. In regions where data for only a few countries are available, country names are listed. Where data for countries within a region were reported for different years, the year is listed after the country. For example, (India, Philippines 1980) indicates that sales for the Philippines were reported for 1980 only, while India reported figures for 1980 and 1988.
—: not available.

Source: Institute for Economic Analysis based on MVMA, 1990, and Stark, 1989. Data are sales and new registrations.

transportation are generally set in terms of motor vehicle densities. For these reasons, it is a good choice of parameter.

For the future, we anticipate a significant increase in motor vehicle densities in newly industrializing Latin America, newly industrializing Asia, low-income Asia, and centrally planned Asia based on (Sathaye and Goldman, 1991). These increases in motor vehicle densities result in large percentage increases in the motor vehicle fleet because of population growth. Motor vehicle fleet and density for World Model regions in 1980 and 1988 and projections for 2020 are shown in Table 13.6, and Table 13.7 shows the corresponding annual growth rates.

The fleet-to-sales ratios are shown in Table 13.8. A low ratio may indicate a fast-growing fleet or a high rate of replacement of the existing stock. The latter is more likely the case in developed regions like high-income Western Europe, while the former is more probable in some developing countries.

Table 13.5 Sales of motor vehicles for World Model regions in 1980 and 1988 (in thousands of units and millions of dollars, 1970 U.S. prices)

	1980		1988	
	$	Units	$	Units
High-income North America	42,063	12,523	57,878	17,231
Oceania	2,321	691	2,042	608
High-income Western Europe	34,993	10,418	43,693	13,008
Japan	16,847	5,016	22,576	6,721
Medium-income Western Europe	2,954	879	5,582	1,662
Eastern Europe	2,893	861	2,851	849
Southern Africa	1,360	405	1,202	358
Newly industrializing Latin America	6,355	1,892	4,627	1,378
Soviet Union	7,387	2,199	7,212	2,147
Major oil producers	5,603	1,668	4,011	1,194
Newly industrializing Asia	1,277	380	5,058	1,506
Low-income Latin America	2,683	799	1,687	502
North Africa and other Middle East	845	252	520	155
Low-income Asia	2,446	728	1,879	559
Sub-Saharan Africa	552	164	294	88
Centrally planned Asia	1,013	302	2,475	737
World	131,602	39,179	163,589	48,702

Source: For high-income North America, Oceania, high-income Western Europe, Japan, medium-income Western Europe, and southern Africa and for centrally planned Asia in 1988, data are from Table 13.4. For newly industrializing Latin America and newly industrializing Asia, the numbers listed above are 1.1 times the numbers in Table 13.4 to correct for missing data for Chile, Venezuela, Indonesia, Singapore, and Thailand. For Eastern Europe and the Soviet Union, we assumed that sales were equal to production. The remaining sales were distributed among the other regions.

Table 13.6. Motor vehicle fleet and motor vehicle density for World Model regions in 1980 and 1988 and projections for 2020 (millions of units and motor vehicles per 100 people)

	1980		1988/1990[a]		2020	
	Fleet	Density	Fleet	Density	Fleet	Density
High-income North America	169.1	66.3	201.8	72.2	243.2	73.2
Oceania	9.5	40.1	11.3	40.8	22.8	56.9
High-income Western Europe	104.8	35.8	133.9	45.1	148.8	50.2
Japan	37.9	32.4	52.5	42.5	66.4	51.1
Medium-income Western Europe	15.4	12.3	23.0	16.4	53.0	30.0
Eastern Europe	11.0	9.8	16.6	14.3	25.4	20.0
Southern Africa	3.5	10.8	4.3	10.5	10.0	13.7
Newly industrializing Latin America	21.7	9.4	29.0	10.1	91.9	20.0
Former Soviet Union	15.5	5.8	24.7	8.6	54.9	16.0
Major oil producers	6.0	3.5	11.9	4.8	68.4	12.0
Newly industrializing Asia	4.4	1.6	10.8	3.3	70.4	15.5
Low-income Latin America	3.5	3.2	4.6	3.3	12.1	5.1
North Africa and other Middle East	2.5	1.4	3.4	1.5	13.3	3.0
Low-income Asia	3.4	0.3	5.0	0.4	44.8	2.0
Sub-Saharan Africa	2.1	1.1	2.6	1.0	7.2	1.1
Centrally planned Asia	0.9	0.1	4.3	0.4	30.1	2.0
World	411.1		539.8		962.53	

a. Density is understated because fleet figures are for 1988, while the population figures are for 1990.

Source: Figures for the motor vehicle fleet in 1980 and 1988 are from MVMA, 1990. Motor vehicle densities are based on population figures from Chapter 2. Figures for 2020 are Institute for Economic Analysis estimates based in part on a discussion in Meyers, 1988, pp. 30–31, about cars per capita and on Sathaye and Goldman (1991).

Table 13.7. Annual growth of motor vehicle fleet and motor vehicle densities for World Model regions in 1980 through 1988 and projections for 1988–2020 (percentages)

	1980–1988		1988–2020	
	Fleet	Density	Fleet	Density
High-income North America	2.2	1.1	0.6	0.0
Oceania	2.3	0.2	2.2	1.1
High-income Western Europe	3.1	2.9	0.3	0.3
Japan	4.2	3.5	0.7	0.6
Medium-income Western Europe	5.2	3.7	2.6	1.9
Eastern Europe	5.3	4.8	1.3	1.1
Southern Africa	2.6	−0.4	2.7	0.8
Newly industrializing Latin America	3.7	0.9	3.7	2.1
Former Soviet Union	5.8	5.1	2.5	2.0
Major oil producers	9.0	4.0	5.6	2.9
Newly industrializing Asia	12.0	9.5	6.0	5.0
Low-income Latin America	3.5	0.4	3.1	1.4
North Africa and other Middle East	4.2	0.9	4.3	2.2
Low-income Asia	4.9	3.7	7.1	5.2
Sub-Saharan Africa	2.6	−1.2	3.3	0.5
Centrally planned Asia	21.5	18.9	6.2	5.2
World	3.5		1.8	

Source: Table 13.6.

According to Table 13.8, centrally planned Asia, low-income Asia, and low-income Latin America, as well as newly industrializing Asia, had the lowest ratios among developing countries in 1980; the ratio for Japan was equally low. This is noteworthy because most literature focuses on the growth of the motor vehicle fleet in the two newly industrializing regions.

The fleet-to-sales ratios projected for 2020 are based on historical fleet-to-sales ratios, assumptions about future economic developments, and assump-

Table 13.8. Fleet-to-sales ratios for World Model regions in 1980 and 1988 and projections for 2020

	1980	1988	2020
High-income North America	13.5	11.7	12
Oceania	13.7	18.6	15
High-income Western Europe	10.0	10.3	10
Japan	7.5	7.8	9
Medium-income Western Europe	17.5	13.8	15
Eastern Europe	12.8	19.6	15
Southern Africa	8.6	12.0	12
Newly industrializing Latin America	11.5	21.1	20
Former Soviet Union	7.1	11.5	12
Major oil producers	3.6	10.0	10
Newly industrializing Asia	11.4	7.1	9
Low-income Latin America	4.4	9.2	12
North Africa and other Middle East	9.8	22.2	20
Low-income Asia	4.7	9.0	10
Sub-Saharan Africa	12.8	29.6	20
Centrally planned Asia	3.0	5.9	7

Source: Tables 13.5 and 13.6 and Institute for Economic Analysis projections for 2020.

tions about motor vehicle saturation in the regions. Note that an increasing fleet-to-sales ratio does not necessarily mean that fewer motor vehicles are sold, provided that the fleet is growing.

Finally, projected motor vehicle sales in 2020 are shown in Table 13.9 together with the figures for 1980 and 1988. World Model parameters governing the use of motor vehicles in 1980, 1990, and 2020 were scaled so that computed annual deliveries matched these figures. The parameters were interpolated for years between 1990 and 2020.

Factors Governing Fuel Use by the Motor Vehicle Fleet

In most countries, transport is a major user of petroleum, absorbing 67 percent of petroleum products in the United States, 45 percent in France, 39 percent in West Germany, and 37 percent in Japan (Davis, Shonka, Anderson-Batiste, and Hu, 1989, pp. 1–3). Motor vehicles also use other kinds of fuels, like methanol from coal or natural gas and ethanol from biomass. There is also a lot of discussion about electric cars. The share of these alternatives is so small that their use in past years can be neglected. In the future, some of them may become important sources of transportation energy, but they are not included in this case study.

Use of energy for transport is very unequally distributed worldwide (see Table 13.10*) and about two-thirds is used in OECD countries. Road transport is

* The information in this table is not contained in the UN energy balances which would otherwise be the source of choice as it is used for developing the World Model Data Base.

Table 13.9. Sales of motor vehicles for World Model regions in 1980 and 1988 and projections for 2020 (millions of dollars, 1970 U.S. prices)

	1980	1988	2020
High-income North America	42,063	57,878	68,070
Oceania	2,321	2,042	5,106
High-income Western Europe	34,993	43,693	49,982
Japan	16,847	22,576	24,789
Medium-income Western Europe	2,954	5,582	11,857
Eastern Europe	2,893	2,851	5,677
Southern Africa	1,360	1,202	2,788
Newly industrializing Latin America	6,355	4,627	15,418
Former Soviet Union	7,387	7,212	15,384
Major oil producers	5,603	4,011	22,976
Newly industrializing Asia	1,277	5,058	26,267
Low-income Latin America	2,683	1,687	3,393
North Africa and other Middle East	845	520	2,251
Low-income Asia	2,446	1,879	15,048
Sub-Saharan Africa	552	294	1,209
Centrally planned Asia	1,013	2,475	14,410
World	131,602	163,589	284,642

Source: Table 13.5. Institute for Economic Analysis projection for 2020 based on Tables 13.6 and 13.8.

Table 13.10. Geographic distribution of transportation energy (percentages)

United States	35.5
Canada and Western Europe	23.1
Japan and Oceania	7.8
Eastern Europe and former Soviet Union	14.9
South and East Asia	4.4
China	1.6
Africa	3.6
Latin America	7.3
Middle East	1.8
World	100.0

Source: Walsh, 1990, p. 226.

often the main use of transport energy. In member countries of the International Energy Agency, about 99 percent of transportation energy is provided by oil, and road transport accounts for 77 percent of the oil used for transportation (International Energy Agency, 1991c, p. 10). Some illustrative examples are shown in Table 13.11.

In this section, we establish a relationship between the motor vehicle fleet and fuel use based on three key parameters: size and mix of the fleet, fuel efficiency of the average vehicle, and number of miles driven by the average vehicle. The size of the fleet was estimated in the last section. We now develop projections for the other parameters.

The overall logic used to associate fuel use with the motor vehicle fleet and sales is shown in Figure 13.1. The parameters that are actually incorporated in the World Data Base need to be expressed on a per-unit-of-output basis. Their derivation is indicated, for the case of household consumption, in Figure 13.2. A similar figure could be drawn for transportation services; the actual figures for some parameters, namely, sales per unit of output and share of trucks, would be different from those for household consumption. Figure 13.2 also differs from Figure 13.1 in that a fleet-to-sales parameter is used since the World

Table 13.11. Transport and road transport energy use as shares of total and of oil-based energy consumption for the United States and representative developing countries in the 1980s (percentages)

		Share of total energy		Share of oil-based fuels	
		Transport	Road	Transport	Road
U.S.	1985	28	23	72	59
Taiwan	1987	17	15	34	31
Kenya	1980	10	7	62	40
India	1985	12	7	48	39
China	1987	4	1	18	7
Brazil	1987	31	28	61	53

Source: Institute for Economic Analysis based on U.S. Congress, OTA 1991, pp. 82–87.

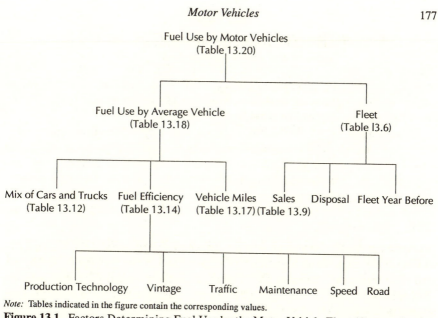

Note: Tables indicated in the figure contain the corresponding values.

Figure 13.1. Factors Determining Fuel Use by the Motor Vehicle Fleet (*Source*: Institute for Economic Analysis)

Model does not directly track all parts of the stock of automobiles. Two entries in Figure 13.2 are identified as World Model parameters. The first is sales of motor vehicles per unit of consumption; the work described earlier in this chapter was used to revise these parameters for future years. The second is energy use for road transport per unit of consumption. Its derivation is described below. We deal with the mix of cars and trucks, technology and fuel efficiency, and vehicle miles traveled, in that order.

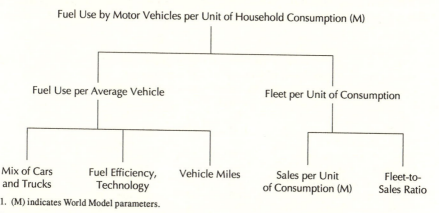

1. (M) indicates World Model parameters.

2. A similar logic governs the derivation of parameters for the Transportation Services sector.

Figure 13.2. Derivation of Parameters Governing Fuel Use by the Household Motor Vehicle Fleet, per Unit of Consumption (*Source:* Institute for Economic Analysis).

Regional Distribution of the Mix of Cars and Trucks

The fuel efficiency of the average vehicle depends on the characteristics of the vehicles in the fleet. The first characteristic to be considered is the mix of trucks* and passenger cars in the motor vehicle fleet; the former generally has lower fuel efficiency than the latter.

Most data on motor vehicle fleets distinguish only between cars and trucks, although there are considerable differences in fuel efficiency among passenger cars, due in part to differences in size. Western European and Japanese cars are in general smaller and more fuel efficient than U.S. cars. In many developing countries, tax systems encourage the purchase of smaller cars (Meyers, 1988, p. 10). Table 13.12 shows the share of trucks in the motor vehicle fleets of the World Model regions.

Data on the the mix of cars and trucks do not distinguish between households and the commercial sector, which typically have different proportions of cars and trucks. The shares of trucks in households and transportation services shown in Table 13.12 are estimated in the following way. For high-income North America we had data on the share of oil used by trucks out of total oil use by households for road transportation. A similar figure was available for transportation services. With those data and data on the annual oil use by the average car and by the average truck (discussed later in this chapter), it was possible to estimate the share of trucks in the household fleet and the share of trucks in the transportation services fleet. For regions other than high-income North

* If not explicitly mentioned, "trucks" includes both trucks and buses.

Table 13.12. Shares of trucks and buses in the motor vehicle fleets of World Model regions in 1980 and 1988 (percentages)

	Total		Households	Transportation services
	1980	1988	1980 and 1988	1980 and 1988
High-income North America	22	24	10	55
Oceania	22	21	10	55
High-income Western Europe	9	10	2	40
Japan	38	41	10	65
Medium-income Western Europe	18	21	5	40
Eastern Europe	20	14	5	55
Southern Africa	30	27	10	65
Newly industrializing Latin America	39	20	15	65
Soviet Union	47	36	15	65
Major oil producers	39	40	15	65
Newly Industrializing Asia	39	42	15	65
Low-income Latin America	40	41	15	65
North Africa and Other Middle East	33	33	10	65
Low-income Asia	42	43	15	65
Sub-Saharan Africa	34	38	15	65
Centrally planned Asia	94	79	25	95

Note: The remaining vehicles are assumed to be cars.

Source: Institute for Economic Analysis projections based on MVMA, 1981, 1990.

America, the data shown in Table 13.12 for the share of trucks in households and transportation services fleets are estimates based on the figures for high-income North America and the share of trucks in the total fleet.

Factors Governing Fuel Efficiency

During the 1970s and early 1980s, the average weight of new American passenger cars decreased substantially, from 4,400 pounds in 1975 to 3,200 pounds in 1982 (National Research Council, 1992, p. 16). This weight reduction was due partly to design changes (Bleviss and Waltzer, 1990, p. 57) and partly to the use of light materials like plastics and aluminum instead of steel. These changes have direct consequences for fuel efficiency because, in general, a lighter vehicle uses less fuel. The fuel efficiency of the average new car increased substantially between 1973 and 1986: from 14 to 28 mpg in 1986 in the United States and from 23 mpg to 32 in Germany, according to Davis, Shonka, Anderson-Batiste, and Hu (1989, pp. 1–11). The potential for further improvement is great.

Although the substitution of light materials continued during the 1980s, the average weight of passenger cars did not fall further. As a result of low gasoline prices in the 1980s, there was growing demand for large, luxury vehicles; the average European and Asian cars became heavier in this period (National Research Council, 1992). In the future, aluminum and plastics are expected to substitute increasingly for steel, not only to reduce weight but also because of their resistance to rust (Stark, 1988, p. 31). In the United States, car manufacturers focus on the use of plastics. In Europe, by contrast, there is more emphasis on aluminum because of concerns about the recyclability of plastics (Bleviss and Waltzer, 1990, p. 57). Other options are to decrease energy loss by friction and waste heat in the vehicle and during braking.

Unfortunately, data on material use in motor vehicles are available only for specific models and specific technologies. Data for the average passenger car, not to mention the average motor vehicle, do not exist. Our estimates for material input changes between 1990 and 2000 are based on technologies known in 1985 that might be adopted even in the absence of major economic or policy changes (Koo, 1985). These are shown in Table 13.13.

The fuel efficiency of a car or truck depends not only on the technical fea-

Table 13.13. Estimated changes in material inputs to the motor vehicle sector between 1980 and 1990 and projected changes for 2020 (percentages)

			1980–1990	1990–2020
High-income North America, Oceania, high-	SE6	Bauxite	+ 0.50	+ 0.56
income Western Europe, Japan, medium-	SE10	Iron	− 0.42	−0.72
income Western Europe, and southern Africa	XX14	Plastic	+ 0.25	+ 0.40
Eastern Europe and former Soviet Union	High-income North America coefficients with ten-year lag			
All other World Model regions	High-income North America coefficients with twenty-year lag			

Source: Institute for Economic Analysis estimates based on Koo, 1985.

tures of the vehicle but also on the circumstances in which it has to operate, including the average age of the fleet, traffic density, maintenance, average speed, and road conditions. Although these factors will not be quantified and therefore are not directly used in generating estimates for fuel efficiency, their identification is useful for this analysis. Fuel use per mile for a given vehicle in developing countries is known to be higher than in OECD countries. Our choice of a specific figure, within a range of possible fuel efficiencies, for a particular World Model region will be influenced by an evaluation of the status of these factors in the region.

Vintage

The fuel efficiency of new passenger cars has changed considerably over the years. In the United States in 1976, the nominal fuel efficiency* of a new passenger car was 17.2 mpg, in 1980 it was 23.2 mpg, and in 1988 it was 28.3 mpg (Davis, Shonka, Anderson-Batiste, and Hu, 1989, pp. 3–19). Clearly, a young fleet tends to have higher fuel efficiency than an old one. Since the average car in the U.S. fleet has become older (Davis, Shonka, Anderson-Batiste, and Hu, 1989, pp. 3–8), the fuel efficiency of the average car in use is much lower than the nominal fuel efficiency of a new car (in the United States in 1987, 18 mpg versus 28.3 mpg, according to Ross, (1989, p. 149). Unfortunately, data on the age composition of a fleet are available only for the United States. In general, vehicles stay in stock longer in developing countries than in OECD countries. Moreover, even new vehicles in developing countries are often old in design compared with OECD purchases (Meyers, 1988, p. 21; OTA, 1991, p. 78).

Traffic and Other Factors

Greater traffic density tends to reduce the fuel efficiency of vehicles. World Bank studies show that in Lagos, Nigeria, and in Bangkok, the average vehicle travels at about half the speed of vehicles in London or Frankfurt due to congestion. In some developing countries, poorly maintained trucks have fuel efficiency levels that are 25–40 percent below those of well-maintained trucks of the same model and vintage (Meyers, 1988, p. 22).

Fuel Efficiency of the Average Car and Truck

Estimates are available for fuel efficiencies of the average car and truck in the United States for the period 1970–87 (Davis et al., 1989, pp. 2–28). The OECD provides estimates of fuel efficiency for the passenger car fleet in several OECD countries. Although the fuel efficiency of new cars increased between 1980

---

* The nominal fuel efficiency is that obtained in official tests. An average car in use has a fuel efficiency which is 15 percent below the nominal fuel efficiency (Ross, 1989, p. 148).

and 1987, the average fuel efficiency did not change in many European countries because of increased sales of larger cars (International Energy Agency, 1991d, p. 34).

Fuel efficiency of trucks is assumed to be similar to that of the United States in other developed countries, while trucks in developing countries use 1.5–2.5 times as much fuel per mile (OTA, 1991, p. 79). The same relationship between developed and developing countries is assumed for passenger cars. One of two fuel efficiencies is assigned to each developing region: high or low. The resulting estimates of fuel efficiencies for 1980 and 1987 are shown in Table 13.14. For lack of data, we assume the same fuel efficiencies for the average car and the average truck in both households and transportation services.

The projections shown in the table for 2020 are based on the following reasoning. In 1987 the average fuel efficiency of cars was $2.35 \ 10^{-4}$ tce/mile (19 mpg) in North America and $2.07 \ 10^{-4}$ tce/mile (21 mpg) in Western Europe. The fuel efficiency of the average new car was 28 mpg in North America (National Research Council 1992, p. 14) and 30 mpg in Europe (Bleviss and Walzer, 1990, p. 55). Volkswagen currently has a test car with a fuel efficiency of 62 mpg (Bleviss and Walzer, 1990, p. 57), and the National Research Council (1992, p. 153) projects for the average new car a fuel efficiency between 34 and 37 mpg for 2006 based on techniques now suitable for mass production. Based on the technological and other considerations discussed earlier, we assume that the average fuel efficiency of cars in high-income North America and southern Africa in 2020 is 40 mpg ($1.13 \ 10^{-4}$ tce/mile). For high-income Western Europe, medium-income Western Europe, Oceania, and Japan, we assume an average fuel efficiency of 45 mpg ($1.00 \ 10^{-4}$ tce/mile). For each region this results in a 52 percent increase in fuel efficiency over the 1987–2020 period. A similar rate of improvement is assumed for trucks (see Table 13.4).

Future fuel efficiences for other regions are very difficult to project, and no reliable estimates could be found. Therefore, these parameters have not been projected in Table 13.14.

The following section estimates vehicle miles and average annual fuel use per vehicle, the remaining parameters identified in Figure 13.2. We have not been able to incorporate the parameters developed in the next section because of the weakness of the data used to distinguish between households and transportation services. For similar reasons, we have made no attempt to project these parameters for the future. Nevertheless, we include this section because it follows the logic of Figure 13.2 and provides the basis for future improvement of this work. The way in which parameters have been incorporated in the data base will be discussed in the final section of this chapter.

Average Miles Driven per Vehicle and Fuel Use per Vehicle

For OECD countries, data on vehicle miles are available for trucks and passenger cars for the years 1970, 1975, and 1980–85 (OECD, 1988, pp. 30–34). These data do not distinguish between private and commercial vehicles. Therefore, we ini-

Table 13.14. Average fleet fuel efficiencies for World Model regions in 1980 and 1987 and projections under the OCF scenario for rich, developed economies for 2020 (miles per gallon)

	1980		1987		2020	
	Trucks	Cars	Trucks	Cars	Trucks	Cars
High-income North America and southern Africa	8.3	15.4	9.6	19.1	20.0	39.8
Oceania, high-income Western Europe, and medium-income Western Europe	8.3	21.7	9.6	21.7	20.0	45.5
Japan	9.6	21.7	9.6	21.7	20.0	45.5
High Efficiency						
Eastern Europe, newly industrializing Latin America, former Soviet Union, newly industrializing Asia, low-income Latin America	5.5	10.2	6.4	12.7		
Low Efficiency						
Major oil producers, low-income Asia, North Africa and other Middle East, Sub-Saharan Africa, centrally planned Asia	3.3	16.3	3.8	7.6		

Notes: 1. High efficiency assumes 1.5 more fuel per mile than high-income North America. Low efficiency assumes 2.5 more fuel per mile than high-income North America.

2. The choice between high and low fuel efficiency for the newly industrializing economies, Eastern Europe, the former Soviet Union, and the other developing economies is based on assumptions about operating conditions and on feedback from the implications for average annual miles driven (described in text and in Table 13.17).

3. Based on feedback from the implications for total energy use, the fuel efficiency for 1987 is assumed for 1980 also in Japan.

4. One gallon of gasoline is about 4.5×10^3 tce. This factor was used to convert to tce, which is the unit used in the World Model.

5. Projections for 2020 have not been m de for the developing countries.

6. The same fuel efficiencies are assumed in households and transportation services.

Source: Institute for Economic Analysis based on Davis et al., 1989, pp. 2–16, 2–28; International Energy Agency, 1991d, p. 34; U.S. Congress, OTA, 1991, p. 79; Institute for Economic Analysis projections for 2020.

tially assumed that the average annual car-miles driven by households are the same as average annual car-miles drived by transportation services. A similiar assumption was made for trucks. The OECD data are shown in Table 13.15.

Data are not available for vehicle-miles in developing countries. Miles driven by the average vehicle might well be larger than in OECD countries. For example, light trucks in Tunisia are driven on average 45,000 kilometers (27,962 miles) per year (Greene, Meddeb, and Liu, 1986, p. 442) compared to about 19,550 kilometers (11,728 miles) in the United States (Davis, Shonka, Anderson-Batiste, and Hu, 1989, pp. 3–35). On the other hand, because of limited roads in many developing countries, average vehicle-miles could also be fewer than in OECD countries. Meyers (1988, p. 13) suggests that the congestion problems in urban areas in developing countries may affect car usage more than ownership and may result in lower average vehicle-miles per year.

Estimates of annual miles driven per average vehicle in the developing regions were made using the following formulas:

$$VM_t = \frac{a \times T}{s \times Rlf_t}$$

$$VM_c = \frac{(1-a) \times T}{(1-s) \times Rlf_c}$$

Table 13.15. Average annual vehicle miles in OECD countries in 1970, 1980, 1985, and 1988 (miles per vehicle)

		Cars		Trucks	
		VM	g (percentages)	VM	g (percentages)
High-income North America	1970	9,949		11,351	
	1980	9,141	−0.8	11,419	0.1
	1985	9,683	1.2	11,528	0.2
	1988	10,036		11,597	
High-income Western Europe	1970	8,374		13,578	
	1980	7,833	−0.7	14,280	0.5
	1985	7,521	−0.8	13,825	−0.6
	1988	7,342		13,578	
Medium-income Western Europe	1970	6,995		11,990	
	1980	5,240	−2.8	9,671	−2.2
	1985	5,093	−0.6	9,215	−0.8
	1988	5,002		8,996	
Japan	1970	8,536		7,503	
	1980	6,342	−2.9	6,672	−1.2
	1985	6,162	−0.6	5,266	−4.6
	1988	6,052		4,572	
Oceania	1970	9,711		10,088	
	1980	8,716	−1.1		1.0
	1985	8,674	−0.1	11,119	−0.5
	1988	8,648		10,837	
				10,675	

Note: VM = vehicle miles; g = average annual rate of change since last period.

Source: Institute for Econornic Analysis based on 1970–1985: OECD, 1988, pp. 30–34; figures for 1988 are extrapolated using the average annual growth rates for 1980–1985.

where

VM_t, VM_c	annual vehicle miles driven by the average truck and car, respectively
a	percent of road transport fuel used by trucks
T	fuel used for road transport
s	share of trucks in total registrations
R	size of the fleet (total registrations)
f_t, f_c	average fuel efficiency of trucks and cars, respectively.

Data on fuel use for road transport do not distinguish between households and transportation services, and data on the size of the fleet do not distinguish between private and commercial motor vehicles. Therefore, it was not possible to apply these formulas separately for households and transportation services. Consequently, we assumed that the average annual car-miles driven by households and transportation services are the same in developing regions. The same assumption was made for trucks.

The formulas were first estimated for individual countries for which the following information was available:

- Fuel use by road transport (OECD, International Energy Agency, *World Energy Statistics and Balances*, 1988b and 1991).
- Total motor vehicle registration and the share of trucks (both from MVMA, 1981, 1990).

We also made use of the estimate that in developing countries trucks account for 50–75 percent of energy consumed by road transport (OTA, 1991, p. 79) and of the fuel efficiencies reported in Table 13.14.

The percentage of road transport energy consumed by trucks was based on the share of trucks, assumed to be 50 percent or 75 percent except in China. In China, trucks account for 80 percent of the motor vehicle fleet, and we assumed that 99 percent of the road transport fuel is used by trucks.

The resulting estimates of average miles driven per vehicle in developing regions are shown in Table 13.16 for countries that are representative of, or dominant in, each World Model region (subject to data availability). Since more data were available for 1988 than for 1980, it was possible to include more countries in each region.

Assuming the same fuel efficiencies (Table 13.14) and average miles driven (See Table 13.17) in households and transportation services for cars and for trucks, average annual oil use in each region can be calculated for all cars and trucks (Table 13.18), and for households and transportation services (Table 13.19).

These averages were multiplied by the fleet to determine total oil use for road transportation and are compared to control totals obtained for OECD countries in Table 13.20. For most of these regions, our estimate and the control totals are close. Oil use calculated for road transportation in all regions is reported in Table 13.21.

The International Energy Agency also publishes similar data for non-OECD countries. These are not shown for comparison, as they have been used in developing our estimates of vehicle-miles driven in developing countries (see Table 13.16).

Table 13.16. Average annual vehicle miles for representive developing countries in 1980 and 1988

	Vehicle miles		Truck energy share	Fuel efficiency
	Trucks	Cars		
1980				
Hungary (6)	7,782	1,285	.75	High
Argentina (2)	9,086	4,840	.50	High
Soviet Union (7)	13,226	7,184	.75	High
Iran (12)	20,608	4,882	.75	Low
Indonesia (10)	12,932	6,996	.75	High
Egypt (13)	13,500	2,453	.75	Low
Colombia (3)	11,966	8,638	.75	High
India (11)	13,145	5,347	.75	Low
Zimbabwe (14)	8,560	671	.75	Low
China (8)	5,408	1,552	.99	Low
1988				
Poland	7,062	3,111	.50	High
Eastern Germany	16,632	2,590	.50	High
Bulgaria	57,705	14,951	.50	High
Hungary	12,278	3,044	.50	High
Average (6)	13,929	4,148		
South Africa (15)	11,601	8,354	.50	High
Argentina	5,895	4,180	.50	High
Brazil	23,587	4,611	.50	High
Chile	7,905	7,810	.50	High
Mexico	7,383	6,472	.50	High
Venezuela	23,625	14,890	.50	High
Average (2)	12,293	5,625		
Soviet Union (7)	10,912	4,010	.75	High
Algeria	9,460	4,154	.75	Low
Gabon	9,854	4,357	.75	Low
Iran	18,661	4,380	.75	Low
Iraq	26,171	18,603	.75	Low
Libya	6,626	3,394	.75	Low
Nigeria	8,152	4,239	.75	Low
Saudi Arabia	3,286	1,895	.75	Low
Average (12)	8,407	3,913		
Hong Kong	5,642	2,442	.75	High
Indonesia	12,052	8,610	.75	High
Malaysia	15,891	2,958	.75	High
South Korea	13,207	7,181	.75	High
Singapore	15,146	4,661	.75	High
Taiwan	14,750	3,245	.75	High
Thailand	7,433	8,496	.75	High
Average (10)	11,376	5,431		
Bolivia	7,291	8,764	.75	High
Colombia	12,433	8,242	.75	High
Ecuador	14,095	24,915	.75	High
Average (3)	11,949	9,656		
Egypt	8,637	3,329	.75	Low
Ethiopia	13,599	4,195	.75	Low
Israel	15,118	2,031	.75	Low
Morocco	841	232	.75	Low
Syria	16,206	12,746	.75	Low
Tunisia	3,142	2,157	.75	Low
Average (13)	6,928	2,571		

Table 13.16. (continued)

	Vehicle miles		Truck energy share	Fuel efficiency
	Trucks	Cars		
India	10,453	6,408	.75	Low
Pakistan	23,878	4,745	.75	Low
Philippines	9,809	2,123	.75	Low
Average (11)	11,493	5,468		
Angola	3,828	853	.75	Low
Benin	7,807	2,824	.75	Low
Cameroon	5,633	3,280	.75	Low
Congo	8,429	4,300	.75	Low
Ghana	7,421	4,219	.75	Low
Ivory Coast	3,641	1,308	.75	Low
Kenya	4,359	3,230	.75	Low
Zimbabwe	2,111	639	.75	Low
Average (14)	4,565	1,979		
China (8)	4,472	1,782	.95	Low

Notes: 1. Truck energy share is the proportion of road transport energy used by trucks.

2. High fuel efficiency is 1.5 less efficient than fuel efficiency in high-income North America; low fuel efficiency is 2.5 times less efficient. See Table 13.15.

3. Region codes are shown in parentheses after the country name: (2) newly industrializing Latin America, (3) low-income Latin America, (6) Eastern Europe, (7) former Soviet Union, (8) centrally planned Asia, (10) newly industrializing Asia, (11) low-income Asia, (12) major oil producers, (13) North Africa and other Middle East, (14) sub-Saharan Africa, (15) southern Africa.

4. See text for derivation of figures.

5. No data are available for China and Egypt in 1988; average vehicle miles driven are assumed to equal the 1980 figures.

Source: Institute for Economic Analysis estimates based on International Energy Agency, *World Energy Statistics and Balances*, 1989 and 1990b; U.S. Congress, OTA, 1991, p. 79; MVMA, 1990; and Table 13.15.

Table 13.17. Average annual vehicle miles for World Model regions in 1980 and 1988

	1980		1988	
	Trucks	Cars	Trucks	Cars
High-income North America	11,419	9,141	11,597	10,036
Oceania	11,119	8,716	10,675	8,648
High-income Western Europe	14,280	7,833	13,578	7,342
Japan	6,672	6,342	5,266	6,162
Medium-income Western Europe	9,617	5,240	8,996	5,002
Eastern Europe	7,782	1,285	13,929	4,148
Southern Africa	11,419	9,141	11,601	8,354
Newly industrializing Latin America	9,086	4,840	12,293	5,625
Soviet Union	13,226	7,184	10,912	4,010
Major oil producers	20,608	4,882	8,407	3,913
Newly industrializing Asia	12,932	6,996	11,376	5,431
Low-income Latin America	11,966	8,638	11,483	8,300
North Africa and other Middle East	13,500	2,453	5,092	1,633
Low-income Asia	13,145	5,347	10,407	5,641
Sub-Saharan Africa	8,560	671	4,565	1,979
Centrally planned Asia	5,408	1,552	4,472	1,782

Note: Average miles driven in southern Africa in 1980 is assumed to equal average miles driven in high-income North America.

Source: Tables 13.15 and 13.16.

Table 13.18. Annual oil use by average vehicle for World Model regions in 1980 and 1988 (tons of coal equivelent)

	1980		1988	
	Trucks	Cars	Trucks	Cars
High-income North America	6.2	2.7	5.4	2.4
Oceania	6.0	1.8	5.0	1.8
High-income Western Europe	7.7	1.6	6.4	1.5
Japan	3.1	1.3	2.1	1.3
Medium-income Western Europe	5.2	1.1	4.2	1.0
Eastern Europe	6.3	0.6	9.8	1.5
Southern Africa	6.2	2.7	5.4	2.0
Newly industrializing Latin America	7.4	2.1	8.0	2.0
Soviet Union	10.7	3.2	7.7	1.4
Major oil producers	27.9	3.6	9.8	2.3
Newly industrializing Asia	10.5	3.1	8.0	1.9
Low-income Latin America	9.7	3.8	8.4	3.4
North Africa and other Middle East	18 3	1.8	8.1	1.5
Low-income Asia	17.8	3.9	13.5	3.2
Sub-Saharan Africa	11.6	0.5	5.3	1.2
Centrally planned Asia	7.3	1.1	5.2	1.1

Source: Tables 13.12, 13.14, and 13.17.

Incorporating Parameters About Transportation in the Data Base

In this section, the incorporation of the parameters reported in this chapter into the data base will be discussed. There remains, however, one final set of parameters: the share of oil used for road transportation in total oil use by households and transportation services. In developed economies, the major alterna-

Table 13.19. Annual oil use by average vehicle in household fleet and in transportation services fleet for World Model regions in 1980 and 1988 (tons of coal equivalent)

	Households		Transportation services	
	1980	1988	1980	1988
High-income North America	3.03	2.67	4.60	4.05
Oceania	2.23	2.11	4.12	3.55
High-income Western Europe	1.74	1.62	4.06	3.45
Japan	1.49	1.34	2.49	1.83
Medium-income Western Europe	1.29	1.19	2.73	2.31
Eastern Europe	0.85	1.88	3.73	6.04
Southern Africa	3.03	2.31	4.95	4.22
Newly industrializing Latin America	2.92	2.89	5.54	5.92
Soviet Union	4.30	2.35	8.09	5.47
Major oil producers	7.22	3.43	19.38	7.20
Newly industrializing Asia	4.19	2.83	7.90	5.86
Low-income Latin America	4.69	4.16	7.65	6.65
North Africa and other Middle East	3.44	2.17	12.50	5.80
Low-income Asia	6.00	4.75	12.93	9.87
Sub-Saharan Africa	2.16	1.79	7.70	3.88
Centrally planned Asia	2.68	2.09	7.01	5.02

Source: Tables 13.12, 13.14, and 13.17.

Table 13.20. Annual oil use by motor vehicle fleet in rich, developed economies according to Institute for Economic Analysis estimates and control totals in 1980 and 1988 (thousands of tons of coal equivalent)

	Year	Institute for Economic Analysis	International Energy Agency	Ratio
High-income North America	1980	583,086	553,422	1.05
	1988	621,537	624,588	0.99
High- and medium-income	1980	255,072	241,280	1.06
Western Europe	1988	309,603	306,384	1.01
Japan	1980	75,396	63,177	1.19
	1988	84,920	81,403	1.04
Oceania	1980	25,673	22,779	1.13
	1988	27,898	28,188	0.99

Note: IEA estimates are the sum of oil-based energy use by trucks (T_t) and oil-based energy use by cars (T_c).
Source: Institute for Economic Analysis estimates based on Tables 13.6, 13.12, and 13.18; OECD IEA, 1984, 1991d.

tive use of oil by households is for space heating; in developing economies, oil is used mainly for cooking and lighting (see Chapter 12). In transportation services, the major alternatives are rail, air, and sea transportation. Estimates of the share of oil used for road transportation for all World Model regions, still very preliminary, are shown in Table 13.22. Direct information about the division of road transportation oil use between households and transportation services was obtained only for the United States and was used, with some adjustments, for other developed regions. Information about nonroad transportation oil use for each sector was obtained for some developing countries form OECD's *Energy Balances* and was combined with estimates in Table 13.21 to calculate the share of oil used for road transportation in these regions. No attempt was made to project changes for the future for this parameter.

Table 13.21. Oil use by road transportation for World Model regions in 1980 and 1988 (thousands of tons of coal equivalent)

	1980	1988
High-income North America	583,086	621,537
Oceania	25,673	27,898
High-income Western Europe	228,117	270,786
Japan	75,396	84,920
Medium-income Western Europe	27,965	38,817
Eastern Europe	18,704	43,404
Southern Africa	12,938	12,393
Newly industrializing Latin America	73,123	92,407
Soviet Union	104,037	89,883
Major oil producers	79,058	63,588
Newly industrializing Asia	26,080	48,034
Low-income Latin America	21,625	25,226
North Africa and other Middle East	17,864	12,672
Low-income Asia	33,707	38,045
Sub-Saharan Africa	8,877	7,169
Centrally planned Asia	6,315	18,887

Source: Institute for Economic Analysis estimates are based on Tables 13.6, 13.12, and 13.18.

Table 13.22. Share of road transportation in oil use of households and of transportation services for World Model regions in 1990 (percentages)

	Households	Transportation services
High-income North America	50	60
Oceania	90	60
High-income Western Europe	50	60
Japan	50	60
Medium-income Western Europe	50	60
Eastern Europe	90	75
Southern Africa	75	80
Newly industrializing Latin America	75	80
Former Soviet Union	55	50
Major oil producers	60	90
Newly industrializing Asia	40	80
Low-income Latin America	40	80
North Africa and other Middle East	50	70
Low-income Asia	35	75
Sub-Saharan Africa	70	70
Centrally planned Asia	26	90

Source: Figures for high-income North America are from the U.S. National Energy Accounts, 1985. Figures for other regions are Institute for Economic Analysis estimates.

Of the many variables and parameters that have been discussed and tabulated in this case study, only a few have been incorporated directly in the World Data Base. Others were utilized, but indirectly. Still others were not used because they had to be based on very little information.

The following discussion identifies the parameters that were used and the ways in which they were incorporated:

1. Each region's coefficients describing the deliveries of motor vehicles to other sectors was scaled to reflect actual motor vehicle densities in 1980 and 1990 and projected densities under the OCF scenario in 2020 (Table 13.9).
2. For years after 1990, the input structures of the motor vehicle sectors in all regions were adjusted to reflect new technology, primarily substitution among material inputs and increased capital requirements (Table 13.3).
3. Improvements in motor vehicle fuel efficiency in transportation services for years after 1990 under the OCF scenario were incorporated for all regions by reducing the oil input coefficient (assuming that uses of oil for other transportation services achieve similar gains in fuel efficiency) according to the figures in Table 13.14.
4. Changes in motor vehicle fuel efficiency from Table 13.14 were incorporated directly in the coefficient governing household use of oil only for developed regions. Because motor vehicle densities in most rich, developed economies are close to saturation and the populations are not projected to grow much, changes in energy use by road transportation depend mainly on changes in average vehicle miles and in fuel efficiencies. We have assumed

that the average miles per vehicle will not increase very much in these regions (except in medium-income Western Europe and southern Africa); therefore, changes in energy use for road transportation depend almost entirely on changes in fuel efficiencies. (See Chapter 12 for further discussion of the method of incorporating these projections.)

5. In developing regions, oil use by households for all purposes was projected directly, without projecting separately each parameter governing oil use, because of a lack of reliable data. (See Chapter 12 for further discussion.)

6. The parameters representing the share of transportation in total oil use by households were also used in calculating the nitrogen emission parameters since mobile and stationary sources of nitrogen emissions had to be distinguished.

Appendix A
Structure of the World Model

The version of the World Model that has been implemented for this study is based on the familiar, static input-output model, which has been extended by the explicit representation of investment and international exchanges. The World Model was designed by Wassily Leontief, and its initial implementation is described in Leontief, Carter, and Petri (1977).

The set of equations presented below is written in succinct matrix form and covers the basic logic of the representation of the world economy. Exceptions and additions to the algebra are noted at the end of the appendix.

Model

Most of the following equations are repeated for each region in each time period. For simplicity, the subscripts distinguishing the time period (t) and region (r) have been dropped, except in equations referring to more than one region or time period. A specific region is identified by the subscript R.

(1)
$$(I-A)\, x = y$$

where $y = c + go + e - m$

(2)
$$c = \hat{\alpha}c + \beta\, POP$$

where $\hat{\alpha}$ is the diagonal matrix with elements of α as the diagonal

(3)
$$go = \gamma \times GDP\, h$$

where $GDP = p_0'\, y$

(4)
$$in = (g + d)(k'x)n$$

(5)
$$m = \hat{M}x \text{ and}$$

$$e = \hat{S}\sum_r m_r \ (e \text{ and } \hat{S} \text{ are region specific})$$

(6) $$BOP = p_N'(e - m) + K_1 + K_2 + K_3$$

(7) $$K_{1,R} = b_{1,R} \sum_r a_{1,r} GDP_r - a_{1,R} GDP_R$$

(8) $$K_{2,R} = a_{2,R} \sum_i in_{R,i} - b_{2,R} \sum_r a_{2,r} \sum_i in_{r,i}$$

(9) $$K_{3,t} = a_3[K_{3,t-10} + (BOP_{t-10} + BOP_t) \times 5]$$

Parameters and Variables

A $n \times n$ matrix of current-account inputs per unit of output

x $n \times 1$ vector of output

y $n \times 1$ vector of total final deliveries

c $n \times 1$ vector of consumption

go $n \times 1$ vector of government spending

in $n \times 1$ vector of gross investment

e $n \times 1$ vector of exports

m $n \times 1$ vector of imports

GDP scalar, gross domestic product

p_0 $n \times 1$ vector of 1970 U.S. prices

α, β $n \times 1$ vectors governing consumption by item as a function of total consumption and population respectively

POP scalar, population

γ scalar, government outlays as a percentage of GDP

h $n \times 1$ vector showing the composition of government spending

g, d scalars, rates of growth and replacement of capital stock, respectively

k $n \times 1$ vector of sectoral capital-to-output ratios

n $n \times 1$ vector showing the composition of gross investment

$\hat{M}$ $n \times n$ diagonal matrix of import coefficients

$\hat{S}$ $n \times n$ diagonal matrix of export shares

BOP scalar, balance of payments (net inflow of short-term capital)

p_N $n \times 1$ vector of current relative U.S. prices

K_1, K_2, K_3 scalars, net inflow of economic aid, long term capital, foreign earnings, respectively

a_i, b_i scalars, where a_1 is aid outflow as a share of GDP; b_1 is aid inflow as a share of the pool; a_2 is capital inflow as a share of investment; b_2 is capital outflow as a share of the pool; and a_3 is the rate of interest on foreign debt

In the model, urban and rural populations are distinguished, and the mix of personal and government consumption goods reflects, in part, the percentage of the population living in cities. For simplicity, this distinction is not reflected in equations 2 and 3. The price vector needs to be used to sum up GDP in the third equation because some commodities are measured in physical units. For those already in value units, the price is simply 1.00.

Investment is represented in equation 4. This equation is a simplification in that, in the model, plant and equipment are treated separately and gross investment is the sum of the two. In each case, there are three kinds of parameters. The total stock is determined by the vector of sectoral capital-to-output ratios for, say, plant. The amount of capital to be put in place that year is calculated by applying the rates of growth and replacement to the total national stock of plant. Finally, the composition of total gross investment is specified.

All regions' imports of a given commodity are delivered from a single world trade pool rather than being specified by bilateral trade arrangements. Imports are computed as a share of domestic production, and a region's exports are a share of the total pool; this is shown in equation 5. In the case of noncompetitive imports, the level of imports is exogenous.

In the balance of payments, defined by equation 6, traded items are revalued in current relative prices (in United States prices) but "normalized" to the overall 1970 price level. This device makes it possible to capture the effects of likely future changes in relative prices (as in the case of petroleum) without requiring a projection of the future price level. In addition to the balance of trade, the equation includes the net inflows of economic aid, of long-term capital, and of earnings on foreign assets. A balance of payments deficit is assumed to be covered by an inflow of short-term capital; a surplus is treated as an outflow of short-term capital.

International flows of economic aid and long-term capital (equations 7 and 8, respectively) are handled by pools like traded commodities. Aid given is a fraction of GDP, and aid received is a share of the pool. Capital inflow is a share of total domestic investment, and capital outflow is a share of the pool.

Earnings on foreign assets (payments on the debt if the figure is negative) are included in the balance of payments and defined in equation 9. The assets at the end of the last period are augmented by an estimate of the ten years' worth of long- and short-term assets accumulated since then.

The model is run for the six time periods between 1970 and 2020 at decade intervals. All of the parameters need to be provided for each region for each year. In this version of the model, exogenous values for two variables, GDP and population, are also required. The stock of foreign assets (or debt) in the base year is also needed.

A number of other calculations are made besides those described above. Notably, three types of emissions are computed once the basic solution has been obtained. These calculations are described in Chapter 4.

Over the last decade, the input-output framework has been extended in a number of new directions. The most important are the dynamic model of physical stocks and flows and the fully integrated dynamic physical, price, and income models (see Duchin, 1988a; Duchin and Szyld, 1985). These extensions can be readily integrated into the World Model.

Appendix B
Building the World Data Base:
Case Study Methodology

The case study, generally covering one or several related sectors of the world economy, serves as the principal organizing device for both the development of scenarios and the construction of the World Data Base. The first objective requires a qualitative analysis of what the important issues are, in the world economy as a whole and on a regional basis, while satisfying the second objective requires the quantification of specific variables and parameters. This work relies mainly on two types of literature. One is the technical literature, in which current and potential future production processes and the characteristics of individual pieces of equipment are described. The second kind of literature offers some information, although usually incomplete and often not internally consistent because of the nature of the undertaking, about consumption, production, and/or trade in the goods and services in question in the different parts of the world. The latter is generally published by international statistical and trade organizations. Some of our early works on building the case study methodology are a study of biomass for fuel (Duchin, 1990) and the design of a data base to organize input-output information about alternative technologies (Duchin, 1988b).

Many types of World Model scenarios can be formulated and successfully executed by nonspecialists using the short *User's Guide* that has been prepared for this and subsequent studies. Conducting a case study of the type described here, however, requires an analyst skilled in both qualitative and quantitative research techniques. Analysts for our case studies have included both experienced researchers and graduate students.

The subject of a particular case study is generally selected because it is considered important for a broader investigation. For this study, for example, we chose those sectors that use a great deal of energy and focused attention on potential technological options for reducing energy requirements. If a preliminary examination suggests that the case may not be as important, from these points of view, as had been anticipated, priority should be given to other case studies.

Besides its qualitative assessment, which is important but difficult to gener-

195

alize, the case study needs to produce the following outputs, which are discussed in turn below:

1. Identification of relevant World Model sectors and determination of relevant units of analysis
2. Control totals and the revision of variables and parameters for the past (if necessary)
3. Description of technology and potential technological change
4. Projection of parameters for the future
5. Documentation of assumptions

Identification of Relevant World Model Sectors and Units of Analysis

The case studies need to be carried out in terms of the classifications, definitions, conventions, and standard units that govern the larger study of which they are part. We will call these, collectively, the *World Model Standards* (wms). Perhaps the greatest shortcoming of the typical case study that appears in the literature is that it makes its own assumptions on these matters; consequently, it is difficult to integrate individual case studies into a common data base.

Complying with standards like the wms imposes a discipline that can be difficult to achieve, and the standards may need to be changed periodically. One of our principal conclusions is that, whenever possible, the output of a sector should be measured in physical units like tons or tons of coal equivalent. It is very difficult to reconcile information from different sources when only value units of measure are utilized. After an initial familiarization with the area, the best choice of physical unit is generally apparent. A standard unit price, for example in dollars of a particular benchmark year, also needs to be estimated.

Control Totals and Revision of Variables and Parameters for the Past

Assuming that one or more World Model sectors have been identified as the subject of analysis, the next step is to develop control totals for the relevant variables for benchmark years. For this study we generally used 1980 and 1988. The relevant variables are sector-specific levels of production, consumption, imports, and exports for each World Model region. The un and other international organizations collect some data of this type, which are geographically comprehensive and more or less consistent, and these should be used when possible. Typically, however, the case study requires more detailed information than is available in this type of source, and the analyst needs to turn to more specialized sources that are often published by the same organizations. Publications of the relevant government agencies of the rich, industrialized countries (such as the U.S. Bureau of Mines) are also extremely valuable sources.

The objective of collecting control totals is to assess whether the existing representation in the World Model is adequate. This, of course, is a matter of judgment and degree, and no rules can be formalized. The analyst needs to inspect the overall volume of world production, the regional distribution of production, the volume of international trade, and the regional distribution of exports and imports. In order to assess the accuracy of the World Model calculations, it is useful to ask: what is the most significant discrepancy with the controls? In perhaps half of the cases, we decided that no revisions, or only minor revisions, were needed. This is true because the original World Data Base already represented a significant body of empirical work, and a great deal of new information had subsequently been incorporated. Nonetheless, the case study provides an opportunity to make improvements that cannot be made in any other, more automatic, way.

The representation of the sector depends on hundreds of parameters. Consequently, if revisions are needed, it is important to be very selective in deciding which parameters to revise. One is not simply trying to match the controls—this would be relatively easy to achieve—but to improve the quality of the underlying parameters for past years so that they serve as a sound basis for projecting the parameters for future years. There are many possible kinds of discrepancies to consider. For example, if the regional distribution of production of a particular sector is close to the controls but the volume of world production is 20 percent too low, the simplest response is to increase all input coefficients representing the use of this sector's output in all regions by 20 percent. A better response, however, especially when a discrepancy is large, is to first identify the major sectors using the output of the sector in question and to determine if their output is systematically underestimated in the World Model calculations. It may seem that this is an endless process, but it turns out to be manageable for several reasons. First, many sectors have only a few major users; second, other case studies in the series may have possibly already addressed the same problem from another angle. When parameters are revised on the basis of having understood the reason for the discrepancy, this can be expected to improve the results. Since by now many case studies have been carried out, subsequent ones should face smaller discrepancies and have more relevant information to draw on. The test of the revision is to rerun the model, check that selected other controls are not violated, ensure that the intended effect has been achieved, and document the changes that have been made.

Description of Technology and Potential Technological Change

The case study has to include a description of the principal production technologies currently in use in the sector or sectors under examination and those that today look like serious contenders for the next several decades. It is important to have an assessment of which technologies are used in which regions and what the underlying reasons are. The two most important factors generally are whether a region is energy-rich and its pattern of development. The analyst needs to identify the principal inputs, per unit of output, that distinguish the alternative technologies. Often these will be capital goods, electronics, skilled

labor, energy, and the degree of recycling of materials. The next step is to identify the technologies likely to be adopted in each region, or group of regions,
over the time horizon of the scenario.

Projection of Parameters for the Future

In the future it may be possible, in working directly with specialists in a given
area, to project directly the numerical values of parameters for future years that
correspond to the assumption that a given technology will be adopted. For now,
however, it is convenient to take as the point of departure the input vector such
as it is after any revisions that have been made because of discrepancies with
control totals. In studying the technology, the analyst has already identified the
parameters that will change the most, and these changes now need to be quantified. The parameters in question include all the current-account inputs, capital
requirements per unit expansion of capacity, rate of replacement of existing
capacity, and the structure of capital requirements. In some cases, the technological change may be directly related to changing trade parameters.

It is often possible to find specific numerical estimates in the literature
(e.g., energy use will be 30 percent lower than under the current technology, and
half of the steel will be substituted for by aluminum). In other instances, the
analyst will have to make a rough estimate.

Documentation of Assumptions

Documentation of assumptions is critical and should take the form of tables
showing the actual values of variables and parameters. These need to be
expressed, of course, in WMS.

Appendix C
World Model Geographic Classification

1. High-income North America
   British Virgin Islands
   Canada
   Puerto Rico
   United States of America
   Virgin Islands

2. Newly industrializing Latin America
   Argentina
   Brazil
   Chile
   Mexico
   Venezuela

3. Low-income Latin America
   Anguilla
   Antigua and Barbuda
   Aruba
   Bahamas
   Barbados
   Belize
   Bermuda
   Bolivia
   Cayman Islands
   Columbia
   Costa Rica
   Cuba
   Dominica
   Dominican Republic
   Ecuador
   El Salvador
   Falkland Islands
   French Guiana
   Grenada
   Guadaloupe
   Guatemala
   Guyana
   Haiti
   Honduras
   Jamaica
   Martinique
   Montserrat

   Netherlands Antilles
   Nicaragua
   Panama
   Paraguay
   Peru
   St. Kitts and Nevis
   St. Lucia
   St. Pierre and Miquelon
   St. Vincent
   Surinam
   Trinidad and Tobago
   Turcs and Caicos Islands
   Uruguay

4. High-income Western Europe
   Andorra
   Austria
   Belgium
   Channel Islands
   Denmark
   Faero Islands
   Finland
   France
   Germany, Federal Republic of (former)
   Greenland
   Iceland
   Ireland
   Isle of Man
   Italy
   Lichtenstein
   Luxembourg
   Monaco
   Netherlands
   Norway
   San Marino
   Sweden
   Switzerland
   United Kingdom

5. Medium-income Western Europe
   Cyprus
   Gibraltar

Greece

Malta

Portugal

Spain

Turkey

Yugoslavia (former)

6. Eastern Europe

Albania

Bulgaria

Czechoslovakia

German Democratic Republic (former)

Hungary

Poland

Romania

7. Former Soviet Union

8. Centrally planned Asia

China

Democratic People's Republic of Korea

Mongolia

9. Japan

10. Newly industrializing Asia

Hong Kong

Indonesia

Malaysia

Republic of Korea

Residual Asia (Taiwan)

Singapore

Thailand

11. Low-income Asia

Afghanistan

Bangladesh

Bhutan

Burma

Democratic Kamputchea

Democratic Republic of Vietnam

East Timor

India

Laos

Macao

Maldive Islands

Nepal

Pakistan

Papua New Guinea

Phillipines

Sri Lanka

12. Major oil producers

Algeria

Bahrain

Brunei

Democratic Yemen

Gabon

Iran

Iraq

Kuwait

Libyan Arab Republic

Nigeria

Oman

Quatar

Saudi Arabia

United Arab Emirates

Yemen

13. Northern Africa and other Middle East

Burkina Faso

Chad

Egypt

Ethiopia

Israel

Jordan

Lebanon

Mali

Mauretania

Morocco

Niger

Somalia

Sudan

Syrian Arab Republic

Tunisia

Western Sahara

14. Sub-Saharan Africa

Angola

Benin

Burundi

Cameroon

Cape Verde

Central African Republic

Comoro Islands

Congo

Cote d'Ivoire

Djibouti

Equatorial Guinea

Gambia

Ghana

Guinea

Guinea-Bissau

Kenya

Liberia

Madagascar

Malawi

Mauritius

Mozambique

Reunion

Rwanda
São Tome and Principe
Senegal
Seychelles Islands
Sierra Leone
St. Helena
Tanzania
Togo
Uganda
Zaire
Zambia
Zimbabwe

15. Southern Africa
    Botswana
    Lesotho
    Namibia
    South Africa
    Swaziland

16. Oceania
    Australia
    New Zealand
    Pacific territories not included elsewhere

Appendix D
World Model Sectoral Classification

1. ISIC Codes

World Model code	Title of sector	ISIC Revision 2 codes
SE1	Livestock	11100, 111010
SE2	Oil crops	111059, 111061, 111062, 111063, 111065, 111066, 111067, 111069, 111070, 111071, 111073
SE3	Grain	111011, 111013, 111014, 111015, 111017, 111018, 111019
SE4	Root crops	111035, 111046, 111047
SE5	Copper ore	230201
SE6	Bauxite	230207
SE7	Nickel ore	230204
SE8	Zinc ore	230213
SE9	Lead ore	230210
SE10	Iron and other ores	230101, 230216, 230219, 230222, 230225, 230228, 230231, 230234, 230237, 230240, 230243, 230246, 230249, 230252, 230255
SE11	Crude petroleum	220001, 220004
SE12	Natural gas	220010, 354013
SE13	Coal	210001, 354001, 210004, 290916, 354004, 354007, 354010
FS1	Fishing	13
XX1	Other agriculture	11102, 111030, 111031, 111033, 111034, 111037, 111038, 111039, 111041, 111042, 111043, 111045, 111049, 111050, 111051, 111053, 111054, 111055, 111057, 111058, 111074, 111075, 111077, 111078, 111079, 111081, 111082, 111083, 111085, 112, 113, 12
XX2	Other mining	290– 290916
XX3	Food processing	311, 312, 313, 314
XX4	Petroleum refining	220007, 35300, 35301, 35302, 35303
XX5	Primary metal processing	371, 372
XX6	Textiles and apparel	321, 322, 323, 324
XX7	Wood and cork products	331
XX8	Furniture and fixtures	332
XX9	Paper and paper products	341

1. ISIC Codes (continued)

World Model code	Title of sector	ISIC Revision 2 codes
XX10	Printing and publishing	342
XX11	Rubber products	355
XX12	Industrial chemicals	3511
XX13	Fertilizer and agricultural chemicals	3512
XX14	Miscellaneous chemicals	3513, 352, 356
XX15	Cement	3692
XX16	Glass, stone, and clay products	361, 362, 3691, 3699
XX17	Motor vehicles	3843, 384401
XX18	Aircraft and parts	3845
XX19	Other transportation equipment	3841, 3842, 384404, 3849
XX20	Metal products	381919, 3811, 3812, 3813, 381901, 381904, 381907, 381910, 381913, 381916
XX21	Machinery	3821, 3822, 3823, 3824, 3829
XX22	Electrical and electronic machinery and equipment	383225, 383228, 382507 383301, 383304, 383310, 383901, 383922, 382925, 382907, 382901, 382904, 382910, 382958, 382964, 383916, 383919 382501, 382504, 382510, 382928, 383101, 383104, 383107, 383110 383113, 383116, 383119, 383122, 383125, 383201, 383204, 383207, 383210, 383213, 383216, 383219, 383222, 383231, 383234, 383237, 383240, 383307, 383904, 383907, 383910, 383913
XX23	Professional and scientific instruments	3851, 3852
XX24	Miscellaneous manufacturing	3853, 390
XX25	Electric utilities	410101, 410300, 410202, 42, 92
XX26	Construction	50
XX27	Trade	61, 62
XX28	Transportation services	71
XX29	Communication services	72
XX30	Other services	63, 81, 82, 83, 91, 93, 94, 95

2. SITC Codes

World Model code	Title of sector	SITC Revision 2 codes
SE1	Livestock	00, 0223, 025
SE2	Oil crops	221
SE3	Grain	041, 042, 043, 044, 045
SE4	Root crops	054101, 054811, 054812
XX1	Other agriculture	051, 0544, 0545, 05421, 054822, 054841, 071101, 072101, 074101, 121001, 121002, 261, 262, 263101, 264, 265, 231101, 231102, 244011, 242100, 242200, 242300
FS1	Fishing	031101, 031301, 031102
SE5	Copper ore	28311
SE6	Bauxite	28330
SE7	Nickel ore	28321
SE8	Zinc ore	28350
SE9	Lead ore	28340
SE10	Iron and other ores	2813, 2836, 2837, 2839, 285, 286
SE11	Crude petroleum	331
SE12	Natural gas	341101, 3412
SE13	Coal	3214, 3215, 3216, 3217, 3218
XX2	Other mining	27, 667201
XX3	Food processing	011, 012, 013, 09, 211100, 211200, 023, 024, 052, 053, 054610, 055, 031103, 0312, 032, 411, 421, 422, 046, 047, 048, 061, 062, 072200, 072320, 073000, 071300, 081, 112, 111, 122100, 121002, 121003, 122200, 122300
XX4	Petroleum refining	3321, 3322, 3323, 3324, 3325, 3326, 3329, 341102
XX5	Primary metal processing	561210, 67, 68, 731701
XX6	Textiles and apparel	263200, 6512, 6513, 6515, 651641, 6519, 652, 653, 656, 655, 657, 841, 611, 85102, 85104
XX7	Wood and cork products	243, 631
XX8	Furniture and fixtures	82
XX9	Paper and paper products	2512, 2513, 2516, 2517, 2518, 2519, 641, 642
XX10	Printing and publishing	
XX11	Rubber products	621, 629, 231300, 851011
XX12	Industrial chemicals	274102, 274103, 512, 51321, 51331, 51333, 51334, 51335, 51339, 513421, 513511, 51355, 51356, 51361, 51362, 51365, 514, 531, 532, 5331, 5999
XX13	Fertilizer and agricultural chemicals	5611, 56129, 5613, 5619, 599200
XX14	Miscellaneous chemicals	2312, 266, 581, 65160, 6517, 5332, 5333, 554, 51327, 57112, 59955, 862
XX15	Cement	661101, 661200
XX16	Glass, stone, and clay products	666, 8122, 661830, 662, 663, 664, 665
XX17	Motor vehicles	711504, 711505, 732, 733301
XX18	Aircraft and parts	7114, 734101
XX19	Other transportation equipment	735, 7312, 7313, 7314, 7315, 891400, 733111

2. SITC Codes (continued)

World Model code	Title of sector	SITC Revision 2 codes
XX20	Metal products	812101, 696, 698, 692, 693, 694, 711100, 731631
XX21	Machinery	715, 71711, 71712, 718, 7192, 7193, 71952, 7197, 71132, 711501, 711502, 711503, 711600, 711811, 712, 71964
XX22	Electrical and electronic machinery and equipment	729301, 729302, 714301, 72503, 72504, 725022, 722201, 729600, 719170, 717151, 697102, 717300, 719420, 725020, 729201, 729202 714101, 714201, 714302, 719150, 7221, 729510, 7299, 724, 726200, 8911, 891201, 725051, 722202, 723101, 7291
XX23	Professional and scientific instruments	719631, 719632, 861
XX24	Miscellaneous manufacturing	864, 891411, 894120, 891810, 891830, 894220, 895210, 895230, 899530
XX25	Electric utilities	351000, 341022

Trade for sectors XX26–30 is not reported in the UN COMTRADE data base.

References

Andersson, C. 1989. "Poland's Biggest Fossil Fuel Power Station." *Acid Magazine* No. 8: 9–11.

Ando, J. 1989. "Recent Developments in SO_2 and NO_x Abatement Technology for Stationary Sources." In L.J. Brasser and Mulder, eds., *Man and His Ecosystem, Proceedings of the 8th World Clean Air Congress 1989*. Amsterdam: Elsevier.

Asian Development Bank. 1990. *Power Utilities DataBook for the Asian and Pacific Region*. Bangkok: Asian Development Bank.

Berman, S. 1985. "Energy and Lighting." In D. Hafemeister, H. Kelly, and B. Levi, eds., *Energy Sources: Conservation and Renewables*. New York: American Institute of Physics.

Bevington, R., and A. Rosenfeld. 1990. "Energy for Buildings and Homes." *Scientific American* 263: 77–86.

Bhagavan, M. R. 1985. "The Energy Sector in SADCC Countries." *Ambio* 14(4–5): 214–19.

Bjorklund, S. 1989a. "Big Sacrifices Needed to Cut East Germany's Sulfur Emissions," *Acid Magazine* No. 8: 20–21.

———. 1989b. "Inefficient Energy at Root of Poland's Environmental Problems." *Acid Magazine* No. 8:20–21.

Bleviss, D. L, and P. Walzer. 1990. "Energy for Motor Vehicles," *Scientific American* 263: 55–61.

Boyd, G. A., and M. H. Ross. 1989. "The Role of Sectoral Shift in Trends in Electricity Use in United States and Swedish Manufacturing and in Comparing Forecasts." In *Electricity: End-Use and New Generation Technologies*. See Johansson, Bodlund, and Williams (1990).

Brown, M., and B. McKern. 1987. *Aluminium, Copper and Steel in Developing Countries. Development Center Studies*. Paris: OECD, Development Center.

Campbell, R. W. 1980. *Soviet Energy Technologies*. Bloomington: Indiana University Press.

Carter, A., P. Petri, F. Drost, and F. Jordon-Rozwadewski. 1970s. "United Nations World Model Data Documentation." 3 volumes, unpublished.

Casler, S. D. 1989. "Energy Flows Through the U.S. Economy: 1980, 1982, and 1985." Unpublished report prepared for the U.S. Congress Office of Technology Assessment.

Chandler, W. U., H. Geller, and M. Ledbetter. 1988. *Energy Efficiency: A New Agenda*. Washington, DC: American Council for an Energy-Efficient Economy.

Chesire, J., and M. Robson. 1985. "UK Industrial Energy Demand: Economic and Technical Change in the Steam Boiler Stock." Occasional Paper No. 19, Sussex Policy Research Unit, University of Sussex.

Claridge, D. E., and R. J. Mowris. 1985. "Passive Solar Heating." In D. Hafemeister, H. Kelly, and B. Levi, eds., *Energy Sources: Conservation and Renewables*. New York: American Institute of Physics.

Davis, S. C., D. B. Shonka, G. J. Anderson-Batiste, and P. S. Hu. 1989. *Transportation Energy DataBook*, 10th ed. Oak Ridge, TN: Oak Ridge National Laboratory, ORNL-656.

Devitt, T., P. Spaite, and L. Gibbs. 1979. "The Population and Characteristics of Industrial/Commercial Boilers." EPA-600/7–79–178a. Washington, DC: Environmental Protection Agency.

Dienes, L., and T. Shabad. 1979. *The Soviet Energy System*. New York: John Wiley and Sons.

Dorian, J. P., and D. G. Fridley. 1988. *China's Energy and Mineral Industries*. Boulder, CO: Westview Press.

Douglas, J. 1988. "The Challenge of Packaged Cogeneration." *EPRI Journal* 13(6):28–37.

Drake, R. H., and A. Y. Turpin. 1988. "Industrial Steam Raising Fuel Switching Analysis." Los Alamos, NM: Los Alamos National Laboratory, LA-UR-88–2473.

Duchin, F. 1990. "The Conversion of Biological Materials and Wastes to Useful Products," *Structural Change and Economic Dynamics* 1(2) 243–61.

———. 1988a. "Analyzing Structural Change in the Economy." In Maurizio Ciaschini, ed., *Input-Output Analysis: Current Developments*. London: Chapman and Hall.

———. 1988b. "Analyzing Technological Change: An Engineering Database for Input-Output Models of The Economy." *Engineering with Computers* 4:99–105.

Duchin, F., G. Lange, K. Thonstad, and A. Idenburg. 1992. "Environmentally Sound Strategies for Economic Development: An Input- Output Analysis." Final Report to the United Nations under contract #CTPS/CON/112/91.

Duchin, F., and D. Szyld. 1985. "A Dynamic Input-Output Model with Assured Positive Output." *Metroeconomica* 37:269–82.

Edmonds, Jae, and John M. Riley. 1985. *Global Energy*. New York: Oxford University Press.

Eketorp, Sven. 1989. "Electrotechnologies and Steelmaking." In *Electricity: End-Use and New Generation Technologies*. See Johansson, Bodlund, and Williams (1990).

Electric Power Research Institute (EPRI). 1991. "Research Update." *EPRI Journal* 16(3):40–43.

———. 1988. *Technical Assessment Guide*, Vols. 2 and 4. Palo Alto, CA.

———. 1987. *Electricity*. Palo Alto, CA.

EPA. See U.S. Environmental Protection Agency.

EPRI. See Electric Power Research Institute.

Eskinazi, D. 1989. "Full-Scale Retrofit of a Low-Nox Burner System." *EPRI Journal* 14(3)40–41.

FAO. See United Nations Food and Agriculture Organization.

Fickett, A. P., W. G. Clark, and A. Lovins. 1990. "Efficient Use of Electricity." *Scientific American*. 263:65–74.

Flavin, C. 1986. "Electricity for a Developing World." Worldwatch Institute, Worldwatch Paper No. 70.

Foell, W. K., and C. W. Green. n.d. "Acid Rain in Asia: An Economic, Energy and Emissions Overview." Madison, WI: Resource Management Associates of Madison.

Fulkerson, W., R. R. Judkins, and M. K. Sanghvi. 1990. "Energy from Fossil Fuels." *Scientific American* 263:129–35.

Gamba, J., D. Caplin, and J. Mulckhuyse. 1986. *Industrial Energy Rationalization in Developing Countries*. Baltimore: Johns Hopkins University Press.

Geller, H. S. 1989. "Implementing Electricity Conservation Programs." In *Electricity: Efficient End-Use and New Generation Technologies*. See Johansson, Bodlund, and Williams (1990).

———. 1988. *Residential Equipment Efficiency: 1988 Update*. Washington, DC: American Council for an Energy Efficient Economy.

———. 1985. "Progress in Energy Efficiency of Residential Appliances and Space Conditioning Equipment." In D. Hafemeister, H. Kelly, and B. Levi., eds., *Energy Sources: Conservation and Renewables*, New York: American Institute of Physics.

Goldemberg, J., T. Johansson, A. Reddy, and R. Williams. 1987. *Energy for Sustainable Development*. Washington, DC: World Resources Institute.

Goldman, C. 1984. "Measured Energy Savings from Residential Retrofits: Updated Results from the BECA-A Projects." In *Proceedings of the 1988 ACEEE Summer Study on Energy Efficiency in Buildings*. Washington, DC: American Council for an Energy Efficient Economy.

Greene, D. L., N. Meddeb, and J. Liu. 1986. "Vehicle Stock Modelling of Highway Energy Use." *Energy Policy* 14:437–46.

Guzman, O., A. Yunez-Naude, and M. Wionczek. 1987. *Energy Efficiency and Conservation in Mexico*. Washington, DC: World Bank.

Hafemeister, D., H. Kelly, and B. Levi, eds. 1985. *Energy Sources: Conservation and Renewables*. New York: American Institute of Physics.

Hannon, B. and J.J. Joyce. 1980. "Energy Conservation through Industrial Cogeneration," *Energy* 1:343-54.

Herman, R., S. A. Ardekani, and J. H. Ausubel. 1989. "Dematerialization." In J. H. Ausubel and H. E. Sladovich, eds., *Technology and Environment*. Washington, DC: National Academy Press.

Hirst, E., J. Clinton, H. Geller, and W. Kroner. 1986. *Energy Efficiency in Buildings: Progress and Promise*. Washington, DC: American Council for an Energy Efficient Economy.

Hirst, E., and B. Hannon. 1979. "Effects of Energy Conservation in Residential and Commercial Buildings." *Science* 205:656–61.

Hoekstra, Pat L. 1991. "Paper Recycling Creates Its Own Set of Environmental Problems." *American Papermaker* 54(4):30–33.

Hogan, T. 1989. "Description of the Industrial Combustion Emissions Model." EPA Contract No. 68–02–4384. Report prepared for the U.S. Environmental Protection Agency, Office of Research and Development.

Hunter, L. C., and J. R. Markusen. 1989. "Per-capita Income as a Determinant of Trade." In R. Feenstra, ed., *Empirical Methods for International Trade*. Cambridge, MA, and London: Massachusetts Institute of Technology Press.

Idenburg, A.M. 1993. *Gearing Production Models to Ecological Economic Analysis: A Case Study, within the Input-Output Framework, of Fuels for Road Transport*. Doctoral dissertation. Enschede: Faculteit der Bestuurskunde, Universiteit Twente.

Ierland, E. C., and T. Hutton. 1988. "Emission Scenarios for SO_2 and NO_x for West Germany, France, Belgium, and the United Kingdom." Wageningen, the Netherlands: Agricultural Economic Research Institute, Agricultural University.

International Energy Agency. 1991a. *Coal Information 1991*. Paris: OECD.

———. 1991b. *Energy Statistics and Balances of Non-OECD Countries 1988–1989*. Paris: OECD.

———. 1991c. *Energy Balances of OECD Countries 1980/1989*. Paris: OECD.

———. 1991d. *Fuel Efficiency of Passenger Cars*. Paris: OECD.

————. 1990a. *Coal Information 1989*. Paris: OECD.

————. 1990b. *World Energy Statistics and Balances 1985–1988*. Paris: OECD.

————. 1989. *World Energy Statistics and Balances 1971–1987*. Paris: OECD.

————. 1984. *Energy Balances of OECD Countries 1970/1982*. Paris: OECD.

————. 1982. *The Use of Coal in Industry*. Paris: IEA/OECD.

Jack Fawcett Associates. 1987. "Capital and Operating Inputs for Alternative Energy Technologies." Bethesda, MD: Jack Fawcett Associates.

Jaczewski, M. 1991. "Eastern European Energy," *World Energy Council Journal* 12–18.

Jannsen, R., and A. Milkop. 1987. "Energy Intensity/Efficiency Indicators." Paper presented at the Asian Development Bank/International Energy Agency Energy Data Workshop, Tokyo, September.

Johansson, T., B. Bodlund, and R. Williams, eds. 1990. *Electricity: Efficient End-Use and New Generation Technologies and Their Planning Implications*. Lund, Sweden: Lund University Press.

Kahane, A. 1989. "Technological Change and Industrial Electricity Use." In *Electricity: End-Use and New Generation Technologies*. See Johansson, Bodlund, and Williams (1990).

————. 1986. "Industrial Electrification: Case Studies of Four Industries Steel, Paper, Cement and Motor Vehicles Production in the United States, Japan and France." Berkeley: Lawrence Berkeley Laboratory, University of California.

Kanoh, T. 1987. "Effective Utilization of Energy and Its Policy Implications." Paper presented at the Asian Development Bank/International Energy Agency Energy Data Workshop, Tokyo, September.

Keeling, C. D. 1973. "Industrial Production of Carbon Dioxide from Fossil Fuels and Limestone," *Tellus* 25(2):174–98.

Koo, Chi-Ming. 1985. "The Economic Impact of Changing Automotive Materials Use." Doctoral dissertation, Department of Economics, New York University.

Lamarre, L. 1990. "New Push for Energy Efficiency." *EPRI Journal* 15(3):4–17.

Leach, Gerald. 1987. *Household Energy in South Asia*. London: Elsevier.

Ledic, M. 1991. "China: CO_2 Emissions and Energy Policies: Scenarios for the Years 2000 and 2030." *World Energy Council Journal* 26–36.

Leontief, W., A. Carter, and P. Petri. 1977. *Future of the World Economy*. New York: Oxford University Press.

Levine, M., A. Gadgil, S. Meyers, J. Sathaye, J. Stafurik, and T. Wilbanks. 1991. "Energy Efficiency, Developing Nations, and Eastern Europe." A report to the U.S. Working Group on Global Energy Efficiency.

Lin, Xiannuan. 1991. *Declining Energy Intensity in China's Industrial Sector*. Cambridge, MA: Massachusetts Institute of Technology.

Marland, G. 1983. "Carbon Dioxide Emission Rates of Conventional and Synthetic Fuels." *Energy* 8(12):981-92.

Marland, G., and R. Rotty. 1984. "Carbon Dioxide Emissions from Fossil Fuels: A Procedure for Estimation and Results for 1950–1982." *Tellus* (36B):232–61.

McCormick, J. 1985. *Acid Earth*. Washington, DC: International Institute for the Environment.

McGowan, Terry. 1990. "Energy-Efficient Lighting." In *Electricity: End-Use and New Generation Technologies and Their Planning Implications*. See Johansson, Bodlund, and Williams (1990).

Meagher, G.A. 1994. "The International Comparison Project as a Source of Private Consumption Data for a Global Input-Output Model." *Structural Change and Economic Dynamics* 5(2).

Merrick, D. 1984. *Coal Combustion and Conversion Technology*. New York: Elsevier.

Meunier, M. Y., and O. de Bruyn Kops. 1984. "Energy Efficiency in the Steel Industry with Emphasis on Developing Countries." World Bank Technical Paper, No. 22. Washington, DC: World Bank.

Meyers, R. A., ed. 1983. *Handbook of Energy Technology and Economics*. New York: John Wiley and Sons.

———. 1981. *Coal Handbook*. New York: Marcel Dekker.

Meyers, S. 1988. "Transportation in the LDCs: A Major Area of Growth in World Oil Demand." Applied Science Division of Lawrence Berkeley Laboratory, LBL-24198.

Moldan, Bedich, and Jerald L. Schnoor. 1992. "Czechoslovakia: Examining a Critically Ill Environment." *Environmental Science and Technology* 26(1):14–21.

Moller, D. 1984. "Estimation of Global Man-Made Sulfur Emissions." *Atmospheric Environment* 18(1):19–27.

Moore, T. 1991. "Adjustable Speed Drives in Power Plants," *EPRI Journal* 16(4):32–37.

Motor Vehicle Manufacturers Association of the United States (MVMA).1981, 1990. *World Motor Vehicle Data*. Detroit, MI.

———. 1975. *Automobile Facts and Figures*. Detroit, MI.

Munasinghe, M. 1986. *Current Power Sector Issues in Developing Countries*. Washington, DC: World Bank.

National Research Council. 1992. *Automotive Fuel Economy: How Far Should We Go?* Washington, DC: National Academy Press.

New York Times. 1991. "Buyers Insist a Bigger House Is Better." November 24, Section 10, p. 1.

Norgaard, Jorgen S. 1989. "Low Electricity Appliances Options with Present and Forthcoming Technology." In *Electricity: End-Use and New Generation Technologies*. See Johansson, Bodlund, and Williams (1990).

OECD. 1991. *Development and Co-operation: 1991 Report*. Paris.

———. 1989. *The Role of Technology in Iron and Steel Developments*. Paris.

———. 1988. *Transport and the Environment*. Paris.

———. 1985a. *The Clean Use of Coal*. Paris.

———. 1985b. *Environmental Effects of Electricity Generation*. Paris.

———. 1983a. *Aluminum Industry: Energy Aspects of Structural Change*. Paris.

———. 1983b. *Control Technology for Nitrogen Oxide Emissions From Stationary Sources*. Paris.

———. 1982. *The Use of Coal in Industry*. Paris.

———. 1981a. *Costs and Benefits of Sulfur Oxide Control*. Paris.

———. 1981b. *Development and Co-operation: 1981 Review*. Paris.

OECD, International Energy Agency. 1991. *World Energy Statistics and Balances*. Paris: OECD.

———. 1990. *Energy Policies and Programmes of OECD Countries*. Paris: OECD.

———. 1987. *Flows and Stocks of Fixed Capital*. Paris: OECD.

———. 1989. *Projected Costs of Generating Electricity: From Power Stations for Commissioning in the Period 1995–2000*. Paris. OECD.

———. 1988a. *Emission Controls in Electricity Generation and Industry*. Paris: OECD.

———. 1988b. *World Energy Statistics and Balances*. Paris: OECD.

———. 1972. *Development and Co-operation: 1972 Review*. Paris: OECD.

OTA. See U.S. Congress, Office of Technology Assessment.

Pape, R. 1990. "Poland's Coming Needs." *Acid News* No. 3: 14–15.

Paszynski, J. 1990. "Energy and Atmospheric Environment in Post-communist Countries: The Case of Poland." Paper presented at the International Symposium on the Global Environment, Gotenba, Japan, October 21–24.

Rind, D., A. Rosenzweig, and C. Rosenzweig. 1988. "Modelling the Future: A Joint Venture," *Nature* 334(6182): 483–86.

Romain-Frisch, J. 1989. *World Energy Horizons 2000–2020*. Paris: Editions Technip.

Rosenfeld, A. H. 1985. "Residential Energy Efficiency: Progress Since 1973 and Future Potential." In *Energy Sources: Conservation and Renewables*. See Hafemeister, Kelly, and Levi (1985).

Rosenfeld, A. H., and D. Hafemeister. 1985. "Energy Conservation in Large Buildings." In *Energy Sources: Conservation and Renewables*. See Hafemeister, Kelly, and Levi (1985).

Ross, M. 1989. "Energy and Transportation in the United States." *Annual Review of Energy* 14:131–71.

Sagoff, M. 1988. *The Economy of the Earth: Philosophy, Law, and the Environment*. New York: Cambridge University Press.

Sathaye, Jayant and Nina Goldman, eds. 1991. "CO_2 Emissions from Developing Countries: Better Understanding the Role of Energy in the Long Term." Lawrence Berkeley Laboratory, No. LBL-30060.

Schipper, L., A. Ketoff, and A. Kahane. 1985. "Explaining Residential Energy Use by International Bottom-Up Comparisons." *Annual Review of Energy* 10:341–405.

Schipper, L., S. Meyers, and H. Kelly. 1985. *Coming in From the Cold: Energy-Wise Housing in Sweden*. Washington, DC: Seven Locks Press.

Schrieber, H. 1986. "Socialist State in Lignite Trap." *Acid News* No. 1:18.

Schurr, S., C. Burwell, W. Devine, and S. Sonenblum, eds. 1990. *Electricity in the American Economy*. Westport, CT: Greenwood Press.

Simoes, J. T. C. 1984. *SADCC: Energy and Development to the Year 2000*. Uppsala: Beijer Institute and the Scandinavian Institute of African Studies.

Smil, Vaclav. 1988. *Energy in China's Modernization*. Armonk, NY: M. E. Sharpe.

———. 1985. *Carbon-Nitrogen-Sulfur*. New York and London: Plenum Press.

Stark, H. A., ed. 1981, 1988, and 1989. *Ward's Automotive Yearbook*. Detroit: Wards Communications.

Sterner, T. 1990. "Energy Efficiency and Capital Embodied Technical Change: The Case of Mexican Cement Manufacturing." *The Energy Journal* 11(2):155–67.

Stewart, D. F., and B. Muhegi. 1989. "Strategies for Meeting Tanzania's Future Cement Needs." *Natural Resources Forum* 14:294–302.

Strout, A. M. 1985. "Energy-Intensive Materials and the Developing Countries." *Materials and Society*, 9(3):281–330.

Suprenant, N. F., R. Hall, and L. Seale. 1976. *Preliminary Emissions Assessment of Conventional Stationary Source Combustion Systems*. Washington, DC: GPO.

Thunberg, B. 1989. "Emissions as High as All of Sweden's!" *Acid Magazine* No. 8:15–18.

Trengove, C. D. 1986. *Australian Energy Policy in the 80's*. North Sydney: Allen and Unwin Australia.

UNCTAD. See United Nations Conference on Trade and Development.

UN/DIESA. See United Nations Department of International Economic and Social Affairs.

UN/ECE. See United Nations Economic Comission for Europe.

UN/FAO. See United Nations Food and Agriculture Organization.

UNIDO. See United Nations Industrial Development Organization.

United Nations. COMTRADE Data Base.

———. Various years. *Construction Statistics Yearbook*. New York.

———. Various years. *Industrial Statistics Yearbook*. New York.

———. Various years. *Yearbook of Energy Statistics*. New York.

———. 1991a. *Annual Bulletin of Housing and Building Statistics for Europe*. New York.

————. 1991b. *National Accounts Statistics: Main Aggregates and Detailed Tables, 1989, Parts I and II*. New York.

————. 1989. *National Accounts Statistics: Main Aggregates and Detailed Tables, 1986*. New York.

————. 1988. *Electricity Balances and Electricity Profiles 1986*. New York.

United Nations Conference on Trade and Development. Various years. UNCTAD *Commodity Yearbook*. New York.

United Nations Department of International Economic and Social Affairs (DIESA). MEDS Data base.

United Nations Division of Natural Resources and Energy. 1984. *Energy Planning in Developing Countries*. New York.

United Nations Economic Commission for Europe. Various years. *The Steel Market in (year)*. New York.

————. 1987. *National Strategies and Policies for Air Pollution Abatement*. New York.

————. 1983. *Energy Transition in the ECE Region*. Geneva.

United Nations Environment Programme and World Health Organization. 1988. *Assessment of Urban Quality*. New York.

United Nations Food and Agriculture Organization. 1990a. FAO *Fertilizer Yearbook*. New York.

————. 1990b. FAO *Production Yearbook*. New York.

————. 1990c. The State of Food and Agriculture. New York and Rome.

————. 1989 and 1983. FAO *Trade Yearbook*. New York.

————. Various years. *Yearbook of Fishery Statistics*. New York and Rome.

United Nations Industrial Development Organization. Various years. *Industry and Development Global Report* (for 1987–88, 1988–89, 1989–90, 1990–91). Vienna.

————. 1985a. "Electric Power Equipment in Developing Countries: Options and Strategies." Sectoral Working Paper No. 25. Vienna: United Nations.

————. 1985b. "The Economic Use of Aluminum." *Development and Transfer of Technology Series*, No. 21, ID/324.

————. 1985c. "The Building Materials Industry in Developing Countries: An Analytical Appraisal." *Sectoral Studies Series*, No. 16, Vol. I, Sectoral Studies Branch, Division for Industrial Studies (UNIDO/IS. 512).

————. 1985d. "The Building Materials Industry: The Sector in Figures." *Sectoral Studies Series* No. 16, Vol. II, Sectoral Studies Branch, Division for Industrial Studies (UNIDO/IS. 512/Add. 1).

————. 1985e. "Use and Conservation of Energy in the Cement Industry." *Sectoral Working Paper Series* (31). Sectoral Studies Branch, Division for Sectoral Studies (UNIDO/IS. 540).

————. 1983a. "First World-Wide Study of the Wood and Wood Processing Industries." *Sectoral Studies Series*(2). Sectoral Studies Branch, Division for Industrial Studies, Vienna. UNIDO/IS 398.

————. 1983b. "Wood Resources and Their Use as Raw Material." *Sectoral Studies Series* (3). Sectoral Studies Branch, Division for Industrial Studies. UNIDO/IS 399.

United Nations Statistical Commission and the Economic Commission for Europe. 1987. *Environmental Statistics in Europe and North America*. New York: United Nations.

U.S. Congress, Office of Technology Assessment (OTA). 1991. *Energy in Developing Countries*. Report No. OTA-E-486. Washington, DC: GPO.

————. 1990. *New Electric Power Technologies: Problems and Prospects for the 1990s*. Report No. OTA-E-246. Washington, DC: GPO.

———. 1983. "The Chemicals Industry." in *Industrial Energy Use*. Report No. OTA-E-198. Washington, DC: GPO, pp. 115–38.

U.S. Department of Commerce. 1990. *Statistical Abstract of the United States, 1990*. Washington, DC: GPO.

———. 1984, "National Income and Product Accounts." *Survey of Current Business* 64(10):9–19.

———. 1989. "National Income and Product Accounts." *Survey of Current Business* 69(10):9–19.

U.S. Department of Commerce, Bureau of Economic Analysis (BEA). 1991. *Survey of Current Business*, pp. 50–51.

U.S. Department of Commerce, International Trade Division, and U.S. Department of the Interior, Bureau of Mines. 1990. *A Cost Comparison of Selected U.S. and South African Coal Mines*. Washington, DC: GPO.

———. 1989. *A Cost Comparison of Selected U.S. and Australian Coal Mines*. Washington, DC: Depts. of Commerce and Interior.

———. 1988. *A Cost Comparison of Selected U.S. and Canadian Coal Mines*. Washington, DC: Depts. of Commerce and Interior.

———. 1986. *A Cost Comparison of Selected U.S. and Colombian Coal Mines*. Washington, DC: Depts. of Commerce and Interior.

U.S. Department of Energy. 1988. *Annual Energy Review*, Washington, DC.

———. Annual. *Historical Plant Cost and Annual Production Expenses for Selected Electric Plants*. Washington, DC.

U.S. Department of Energy, Energy Information Administration. Various years. *Cost and Quality of Fuels for Electric Utility Plants 1987*. Washington, DC: Department of Energy.

U.S. Department of the Interior, Bureau of Mines. Various years. *Minerals Yearbook*. Washington, DC: GPO.

———. Various years. *Mineral Commodity Profiles*. Washington, DC: GPO.

U.S. Department of Labor, Bureau of Labor Statistics (BLS). 1990. "Time Series of Input-Output Industries." Unpublished data base.

———. 1980. *Historical and Projected Input-Output Tables of the Economic Growth Project: Volume l. Direct Requirement Tables*. Bulletin 2056. Washington, DC: GPO.

U.S. Environmental Protection Agency. 1990. *Policy Options for Stabilizing Global Climate*. Washington, DC.

———. 1989. "1985 National Utility Reference File. " Unpublished data base. Research Triangle Park, NC.

———. 1985. *Compilation of Air Pollutant Emission Factors*, 4th ed. Research Triangle Park, NC.

———. 1983. *Control Techniques for Nitrogen Oxides Emissions from Stationary Sources*, 4th ed. Research Triangle Park, NC.

———. 1981. *Control Techniques for Sulfur Oxide Emissions from Stationary Sources*. Research Triangle Park, NC.

Vernon, J. 1990. "Dealing with Sulfur Dioxide." *Acid News* 1:14–17.

Veverka, A. C. 1991. "Economics Favor Increased Use of Recycled Fiber in Most Furnishes." In K.L. Patrick, ed., *Paper Recycling: Strategies, Economics and Technologies*. San Francisco: Miller Freeman.

Volfberg, D. 1991. "The Future of the Soviet Energy Economy." *World Energy Council Journal* 19–25.

Wald, M. L. 1990. "A New Geography for the Coal Industry." *New York Times*, November 25, p. F5.

Walsh, M. 1990. "Global Trends in Motor Vehicle Use and Emissions." *Annual Review of Energy* 15:217–43.

Williams, R. H. 1990. "Innovative Approaches to Marketing Electric Efficiency." In *Electricity: Efficient End-Use and New Generation Technologies and Their Planning Implications. See* Johansson, Bodlund, and Williams (1990).

Williams, R. H., and E. D. Larson. 1989. "Expanding Roles for Gas Turbines in Power Generation." In *Electricity: Efficient End-Use and New Generation Technologies and Their Planning Implications. See* Johansson, Bodlund, and Williams (1990).

Williams, R. H., E. D. Larson, and M. H. Ross. 1987. "Materials, Affluence, and Industrial Energy Use." *Annual Review of Energy* 12:99–144.

Wilson, D. 1983. *The Demand for Energy in the Soviet Union.* Totowa, NJ: Rowman and Allanheld.

World Bank. 1990. Socio-Economic Time Series Access and Retrieval System.

———. 1985. *China: The Energy Sector.* Washington, DC.

———. 1984a. *Energy Issues and Options in Thirty Developing Countries.* Report of the Joint UNDP/World Bank Energy Sector Assessment Program, Report No. 5230. Washington, DC.

———. 1984b. *India: Economic Issues in the Power Sector.* Washington, DC.

———. 1983. *The Energy Transition in Developing Countries.* Washington, DC.

World Commission on Environment and Development. 1987. *Our Common Future.* Oxford and New York: Oxford University Press.

World Energy Conference. 1974, 1978. *Survey of Energy Resources.* London.

Xia, S., and R. Fong. 1990. "Project Proposal: An Application of Input-Output Analysis and the LINK Model in the Energy and Environment System of China." Beijing: Tsinghua University.

Yannis, Karmokolias. 1990. "Automotive Industry Trends and Prospects for Investment in Developing Countries." International Finance Corporation Discussion Paper No. 7. Washington, DC: World Bank.

Index

217